ML Upham

Revolution and the Rebirth of Inequality

Revolution and the Rebirth of Inequality

A Theory Applied to the National Revolution in Bolivia

Jonathan Kelley
Herbert S. Klein

University of California Press   Berkeley • Los Angeles • London

University of California Press
Berkeley and Los Angeles, California

University of California Press, Ltd.
London, England

Library of Congress Cataloging in Publication Data

Kelley, Jonathan.
    Revolution and the rebirth of inequality.

    Includes bibliographical references and index.
    1. Revolution.   2. Equality.   3. Elite (Social
sciences)   4. Bolivia—History—Revolution, 1952.
I. Klein, Herbert S., joint author.   II. Title.
HN281.K44   984′.052   80-51239
ISBN 0-520-04072-4

Printed in the United States of America

1   2   3   4   5   6   7   8   9

To

J. L. Kelley *père*

and

Daniel Charles Klein

Contents

Introduction

THE QUESTION

The violent overthrow of traditional elites by a revolution from below is probably the most shattering and fundamental transformation of human society. The French Revolution, the Russian Revolution of 1917, and the Communist Revolution in China are only the most conspicuous examples of a phenomenon which has appeared through history, most often in the preindustrial, predominantly peasant societies in which the majority of mankind has long lived. Such revolutions are rare but they are more common in recent years than in the past, and no society is immune. Revolutions are fundamentally about redistribution, about ending the exploitation of the old elite and providing new opportunities for the poor and the oppressed. Revolutions redistribute land and wealth, reorganize the economy, and restructure the society in ways that lead irreversibly away from the prerevolutionary past toward a different and presumably more egalitarian future. This book is about the changes that follow from revolution and the new society that emerges. We offer a general theory of inequality and inherited privilege in postrevolutionary society and a detailed empirical analysis of the Bolivian National Revolution.

Revolutions are not only fascinating in themselves but provide an unparalleled opportunity to observe the inner workings of a society. By stripping away the custom, convention, tradition, and routine that had accumulated over the generations and abruptly trying to impose a new organization on society, revolution enables us to distinguish the more ephemeral elements of the social order from its primary components; to see what changes cannot be made in a society and what changes can, and with what result. Too much of our social theory has grown out of the analysis of a few stable industrial societies, with little attempt to evaluate fully the processes of change or the more fundamental institutions that are present in all societies. Revolution gives us a chance to observe fundamental changes in a society and add a dynamic element to our static understanding.

But we know very little about them. Elites are swept aside, dogmas replaced, and masses mobilized, but the inner dynamics and long-run consequences of change are only poorly perceived. To be sure, we know something, often a fair amount, about the origins of revolution. The economics of exploitation, the politics of governments dominated by landed elites, the recruiting of revolutionary cadres, the historical details of revolt, and the causes that lead to success or failure are reasonably well understood. We also know a fair amount about the consequences of radical revolutions that failed. But we know remarkably little about the consequences of a successful radical revolution. We know what happens to the most prominent of the old elite but for the lesser ranks of the elite, for the middle classes, and for the exploited masses themselves, we know almost nothing. The consequences of revolution for ordinary people are obscure. Revolutions generally promise peasants freedom, justice, and at least some relief from rent, taxes, usury, and restrictions on their movement. They surely benefit from that and, at least in the short run, from the more open and equalitarian society that results. But it is unclear whether some benefit more than others, and why. And the long-term effects are even less clear. Does equality endure, or does inequality reemerge? Does social mobility grow or decline? Who benefits from the forces unleashed by the revolution, how do they benefit, and why? What is the intrinsic logic of postrevolutionary society and what is the evidence about how it actually works out in practice?

These are the questions that we seek to answer in this book. In our answer we take two directions, one theoretical and one empirical.

THEORY

We offer a theory about revolution's effects on stratification among ordinary people, about its effects on income, on inequality, and on inherited privilege for everyone except the tiny traditional elite. We deal with revolutions in which an exploitative elite is overthrown by rebellion from below, by a revolution of exploited peasants and rural craftsmen, of small town workers, traders, and clerks. We are concerned with revolutions of the exploited and with the effects that such revolutions have on the vast majority of the population. We argue that such a revolution improves standards of living for the majority, reduces inequality, and causes inherited privilege to decline. But education and skills remain valuable and revolution does not benefit the poorest of its supporters as much as those who were better off before.

In the longer run, in the generation or two following the revolution, the majority still benefits. But we argue that revolution provides new opportunities for those among them with education or skills, land or capital, ability, motivations, or other resources. As they take full advantage of their resources, they move ahead of their less fortunate peers and inequality grows apace. And because they have growing advantages to pass on to their children, inherited privilege among the previously exploited majority grows as well. In addition to these changes among the previously exploited, we argue that inequality and inherited privilege may even grow in the society as a whole, depending on what the new postrevolutionary elite is like, and whether or not the revolution leads to long-term economic growth.

This is basically a theory about revolutions but many of the predictions about long-term consequences apply more generally to any social changes that reduce exploitation or increase economic opportunities. These include the various changes that led to the end of feudalism, the introduction of cash crops or a market economy in a nonmarket society, the "Green Revolution" in agriculture, and the political changes which have increased opportunities for ethnic and linguistic minorities in many countries. In the body of the book we will deal with these generalizations only in passing but return to them in the conclusion.

The theory is basically straightforward and we present it in a simple and conventional manner. But there are some complexities lurking under the surface, ones that lead to interesting conclusions, and so we also present the results of a computer simulation of the theory. For readers who prefer a more rigorous presentation, the argument is developed formally in Appendix 1. The theory is not post hoc, but was developed prior to the data analysis.

DATA

To test this theory requires reliable empirical data on a revolutionary society and they are very hard to come by. Although a question of profound interest and importance, few systematic data exist and, forced to rely on scattered and fragmentary sources, interpretations of the revolution's impact on society have been diverse, with relatively little agreement between one analysis and another. The problem, of course, is that societies in the midst of revolution are not the place for the kind of large-scale, systematic survey research needed reliably to assess the effects on the population at large of any social change, even a change as dramatic as revolution. Indeed, reliable data are especially important for revolutions since feelings run high and preconceptions are strong. But survey research is rarely permitted in revolutionary societies and, even if allowed, is rarely possible in practice, especially since most revolutions occur in underdeveloped countries where such studies are difficult to carry out even in the best of times. Fortunately, however, the Bolivian Revolution of 1952 is an exception. We have detailed survey materials on Bolivia, data that are, to the best of our knowledge, the most complete such data on politics and stratification available concerning ordinary people in a society recently transformed by revolution. The second aim of this book is therefore to provide a rigorous empirical analysis of the effect of one radical revolution, the Bolivian Revolution, both for its own sake and as a means of testing our theory.

The Bolivian data are very suitable for these purposes. The Bolivian National Revolution marked a fundamental and irreversible trans-formation of Bolivian society. Led by the Movimento Nacionalista Revolucionario, a socialist party with strong support in both working and middle classes, armed rebels seized Bolivia's capital after three days of heavy fighting in April 1952. The national government col-lapsed and the army surrendered to the rebels. They promptly dis-banded the army and distributed its weapons to the civilian population who remained the dominant military force for years afterward. The government nationalized the mines and much of such modern indus-try as existed, seizing control of some two-thirds of the nation's capital stock. In the previously quiescent countryside, Marxist radicals in the revolutionary movement distributed arms to the peasants; with the army disbanded this left military control of the countryside in the peasants' hands and they promptly used their power to overthrow the landed elite, one of the most backward and exploitative in the world. They killed or exiled the old elite, abolished traditional work obliga-tions and monopolistic privileges, and redistributed the land. It was much like the "Great Fear" period of the French revolution. In the course of a year or two, an exploitative elite dating back to the Spanish conquest four centuries before was abolished, never to reappear.

To have extensive quantitative and qualitative data on a society that has recently undergone a revolution of this magnitude is exceedingly rare and we are fortunate to have data from the definitive study conducted by the Research Institute for the Study of Man and kindly made available to us by Vera Rubin and Lambros Comitas. It includes extensive ethnographic fieldwork in six carefully selected rural areas in different parts of Bolivia, a census of all inhabitants of the areas, and an extensive social survey of 1,130 heads of households in the areas. The social survey includes detailed information, both current and retro-spective, on stratification, politics, and related topics and is our main source of data. For various personal and financial reasons, the survey data have never been analyzed and this is the first report on them.

ORGANIZATION OF THE BOOK

We begin with our theoretical model of revolution's effects on in-equality and inherited privilege in chapter 1. The next chapter de-scribes Bolivia, the setting in which we will test this theory, and the measures and methods we use in our analysis. The third chapter offers an analysis of the economic, social, and political organization of prerevolutionary Bolivia, providing a baseline against which revolutionary changes can be measured. We then describe the revolution itself in the fourth chapter.

Having established the revolutionary character of the Bolivian experience, as well as some of its limitations, the rest of the book deals with the consequences that slowly unfolded from this abrupt and violent beginning. In the fifth chapter we provide an appreciation of the revolutionary experience as perceived by ordinary Bolivians looking back over fourteen years of revolutionary change. After this subjective view of the revolution, we then turn in the sixth chapter to an analysis of objective data on its consequences for the economy and the distribution of income, paying particular attention to the issues that were central to our theoretical analysis. Finally, we analyze revolution's effects on inherited privilege, testing our predictions in all their detail in the seventh chapter. In the conclusion we assess the limitations and the possibilities of our model for both the historical experience of the Bolivian revolution as well as for revolutions (and certain other kinds of social changes) in other times and other places.

ACKNOWLEDGMENTS

In undertaking this research we have incurred many debts. Lambros Comitas called the Bolivian survey materials to our attention and we would like to thank him, Vera Rubin, and William J. McEwen, who were responsible for collecting and coding these extensive and valuable data, for their permission to use them and for their constant advice. Donald J. Treiman first suggested we study the revolution, provided wise advice throughout the project, allowed us access to his unpublished materials, and read the final manuscript; we thank him warmly. The difficult task of coding the open ended questions was successfully carried out by the Bolivian scholar Antonio Mitre. Robert V. Robinson supplied vital statistical and programming assistance throughout the project. Accurate typing and clear tables came from Betty Gamble, and the figures from Marilyn Hinsby. We thank the National Science Foundation for support under grant SOC74-21514, which was efficiently administered for us by the Center for Policy Research, and we thank the Australian National University for computer time and art work.

Throughout the study we have relied heavily on the advice of friends and colleagues and we would like to thank Richard N. Adams, Xavier Albó, Daniel Bell, Donald J. Black, Leonard Broom, Paul Burstein, Robert G. Cushing, Dorothy B. Darroch, Susan Eckstein, Stanley L. Engerman, George A. Farkas, Louis Wolf Goodman, Archibald O. Haller, John Higley, F. L. Jones, J. L. Kelley *père*, Harriet Manelis

Klein, Marijke Saltet, Arthur L. Stinchcombe, and Sandy Stuart for their help. Much that is good in the manuscript should be laid at their door. Finally, we thank the American Association for the Advancement of Science for awarding their Socio-Psychological Prize to an earlier version of this study.

Canberra   J.K.
New York   H.S.K.

1
A Theory of Revolution's Effects on Inequality and Inherited Privilege

> Humanity left to its own does not necessarily re-establish capitalism, but it does re-establish inequality. The forces tending toward the creation of new classes are powerful. *Mao Zedong, 1965*

Revolutions have appeared throughout the history of mankind, but we still know very little about their consequences. What happens to the old elite is evident but the consequences for the great bulk of the population, for peasants and laborers, for craftsmen and small traders, for clerks and bureaucrats, and for the lesser ranks of the old ruling class are far from clear. While we know a great deal about what the revolution's leaders would like to happen and about the policies adopted by the revolutionary government and their foreign friends and foes, there is still a wide gap between what leaders want and what actually happens in the real world to ordinary people far removed from the centers of power, especially in the less developed, largely peasant societies where most revolutions have occurred. Even at the best of times their governments and bureaucracies are often inefficient and self-serving while, disrupted by the revolution, with conflicting loyalties, new personnel, and an uncertain future, the years following a revolution are hardly the best of times. Moreover, a revolution sets loose a myriad of new forces, some of which contain within themselves the seeds of profound change. As well as redistributing wealth from the rich to the poor, revolution destroys many of the commercial and political privileges of the old elite and thus eliminates many of the restraints with which the elite had fettered the bulk of the population, opening up new opportunities for the previously exploited population. They surely benefit from these changes, at least in the short run, and from the more open and equalitarian society that results. But whether and why some benefit more than others is unclear. The long-term effects are even less evident. Does equality endure or does inequality reemerge, perhaps in new and more virulent forms? Does social mobility grow or decline? Who benefits from the forces unleashed by revolution and how?

In this chapter we propose a theory about these questions. We show that, in the short run, a revolution can be expected to reduce economic inequality and status inheritance but also to benefit its prosperous and well-educated supporters more than its poorer ones. In the long run previously exploited groups will still be better off but economic inequality and status inheritance will grow steadily, in some circumstances eventually exceeding their prerevolutionary levels.

SCOPE OF THE THEORY

Our theory deals with the predominantly rural, poor, preindustrial, peasant-dominated societies in which most revolutions have occurred.[1] We offer a general theory about the effect of revolution on inequality and social mobility, not a theory about the Bolivian revolution alone, or about any other specific revolution. To be sure, there are unique features in all revolutions, in the countries in which they occurred, and in the historical and international settings surrounding them. While understanding a specific revolution requires a close and detailed analysis of its particular circumstances, there are nonetheless general patterns common to all radical revolutions. It is with these general patterns that we are concerned.

We believe that our theory applies to any revolution satisfying two conditions: first, a politically and economically dominant traditional elite has previously been able to expropriate a large fraction of the surplus produced by peasants and other subordinate groups and, second, the revolution liberated subordinate groups from their traditional exploitation. We call this combination of events a *radical* revolution and claim that our theory applies to any radical revolution.

We deal with the apolitical mass of the population, deliberately excluding the revolution's political and military leaders, the revolutionary intelligentsia, and other revolutionary elites. Nonetheless, their ideology and the policies of the government they establish are extremely important. The peasants' goals will generally be what they regard as simple justice—personal (or communal) control over their land, minimal taxation, and the right to sell their produce on the open market. That leads to a predominantly market economy with peasants (or peasant communities) functioning essentially as small capitalist entrepreneurs accumulating income and property. In that case our model applies with full force. But the revolutionary elite may oppose the emergence of a classical peasant economy, instead pursuing more radical and collectivist goals. If successful this will mean, as Wolf (1966; 1969) and others have noted, the end of a conventional peasantry and the rise of a rural working class, usually employed in state-owned communal farms. Our model still applies in this case, but the changes will be slower and somewhat attenuated, in ways we specify.

Some Wider Implications.   Our predictions about long-term effects[2] apply not only to radical revolutions but, we believe, to *any* social changes that reduce exploitation or increase economic opportunities.

Such changes include economic "revolutions" that liberate people from stifling restrictions or increase their productivity by technical means: specifically, the gradual changes that destroyed feudalism, the Green Revolution in agriculture, the introduction of cash crops or a market economy in nonmarket societies, and the like. They also include political changes that have increased opportunities for blacks and women in the United States, untouchables in India, nationalists in ex-colonies throughout the world, and other previously subordinate groups. All these social changes have what we believe is the key *long-term* characteristic of radical revolutions: they increase economic opportunities for previously subordinate groups. But political revolutions have unique short-term characteristics that greatly influence inequality and social mobility in the five or ten years immediately following the revolution and recognizable effects decades later. We will therefore confine our attention here largely to political revolutions, a large enough topic in itself, and return to the wider questions raised by other kinds of social changes once again in the concluding chapter.

DEFINITIONS

Before setting out our theory of how a radical revolution affects inequality and inherited privilege we should say just what we mean by these terms.

Radical Revolution. A revolution, as we use the term, is an abrupt, usually violent, transfer of political power and government office from one elite to another by illegal means. A *radical* revolution, as we define the term, is a revolution that liberates a previously exploited population. Specifically, it is a revolution in a society where a politically and economically dominant traditional elite was able to expropriate a large fraction of the surplus produced by peasants, small town workers, craftsmen, traders, clerks, and other subordinate groups (for example, by control of land, forced labor, discriminatory taxation, usury, control of government or commercial employment, or through monopoly privileges in agriculture, trade, or government) and a revolution that liberates subordinate groups from their traditional exploitation (by destroying the old elite's economic privileges, reducing taxes or interest rates, redistributing land, allowing free access to opportunities in farming and business, expropriating or destroying accumulated wealth, or in other ways). Examples of radical revolutions include, among many others, the French Revolution, the Mexican Revolution of 1910, the Russian Revolution of 1917, the Communist Revolution in China, and the Bolivian Revolution of 1952.

Income. When we discuss income we mean to include not only money income, the main form in market economies, but all other forms of income. This includes income in kind (for example, the value of food that farmers grow and consume themselves), income imputed from property (for example, the rental value of a homeowner's house), and the value of other rights (for example, the right to a company car, rights to free medical care, the rights that feudal landlords had to free services from their serfs). It also includes the diverse nonmonetary privileges common in modern socialist societies (for example, rights to better housing, subsidized vacations, foreign travel, or to shop at special "hard currency" stores [Lipset and Dobson 1973:128–130]). All these provide goods and services of the sort that are bought with money in other circumstances and we will think of income as including them.

Inequality. Income (or analogously, educational) inequality is a more difficult concept mainly because it has many different, although related, aspects. This leaves a wide choice of measures depending largely on which aspect one wants to stress (Allison 1978; Kondor 1975; Sen 1973). We have in mind a very simple notion of inequality, and one that seems politically as well as theoretically germane: the idea that inequality is greater when differences in income between one person and another are large and widespread. Thus if one person has an income of $4,000 and the other has $8,000 we wish to say that there is more inequality than in a situation where one has $5,000 and the other $7,000. This simple notion seems to underly much of the political concern with inequality where one is typically concerned with the size of the gap between rich and poor. A very natural, and politically important, thing to ask about revolution is whether the gap between rich and poor has grown or narrowed, and by how much. This is what we would like to measure. It is a familiar and intuitively reasonable idea and is easily measured in conventional ways. What we do in effect is look at the differences between all possible pairs of people in the society and see how large they are on the average. When there are large differences between people we define inequality as large and when the differences between people are small on the average, we say there is little inequality.[3] There is a familiar and reasonable index of this kind of inequality, the *standard deviation*. It is now widely used in measuring inequality in education and income (for example, Jencks et al. 1972; Mincer 1974) and we use it for both purposes.

In previous work, inequality was more often measured by the Gini and related coefficients. But the Gini is in fact directly comparable to, and monotonically related to, the standard deviation, the chief difference being that the Gini adjusts for differences in the mean while the standard deviation does not (Paglin 1975:601). Thus, for example, if everyone's income doubles the Gini is unaffected but the standard deviation is doubled. Doubling income also doubles the gap between rich and poor—so a poor man has twice as large a gap to overcome if he is to live like a rich one and his son has twice the handicap to overcome if he is to compete with a rich man's son—and that increases inequality in a familiar and reasonable sense of the term. So we prefer a measure, like the standard deviation, that reflects such changes. With this exception, the choice of measure in practice makes little difference since different measures lead to much the same substantive conclusions.[4] Later in this chapter we will show that our theoretical conclusions are essentially unchanged if inequality is measured by the Gini coefficient rather than the standard deviation.[5]

Note that inequality in the sense we define it, or in the sense measured by Gini coefficients or most other inequality measures, is not necessarily a bad thing. It is possible for a society to change in a way that leaves everyone with a higher income than before (which is presumably a good thing) but also leaves it with a more unequal distribution of income. Indeed, there is some reason to think that this will be a common pattern when a poor society begins to develop economically (Fields 1979; Robinson 1976). And our theory implies that a radical revolution does it as well, leaving everyone in the previously exploited population better off than they were before but also creating more inequality among them.

Inherited Privilege.   We are concerned not only with inequality but also with inequality of opportunity, with the way in which privileges are passed from one generation to the next. In most societies parents with wealth and high status are able to give their children an advantage in life, helping them get more education, better jobs, and higher incomes than children born into less privileged families. These inherited privileges are almost always a source of deep resentment to the majority of the population and their destruction is usually a central goal of radical revolutions. We will try to show how revolution affects inherited privilege. Conceptually this is fairly simple; we want to know how much an advantage in education, occupation, or income a child born into a privileged home has compared with a child born into a poor family. The most appropriate measures of this, which are also the conventional ones, are based on regression analysis. However, the intuitive concept is all we need for the moment so we will leave the technical details for later.

Short Run versus Long Run.   We will distinguish the effects that revolution has in the short run from those it has in the long run. Just what is short run and what is long run will vary from revolution to revolution but as a rough approximation we might think of the first decade or so as the short run and the first generation or two as the long run.

REVOLUTION AND INEQUALITY

The effects that revolution has in the short term are rather different from those it has in the long run and so we will take them up separately. Let us begin with the short-run consequences for inequality.

SHORT-TERM EFFECTS ON INEQUALITY

Revolutions profoundly alter inequality. We are dealing with radical revolutions which, by definition, at least partly free peasants and the rest of the subordinate population from their traditional exploitation and thereby improve their economic position at the expense of the traditional elite. Transferring resources from the rich to the poor clearly reduces inequality in the society as a whole. That is, of course, typically one of the revolution's main goals. In practice, the redistribution is often extensive. Radical revolutions often redistribute land, the fundamental fixed asset in peasant societies, and hence redistribute income. They usually redistribute liquid capital as well, expropriating or destroying rents, savings, debts, pensions, and monopolies; this reduces inequality, more so in the rare cases where the proceeds are directly redistributed to the poor. In many revolutions the expropriation is partly inadvertent. Property is abandoned during the crisis, and the collapse of the old government often leads to dramatic inflation that destroys the value of savings, pensions, salaries, and rents; these are more damaging to the old rich.[6] Taxes and rents that fall most heavily on the poor are often reduced or eliminated. In precapitalist societies, the main form of exploitation is often through labor taxes extracted by the state or by landlords, and their abolition increases the time peasants have to work for their own benefit, leading to further equalization (Burke 1971:317–333; Klein 1969). In modern times, revolutionary governments usually establish new health, education, and welfare programs that result in major transfers of resources to the poor and further reduce inequality.

Human Capital.   In the short run we predict that radical revolutions will not destroy the value of human capital but will, if anything, make it more valuable since the range of opportunities for utilizing education, knowledge, technical skills, and other forms of human capital in practice increases. First, especially in previously isolated and traditional rural areas, rapid changes in marketing and the expansion of the money economy upset traditional economic arrangements and reward the adaptability, rationality, and cosmopolitan orientations that education provides (Schuman, Inkeles, and Smith 1967). Literacy and elementary bookkeeping skills are valuable even in a very primitive market economy (Pirenne 1936:13; Kelley and Perlman 1971:216–220). Second, new political and economic power creates new opportunities for cultural brokers and go-betweens (politicians, lawyers, expediters, etc.) to mediate between peasant communities and non-peasant society (Bailey 1963). To do so requires knowledge, contacts, and linguistic and political skills. Modern revolutions generally create numerous new positions in schools, health and welfare agencies, the government bureaucracy, and nationalized industry. Economic growth, a goal of almost all modern revolutions, expands the market economy and increases employment in professional, managerial and clerical jobs, and in transportation (Moore 1966; Kuznets 1966), and success in these requires educational, technical, and linguistic skills. Third, educational credentials may become more important quite apart from any real connection with performance, since requiring fixed levels of education is an effective and convenient way of restricting access to jobs (Collins 1971), especially in the expanding bureaucracies. Finally, in societies where there are several languages (or where the educated classes speak a different dialect) skills in the dominant language often become more valuable after the revolution. They give access to new opportunities in education and commerce and are useful in dealings with the bureaucracy. With increasing contact between urban and rural areas and the atrophy of the old elite's role as intermediary, facility in the national language helps in dealing with the police, bureaucracy, merchants, and employers.

These new opportunities will, we predict, make education, technical and linguistic skills, and other forms of human capital more valuable, giving a larger return in occupational status and income. Some will be able to take direct advantage of their skills by self-employment, taking up more attractive and profitable opportunities than were available before the revolution. To match these new opportunities in self-employment, employers will have to offer more to attract skilled employees. Also the growth in the number of jobs requiring education and linguistic skills increases the demand for skilled personnel, and since the supply can increase only slowly, skilled workers will use their improved bargaining position to extract better wages.

Who Benefits? Radical revolutions benefit the peasants and other previously exploited groups, since their surplus is no longer expropriated by the old elite. Thus all gain something but some gain more than others since revolutions do not overturn the stratification order, putting the poor in place of the rich or the illiterate in place of the educated. Rather, revolution just lops off the top, removing the old elite but leaving everyone else in much the same position they were before.[7] Those with human capital, already better off before the revolution, have a great advantage in commercial agriculture and in the new bureaucratic, commercial, and political jobs (in the Soviet Union, Khrushchev 1970:18−21; in China, Frolic 1978:410−413). In addition, there are typically substantial differences in the amount and value of land peasants worked before the revolution, and they are often able to maintain or strengthen their customary rights afterward (for example in Bolivia, Carter 1964); then with their surplus no longer expropriated, these peasants benefit more from their advantages. Among the revolution's supporters and the rest of the population who were not prime targets of revolution, the old inequalities remain.

LONG-TERM EFFECTS ON INEQUALITY AMONG PREVIOUSLY EXPLOITED GROUPS

A radical revolution allows peasants and other previously exploited groups to obtain a higher return on their land and physical capital since, by definition, it reduces exploitation. By reducing rents or taxes on land, it allows peasants to retain more of what they produce. The destruction of corvée labor obligations—the crucial tax in many agrarian societies, including Bolivia—allows peasants more time to work their own land for their own benefit (an additional one to three days per week in medieval Europe and three or more days in twentieth-century Bolivia; Pirenne 1936:64; Burke 1971:328). Revolution is also likely to reduce the costs peasants pay for goods and services by destroying traditional monopolies on trade, credit, and justice. Monopolies allowed traditional elites to charge exorbitant prices; even where the revolutionary government makes no deliberate attempt to reduce prices, competition is likely to drive them down. Furthermore, prior to the revolution, peasants' opportunities are often restricted to the least profitable sectors of the rural economy. The destruction of serfdom, corvée labor, and other obligations tying peasants to the land, however, provides new opportunities and therefore higher incomes (Olson 1978). They can sell their own produce and take up wage-paying jobs in addition to agriculture, which in some cases increases their income dramatically (for example in Bolivia, Burke 1971:318–331). Some become traders and merchant middlemen, replacing the old elite's commercial monopolies. Finally, economic change may have the same effects, with or without revolution. The introduction of new cash crops or new agricultural techniques, the opening of new markets, and the like all provide new and often profitable opportunities. Ending economic discrimination against blacks, untouchables, Ainu, and the like, opens up opportunities for them.

These new opportunities will, we predict, lead to greater economic inequality among peasants and the rest of the previously exploited population.[8] Even in prerevolutionary times, peasants differ in the amount of property they own (for example, in the size and quality of usufruct landholdings), in human capital (agricultural or linguistic skills, education, experience with the outside world), and in ability, diligence, motivation, luck, and the like. By expropriating the surplus and restricting opportunities to use capital effectively, the old system prevented fortunate peasants from getting the full benefit from their advantages and so restrained the growth of inequality. Revolution removes the restraints, allowing them to take full advantage of their resources.[9] In the long run, we predict, this creates steadily growing inequality among peasants and other previously exploited groups. The fragmentary evidence now available supports this prediction (Chevalier 1967:178, 180–184; Craig 1969:290–291; Lenin 1920:339; Petras and Zemelman 1972:xii, 95–97; Volgyes 1978), and we will see it operate in Bolivia as well. This leads to what might be called the kulak stage—the rise of a newly enriched sector of the peasant population and the emergence of an essentially capitalist rural stratification system.[10] The same reasoning applies to economic revolutions and to social changes that reduce exploitation, and in fact there is evidence that they increase inequality (for example, in agriculture following the Green Revolution, Havens and Flinn 1975).

Human Capital.   In the long run a radical revolution leads to greater investments in human capital among the peasantry and previously exploited groups. First, revolution provides additional reasons for acquiring human capital. Education, linguistic skills, and other forms of human capital are always valuable and, as we argued, revolution if anything makes them more so. Peasants can expect greater benefits from education after the revolution, since they have new opportunities to use it and they can keep more of what they earn. Investing in education therefore becomes more attractive on straightforward economic grounds (Mincer 1974; Burke 1971:324–330). Economic revolutions often have the same effect (Patrick and Kehrberg 1973). Second, modern revolutions supply the means. Whether from conviction or because of peasants' new political power, revolutionary governments generally expand the school system, making education available where it was not before.

These opportunities are not equally available to all but instead go disproportionately to children from privileged families. Throughout the world, well-educated, high status parents are much more successful than other families in getting their children educated (in tribal societies, Kelley and Perlman 1971; in socialist societies, Anderson 1975, Lane 1971:107–120, Dobson 1977; in industrial societies, Treiman and Terrell 1975a); they provide encouragement and role models, teach linguistic and academic skills, force their children to work harder, and so on. Schooling is usually expensive, with both direct costs (fees, supplies, clothing, etc.) and substantial indirect costs in income foregone (income the student could otherwise have earned); prosperous families can better afford these costs.

Educational inequality also increases among peasants and other previously exploited groups. Able and motivated children are able to acquire some education and so rise above their peers, whereas before all would have remained unschooled. As economic inequality grows among peasants, the more prosperous can more easily afford education for their children, so educational inequality grows in the next generation. Since education and other forms of human capital are quite valuable, any growth in inequality in them leads to greater inequality in income and wealth.[11]

Government Intervention.   A revolutionary government can try to restrain these forces by limiting the private accumulation and inheritance of capital. Populist and middle-class revolutionary parties are unlikely to have either the ideological justification or the dedicated cadre with which to do so, although many socialist and communist governments make the attempt. But it is unlikely to succeed. Expropriating large landowners, large capitalists, and foreign investments and thereby securing the "commanding heights" of the economy will not be enough, since accumulation by the mass of upper peasants, the educated middle class, and skilled workers leads, we have argued, to inequality. To restrain these groups, private capital will have to be abolished throughout the economy. In practice this is usually accomplished by socializing the industrial economy and collectivizing the land and sometimes by the physical extinction of the kulaks (as, for example, in Russia). Many people have something to lose from such actions, and they are not without recourse. Small businessmen have money and can threaten to withdraw valuable services; the upper levels of the peasantry know they have much to lose; the educated middle class and party workers newly ensconced in the bureaucracy will want to secure their advantage by accumulating wealth; skilled workers will want to reap full advantage from their skills. To fully overcome the opposition of these groups requires from the party's cadres a level of commitment, dedication, and resistance to temptation that is difficult to maintain over the years; it also requires an extensive and efficient bureaucratic apparatus that can extend its control to the very grass roots, an apparatus few societies have ever possessed. China's cultural revolution may have been in part an attempt to overcome this kind of opposition and prevent the reemergence of inequality (Yueh 1976). Even in China, however, the costs were great, opposition strong, and success ephemeral; other examples are not easy to find.

But the abolition of private capital is not in itself enough to prevent the long-term growth of inequality, since much (indeed most) inequality arises from differences in education, skills, language, and other forms of human capital that are almost immune to redistribution. Human capital is crucial: to run even a moderately complex society requires an educated elite—business, industry, and government require a variety of administrative and technical skills, and even farming and small trading are greatly facilitated by literacy, bookkeeping, and specialized technical skills (Becker 1964; Mincer 1974; Stinchcombe 1961). Although it is sometimes claimed that schools impart few skills of any genuine importance but merely screen or certify or are otherwise dispensable, that claim is inconsistent with detailed evidence for modern industrial societies and with the clear importance of education in societies with very different economic and institutional structures (for industrial societies, see Layard and Psacharopoulous 1974;

and Welch 1975:65–69; for socialist societies, Anderson 1975, Lipset and Dobson 1973; for feudal societies, Pirenne 1936:13; for tribal and developing societies, Lenski 1966, Kelley and Perlman 1971, and Kelley 1976:table 1). Ignoring these skills in favor of political or equity considerations is exceedingly costly (Khrushchev 1970:18–21). To date only China has systematically and persistently attempted it after the revolutionary government was firmly established and even they seem in the end to have abandoned the attempt. Thus a revolution able to abolish private property will slow the long-term growth of inequality but will not prevent it.

STRATIFICATION IN THE SOCIETY AS A WHOLE

In the long run, a radical revolution will, we have argued, create more inequality and status inheritance among peasants and the previously exploited rural masses. But its effects on the society as a whole are less clear. We will argue that inequality and status inheritance first decrease and then remain low for a period; in most circumstances they then increase steadily and, in some circumstances, eventually exceed their prerevolutionary levels.

Economic development itself increases inequality. Even if everyone retains the same relative position, development increases the absolute size of the gap between rich and poor and therefore increases inequality as we define it. If, for example, the introduction of new cash crops doubles everyone's income, it also doubles the gap between poor peasants and rich merchants, so the peasant has twice the obstacle to overcome if he is to live as well as a merchant, and a peasant's son has twice the handicap to overcome if he is to catch up with a merchant's son. In addition, anyone with property, human capital, or other advantages will be better able to take advantage of new opportunities opened up by economic development and that increases inequality by any definition.

The benefits which revolution provides for peasants and the exploited rural masses will at first decrease inequality in the society as a whole. Peasants' income, wealth, and human capital almost always begin well below the average for the whole society, while the commercial and administrative sectors in rural towns and most urban groups are markedly better off initially. The revolution reduces exploitation, improving the economic position of peasants and moving them closer to the mean. This reduces inequality.[12] Most peasants go no farther. But those with human capital, land, physical capital, or other resources will continue to improve their position, especially if the revolution is one that produces economic development. As they draw closer to the mean, inequality continues to decline. But as they surpass the mean in increasing numbers, inequality first stabilizes and then (depending on how many surpass it and by how much) may increase.[13] So there is a standard sequence following the revolution. Inequality first declines, then stabilizes, and then increases again. If peasants continue to improve their economic position, the decline lasts longer, but inequality begins to increase again and eventually may exceed its prerevolutionary level.

How far along this sequence a society proceeds depends not only on what happens to the peasants but also on how high the mean is to begin with and how it changes subsequently. Most prerevolutionary peasant societies are very poor, with a small surplus extracted by a tiny elite (Lenski 1966:chaps. 8, 9). The average is low and, other things being equal, that makes it easier to surpass, and the society will then go through the sequence quickly, perhaps reaching the stage where inequality exceeds prerevolutionary levels. In richer societies (Eastern Europe following the communist revolutions, for example), peasants have farther to go, and the society passes along the sequence more slowly and inequality is unlikely ever to reach prerevolutionary levels. The average also depends on what happens to the urban population and the postrevolutionary elite, but that reflects the power and ideology of the revolutionary leadership, the society's economic and administrative capacity, international political and economic restraints, and a variety of other factors beyond the scope of our theory. It also depends on whether a new ruling elite emerges after the revolution (Djilas 1957; Dahrendorf 1959).

There may be further redistribution after the revolution; this too affects inequality. Particularly where there is no sustained economic growth, gains by rich peasants may be someone else's losses. If they gain entirely at the expense of the elite, there will be more equality. But in practice, their gains will most probably be at the cost of poor peasants and lower and middle classes in the towns. As rich peasants take over marketing, credit, and middleman functions, they displace middle- and lower-class urbanites, and liberated peasants compete for desirable urban jobs. Successful peasants will produce cash crops more efficiently, undercutting poor peasants' market positions and driving them off the land. When rich peasants begin to pass the mean, inequality will eventually increase as long as their gains are mainly at the expense of groups below the average (or, of course, if they are at no one's expense).

A revolution's effects on inequality in the society as a whole thus depend crucially on the speed of economic development, the economic position of urban groups and the postrevolutionary elite, and government policies toward accumulation. We predict that inequality will increase most dramatically if the revolution generates economic development (which directly increases inequality) and if the entire society was poor to begin with (since rich peasants exceed the mean sooner).

Since modern revolutions in poor societies (Mexico in 1910, Bolivia in 1952, for example) almost always promote economic development, we predict that they will eventually create more inequality than existed before the revolution unless governments make strenuous efforts to prevent it. The scattered evidence now available suggests that inequality does increase (Wolf 1956). In contrast, we predict that peasant revolutions in traditional societies in which urban areas remain much richer than the countryside and no economic development results will reduce inequality (Punjab in the late nineteenth century, for example).

SUMMARY

Hypothesis 1. A radical revolution cannot redistribute human capital and hence cannot entirely overturn the old stratification order, but instead leaves those with human capital better off than those without it, both in the short and in the long run.

Hypothesis 2. In the short run a radical revolution produces a more equal distribution of income and property in the society as a whole, but cannot entirely eliminate income inequality.

Hypothesis 3. In the short run a radical revolution causes a shift in the basis of stratification, making human capital more valuable relative to property as a source of income and occupational status.

Hypothesis 4. In both the short and the long run those who were exploited under the old regime are better off after a radical revolution, increasingly so as they come to utilize more fully their human capital, land, physical capital, and other resources.

Hypothesis 5. By allowing them to utilize more fully their human capital, land, physical capital, and other resources, radical revolutions set loose forces which in the long run cause economic inequality among previously exploited groups to increase steadily.

Hypothesis 6. In the long run, a radical revolution leads peasants and other previously exploited groups with little human capital to acquire more but it also causes inequality in the distribution of human capital among them to increase.

Hypothesis 7. In the society as a *whole*, inequality following a radical revolution will first decrease, then begin to increase again and eventually (a) stabilize at a level below its prerevolutionary value if the general population remains well off and there is little economic development among previously exploited groups but (b) continue to increase and perhaps in time exceed its prerevolutionary levels in poor societies in which there is substantial economic development among previously exploited groups.

The predictions about long-term effects (Hypotheses 1, 4, 5, 6, and 7) apply not only to radical political revolutions but with some qualifications to other fundamental social changes which reduce exploitation or increase economic opportunities for other reasons (for example, the end of feudalism, the growth of a market economy in nonmarket societies, the end of colonialism, the Green Revolution in agriculture, political changes that improve opportunities for minorities).[14] We will return to these questions in the concluding chapter.

REVOLUTION AND INHERITED PRIVILEGE

We have argued that a radical revolution will not lead to an equalitarian society but that differences in income will persist and even grow among the previously exploited population, that the new opportunities will be of most benefit to those who already had the training and resources to exploit them, and that the best jobs would go not to the poor and illiterate so much as to those with education, skills, and ability. It is a society with marked inequality, with people rewarded according to the value of their work, not according to their needs. But this inequality of outcome is not the same thing as inequality of opportunity. It might well be that people have an equal opportunity to compete for the good jobs, that all can enter the race on equal terms even though the rewards go only to the victors. But will the children of poor and illiterate peasants, the children of small craftsmen, of unskilled laborers, of sales clerks, miners, and factory workers have an equal chance to rise to the top? Or will positions at the top of society be monopolized by the children of lawyers, government bureaucrats, and managers of nationalized industries; by the children of civil engineers, draftsmen, and skilled machinists; by the children of prosperous farmers and the newly rich? Can a revolution eliminate inherited privilege?

Revolutionaries certainly believe that inherited privilege will end, and their opponents fear that it will. The rhetoric of revolution and reaction is replete with images of society turned upside down, of the elite brought down and the children of the masses elevated to be their equals or their masters; Marx and his successors thought that inherited privilege would end after a communist revolution and so did the Chinese revolutionaries. But good intentions do not necessarily change the world. We might well wonder whether radical revolutions can eliminate inherited privilege any more than they can eliminate income inequality. We now offer a theory about that. Let us begin by stating a little more precisely what we mean by inherited privilege.

DEFINITIONS

The basic idea of inherited privilege is simple enough: we want to know how much of an advantage a child born into a privileged home has compared with one born into a poor, illiterate family. To measure this we need to have some idea of what is a privileged home and what is not, and some way of describing the size of advantage that comes from being born into one kind of home rather than the other. Let us begin with privilege.

Status. The best single indication of where someone ranks in society, whether he or she is at the top or the bottom, among the elite or in the masses, is occupation: people are known by their work. Lawyers and doctors, clergymen and professors, chemists and engineers are at the top together with large landowners and big ranchers, government leaders and business executives, bankers and department heads, politicians, industrialists, and big businessmen. Below them come middle-size farmers, civil servants and secretaries, bookkeepers and office clerks, bank tellers and insurance agents, and those who own or manage small businesses. Lower yet come cashiers and file clerks, mail carriers and telephone operators, stock clerks and policemen, jewelers and master craftsmen, firefighters, hairdressers, and undertakers. Below them come carpenters and plumbers, semiskilled factory workers, bus drivers, and cannery workers. Lower yet are janitors and servants, waiters and bartenders, porters and dockworkers, and un-skilled factory workers. Next come small peasant farmers (by far the largest group in preindustrial societies). Finally, at the very bottom of the hierarchy are farm laborers, together with a scattering of loggers, fishermen, and hunters. This hierarchy is the same throughout the world, in preindustrial societies as well as in industrial ones, in socialist societies as well as in capitalist ones, in the past as well as the present (see the definitive work by Treiman 1977, and chapter 2 below).

A person's position in the hierarchy of jobs is centrally important to his or her life. Work confers prestige or denies it; deference is accorded to those in high ranking jobs and demanded of those in low ranking jobs; honor goes to those who fill the high positions in life. In part this is because high status jobs pay better than low status jobs. They pay better not just in capitalist societies but in all societies and throughout history—in tribal societies and in peasant societies; in Mycenaean Greece and dynastic Egypt; in fifteenth-century Florence, seventeenth-century England, eighteenth-century North America; and throughout the contemporary world. Furthermore, the correlation between status and income is high.[15] And income is desired throughout the world, not because people value the same goods but because money allocates scarce goods and everyone wants something that is scarce—housing, food, art, or temples to the gods. High status jobs are also valued because they involve complex and demanding tasks for which education and skill are required; the correlations are high and are found in every society yet studied.[16] This is, of course, one reason they are highly paid (Mincer 1974). Since complex tasks and those requiring education are more often cognitive than physical, they are likely to be nonmanual, clean, and physically undemanding; there is in fact clear evidence that these characteristics are all highly correlated in a variety of societies.[17] So a man's position in the occupational hierarchy reflects not only his position in the world of work but also his education, his income, his prestige, and many other things about his life. That is why occupational status is the central concept in studies of social mobility, and why revolution's effects on who does and does not obtain high status jobs is a primary issue, both theoretically and to the people themselves.[18]

Inherited Privilege.   Once we have decided to use occupational status as an indicator of a person's rank in society, it is natural to measure inherited privilege by the extent to which high status parents are able to get their children into high status jobs. Specifically, we want to know what status a child born into a family at the top of the status hierarchy can expect and what status a child born to a family at the bottom of the hierarchy can expect. The difference between the status of the first and the status of the second indicates the amount of inherited privilege. An illustration may make this clearer. Consider, for example, a son born into a lawyer's home at the top of the status hierarchy in the United States (his father would have 100 status points according to our way of measuring status where 100 is the top and 0 the bottom).[19] This lawyer's son could expect to get, on the average, a job about the level of a schoolteacher (70 status points). In contrast, a son born into a farm laborer's home (whose father would have 0 status points) could expect to get a job about the level of a semiskilled factory worker (30 status points). It is the difference between these two that indicates inherited privilege, the difference between an expectation of becoming something like a schoolteacher rather than a factory worker, 70 status points rather than 30. This is what we mean by inherited privilege.[20] The study of inherited privilege, defined in this or very similar ways, has become a central concern in sociology in recent decades.[21] It is closely related to the traditional concept of social mobility and, indeed, if for "great inherited privilege" you wish to read "little social mobility" (and vice versa) you will not go far wrong; to avoid confusion we will however avoid the older term.[22]

THE MODEL

To understand how revolution can be expected to affect status inheritance we begin by asking a simple but fundamental question: how are high-status parents able to confer advantages on their children, that is, how are they able to pass status on from one generation to the next? We argue that this comes about primarily because parents are able to give their children *scarce and valuable resources*, concrete and tangible advantages that help the children in the competition for desirable jobs and desirable spouses. These are of two main kinds: *human capital* (education, knowledge, skills in crafts, war, language, and the like) and *property* (wealth and income, land, family businesses, cattle, etc.); as a first approximation, we assume that other resources can reasonably be ignored.

We assume that high status jobs are on the average more desirable than low status ones so that workers would choose them if they could; that, to a reasonable approximation, all forms of property can be aggregated into a single composite (total market value); and that all forms of human capital can analogously be aggregated (into training time, or possibly costs of training; Mincer 1974). The crucial assumption is that workers compete for jobs on the basis of their property, their human capital, and various other things unrelated to their parents' status. A few workers are able to use their wealth to buy occupations (absentee landlords, *rentiers*), and many more are able to advantageously combine skills and wealth (by buying farms, prosperous businesses, or professional practices). Those with appropriate investments in human capital can perform complex jobs (blacksmith, clerk, army officer, lawyer) while those without it cannot do these jobs as well, if at all. Of course many other factors are important (motivation, appearance, intelligence, honesty) and there is a great deal of luck and confusion; we may for simplicity's sake think of these as being combined into a single omnibus "all other" factor. The job market is then very much like a marriage market with a simultaneous matching of workers and jobs; workers prefer the highest status jobs available while employers prefer to hire the most skilled workers (since they perform better) and owners prefer to sell to those who offer the highest price. The result is that workers with the most wealth, human capital, or other advantages get the best jobs. Workers with middling levels of capital and other advantages get middling status jobs since they cannot get better ones (because of competition from more advantaged workers) but need not take worse jobs. The least advantaged workers are left with the worst jobs. The result is that a worker's occupational status is some monotonically increasing function of his property, human capital, luck, and other advantages, each appropriately weighted. We assume that having either property or human capital always confers at least some small advantage. We also assume that in the short run the nature of the economy determines which jobs are available and, since that changes only slowly, that the supply of jobs is therefore fixed, at least to a reasonable approximation.

To understand how status is passed from one generation to the next, we need to know where a child gets his (or her) property, human capital, and other advantages.[23] Property, we argue, comes in part from gift, inheritance, or loan from his parents and through loans on the surety of his parents' wealth or good name. In addition to land or capital from one's parents, a child may acquire it from his own efforts, inherit it from distant relatives, borrow it from banks, partners, or friends, or acquire it in diverse other ways. We assume that having wealthy parents is always an advantage and that having educated parents is either advantageous or irrelevant.

A child's human capital depends on his parents' wealth since they can use it to pay school fees, hire tutors, buy books, and the like. Perhaps more important, prosperous parents can more easily afford to forego the income the child would otherwise contribute to the household by quitting school and going to work. This can be an important consideration in circumstances where young children's labor is valuable (as on farms), for very poor families where even a small increase in income is important, and in any society where children live at home and contribute to the family budget after they finish schooling (as in many socialist societies). Crucially, a child's human capital depends on his parents' human capital; throughout the world well-educated parents are able to get their children more schooling by teaching them linguistic and academic skills, by motivation, example, and encouragement, and by other familiar means (in socialist societies, Dobson 1977; Lane 1971; Lipset and Dobson 1973; in capitalist societies, Treiman and Terrell 1975*a*; Kelley 1978). And of course a variety of other factors unrelated to family background are also important. We assume that there is always some educational advantage in having wealthy or well-educated parents.

With these assumptions, we can derive an approximate expression for the amount of inherited privilege. The argument (which is stated formally in Appendix 1) turns essentially on the size of the advantages in property and human capital that a child can expect from his or her parents. Other things being equal, if some parents are very rich and others very poor, then there is a large advantage to being born into a rich home or, conversely, a large disadvantage to being born into a poor home. So the child of rich parents will acquire substantially more property and human capital to use in the competition for high status jobs whereas the child of a poor family will acquire little. That will give the child of the rich family a substantial advantage, one that will weigh heavily in the outcome. If, however, prosperous parents are only a little richer than poor ones, that is, if inequality of income is modest, then the advantage of being born in the rich home will be smaller since the difference between what a child gets from his rich parents and what another child gets from his poor parents is smaller. This smaller difference in their inherited advantage is then more easily overshadowed by luck, intelligence, motivation, or other factors more or less unrelated to family background, and the link between family background and the child's own status is therefore weaker.

The same argument applies to human capital. If, on one hand, many parents have university degrees while others are illiterate, that is, if inequality in human capital is great, then the advantage of being born into the well-educated home is great and the disadvantage of being born into the poorly educated home grave. If, on the other hand, differences in human capital are modest—if, for example, university graduates are rare and farmers have mostly finished primary or even secondary school—then the advantage of being born into the educational elite is smaller and more easily overshadowed by intelligence, luck, motivation, and other things not closely related to family background. So when there is less inequality in the distribution of human capital, there will be less of a link between family background and occupational status, and when there is greater inequality there will be more inherited privilege.

There is considerable evidence for this theory in other contexts (Kelley 1971; Kelley, Robinson, and Klein 1980; Kelley, Treiman, et al. 1980) but here we are concerned only with its implications for revolution.

IMPLICATIONS

The crucial result for present purposes is that the amount of status inheritance depends on inequality in the distribution of both property and human capital and hence that the changes in inequality created by a radical revolution are mirrored by changes in status inheritance. Let us look at what this implies about revolution's effects on status inheritance.

Short-Run Effects.   Because a radical revolution leads to the redistribution of wealth, we predict that it leads to less inheritance of status—more social mobility—for those who came of age just after the revolution. Since many prerevolutionary elite parents lose their wealth, they have less of an advantage to pass on to their children, whereas some poor parents gain new resources and have more to give theirs. So on the average there is less variation in the wealth different parents have to pass on to their children and hence less status inheritance.

But status inheritance will not disappear. Some economic inequalities will remain after even the most dedicated and efficient attempts at redistribution. But more crucially, human capital remains; education, literacy, technical and linguistic skills, and the like retain or even increase their value and cannot be redistributed. The old elite and others who were better off before the revolution have more of these resources and are able to pass some of their skills on to their children. So an effective means of transmitting status from one generation to the next remains; in the short run a revolution will reduce status inheritance but not eliminate it.[24] It does, however, lead to a shift in the basic pattern of status inheritance with property becoming relatively less important and human capital relatively more important in transmitting privilege from one generation to the next. In this sense revolution leads in the short run to a more modern pattern of status inheritance, shifting away from the great inequality and emphasis on property which is more characteristic of less developed societies toward the lesser inequality and emphasis on human capital more characteristic of advanced societies (Kelley 1978; Kelley, Robinson, and Klein 1980).

Long-Term Effects. In the long run status inheritance among previously exploited groups will, we argue, begin to increase again from its revolutionary low. The reason for this is that revolution sets loose forces that, as we have seen, cause economic inequality among peasants and other previously exploited groups to begin to grow from its revolutionary low. Since fortunate peasants will have increasingly large advantages to pass on to their children, we predict that revolution will in the long run lead also to steadily increasing status inheritance among them. Educational changes also increase status inheritance both indirectly (because they lead to more economic inequality) and directly. We argued that educational inequality would in the long run increase among poor peasants, that the gap between well and poorly educated peasants would increase. It therefore becomes more of an advantage to be born into a well-educated family. The same reasoning applies to those economic revolutions and social changes that reduce exploitation, and in fact there is evidence that they increase status inheritance (for example, among American blacks following the civil rights changes in the late 1960s, Featherman and Hauser 1976).

Status inheritance in the society as a whole will, we argue, follow the pattern we described earlier for inequality in the society as a whole. It will first drop following the revolution since inequality in property declines but then begin to rise once again from its revolutionary low as inequality reemerges. Depending on what happens to inequality (specified in Hypothesis 7), status inheritance may or may not eventually rise above its prerevolutionary levels.

Government Intervention. A revolutionary government can, and often will, try to restrain the reemergence of inherited privilege. But it will be remarkably difficult, since it must first control the inequality that arises from the property of small farmers, small businessmen, skilled workers, and other diverse, numerous, and often powerful groups far removed from the commanding heights of the economy. But even that is not enough since government cannot effectively prevent human capital from being passed from one generation to the next without draconian changes in the family. The knowledge, values, culture, and language skills acquired in elite homes give their children an enormous and enduring advantage in socialist as well as capitalist societies (Anderson 1976; Duncan, Featherman, and Duncan 1972: chaps. 3, 5, 6; Lane 1971: chap. 5; Dobson 1977); selective admissions policies for higher education and government can somewhat reduce the advantage but not eliminate it, save at enormous cost. Thus a revolution that is able to abolish private property will slow the long-term growth of inequality and status inheritance but will not prevent it.

SUMMARY

Hypothesis 8. Because a radical revolution redistributes property but cannot redistribute human capital, in the short run it reduces the advantage of being born into a family with property but not the advantage of being born into a family with human capital, so reducing status inheritance in the society as a whole, but not eliminating it.

Hypothesis 9. By creating greater inequality in property and human capital, in the long run a radical revolution causes status inheritance among previously exploited groups to increase steadily and eventually exceed its prerevolutionary level.

Hypothesis 10. In the society as a *whole*, status inheritance following a radical revolution will first decrease, then begin to increase again and eventually (a) stabilize at a level below its prerevolutionary value if the general population remains well off and there is little economic development among previously exploited groups but (b) continue to increase and perhaps in time exceed its prerevolutionary levels in poor societies in which there is substantial economic development among previously exploited groups.

The predictions about long-term effects (Hypothesis 9 and the latter part of 10) apply not only to radical revolutions but also to any social changes that reduce exploitation or increase economic opportunities for other reasons, just as (and for the same reasons) the predictions about long-term changes in inequality applied to these groups.

This completes the verbal presentation of our theory. We have tried to lay things out as carefully as we could but have inevitably had to assert some conclusions more on the grounds of plausibility than proof. Some readers may reasonably wish to have the underlying model developed more rigorously and completely and that is what we attempt to do in Appendix 1. In the final section, we present some results from a computer simulation of the model, which has the virtue of putting some flesh on the bare mathematical bones and giving a simple, visually clear summary of some of the main predictions.

A COMPUTER SIMULATION OF THE MODEL

In working out the logic underlying our argument, we have taken two somewhat different approaches. The first is a mathematical model. It lays out a simplified version of the underlying model with some precision and has the virtue that the theoretical conclusions in Hypotheses 1 to 10 can be shown to follow logically from a simple and relatively straightforward model. This is particularly useful for the arguments about status inheritance since this lends itself to a straightforward formal exposition that captures the main features of the argument in a tractable form. The results on inequality are not as satisfactory. The model we have developed is mathematically straightforward and expresses some of the main features of the argument but it does so at the cost of a great simplification. This is particularly noticeable in modeling the taxes a prerevolutionary elite was able to extract from the bulk of the population. This is crucial, since many of the consequences of the revolution flow from the lifting of this burden. The difficulty is not in figuring out what the taxes were like, but in finding a way to describe them mathematically which is simple enough to be tractable but complex enough to do justice to reality. We have not had much success in that and have resorted instead to a different strategy: computer simulation.

The advantage of computer simulation is that it is relatively easy to express quite complex theories. What one does, in essence, is to model from the bottom up, beginning with elementary processes such as earnings, savings, death, and taxes. Then the results for the model as a whole are built up from the interaction of all the component processes; for example, an income distribution can be built from the details of earnings, savings, death, and taxes. That is very nice. But with this power come costs, two of which are particularly troubling. The first is that the model becomes so complex it is hard to see what is happening. We have tried to minimize this difficulty by keeping the model simple and by introducing the various elements of the model in stepwise fashion, a few at a time, so that the effect of each can be seen in turn. The second major difficulty is in reaching general conclusions of the sort we have set forth in our hypotheses. We can show that, for a particular set of initial assumptions and parameters, the conclusions follow. But the very complexity that gives the simulation its ability to mimic reality stems in part from its large number of parameters and initial assumptions, far too many to investigate exhaustively. We have attempted to minimize this difficulty by running our model for a very wide range of initial values, only a few of which are presented in text; more are given in Appendix 1, section 3. All of the many dozen simulations we have run seem to produce much the same results, but some uncertainty necessarily remains.

In the following sections, we will first describe the logic of our computer simulation and then show the conclusions implied by the model, showing in this way that our argument does indeed lead to the predictions embodied in our hypotheses about inequality. According to our theory, revolution's effects on inherited privilege follow directly from its effects on inequality and so the particular pattern of changes we will see in the simulation of inequality will follow for inherited privilege as well. Since the logic is, we hope, reasonably clear we have decided to leave the mathematical derivations out of the text, presenting them instead in Appendix 1, section 2.

THE MODEL

The Population. The simulation is based on a hypothetical population with four distinct classes: a small elite to represent the prerevolutionary landowning elite; a larger class to represent the non-agricultural middle and working-class population of small merchants, clerical and sales workers, craftsmen, and small town workers; a small population of prosperous "big" peasant farmers with good sized land-holdings; and finally a large group of poor, small peasant farmers. Of course in the real world there are many more distinctions but this simple four class system should suffice to capture the main outline of the matter. We ignore differences within classes except those that arise from accumulation of property over the life cycle. The effect of this is to ignore differences based on ability, luck, motivation, and the like. These differences are large but not especially important for the questions at hand.

The number of people in each class can vary but our baseline model has a population that is 4 percent elite, 40 percent in the combined nonagricultural middle and working classes, 10 percent prosperous big peasants, and 46 percent poor peasants. These figures are chosen to give a fairly small elite (and, as we will see, a wealthy elite), because that seems typical of prerevolutionary societies. The nonagricultural middle and working class is about the size typical of preindustrial societies (see figure 3.1 below or Kuznets 1966: 404).

Demography. We assume that people in all classes have a thirty-year working life (say, from age twenty to fifty) after which they die or retire. We assume that each is immediately replaced by another person of the same class (for example, an old peasant is replaced by a young one). The replacement has the same working capital as the man he replaces (who might be his father), but the additional savings the older man accumulated over his lifetime are, we assume, used to pay for his retirement, wife, funeral, and the like and not passed on to his successor. The effect of this assumption is that inequality in the society reaches a stable state rather than growing without limit over the years.

Property and Human Capital. We assume that people in different classes are endowed with different amounts of property and human capital. The peasants have mainly land, the middle and working classes have both property and human capital, and the elite have both as well (and also rights to tax the rest of the population, which we treat separately). We assume that people earn something from their investments in property or human capital, how much varying from one simulation to another but usually 10 percent. This is roughly the usual figure for preindustrial societies (Kuznets 1966: 420–423). Following the logic of human capital theory, we generally assume that the same rate of return applies to property and to human capital (Becker 1964; Mincer 1974), except during the revolutionary period when the returns to property are more vulnerable to revolutionary change.

The amount of property and human capital that different classes have, and hence the income they receive from them, varies from model to model. In our baseline model, we assume that everyone, elite and peasant alike, works full time and earns from that, as the unskilled labor component of their income, just barely enough to survive. In effect, we model a society so poor that an unskilled laborer without any land, human capital, or savings would have an income just on the margin of subsistence—a common, if lamentable, situation in poor agrarian societies. We assume that poor peasants have enough land to raise their incomes 20 percent above subsistence and that big peasants have land enough to give them incomes twice the subsistence level plus enough human capital (which would be mostly knowledge and skills rather than formal education) to raise their incomes a further 20 percent above subsistence. The nonagricultural middle and working class in our baseline model has enough property and human capital to raise their total incomes to twice the subsistence level. For the elite, we assume that they have human capital (which will be immune to revolution) enough to give them incomes twice the subsistence level. We treat their property in two parts, a smaller personal component which they are able to keep through the revolution (this models the land that elites are often able to keep for their own use even after land reform as well as the property they are able to successfully hide), and a larger component they lose in the revolution. In the baseline model, the personal component is enough to give them incomes twice the subsistence level. We will describe the second component in a moment, under the heading of taxes.

Savings and Investment over the Life Cycle. We assume that people invest a substantial proportion of the income they have above the subsistence level, and receive a monetary return (10 percent in the baseline model) on past savings. This models not only the accumulation of savings, pensions, rental property, and the like, but also investments in land, equipment, and skills—the kind of investments that underlie the well-known tendency for incomes to rise with age, particularly for those who initially have property or human capital. By making the savings a proportion of income above the subsistence level, we in effect assume that poor peasants save and invest little (since they have little income above subsistence) while big peasants and the nonagricultural middle class invest more, and the elite most of all. In the baseline model, these savings are 30 percent of income above the subsistence level, after taxes; that produces a savings rate of roughly 15 percent for the society as a whole, which seems to be about the usual order of magnitude for preindustrial societies.[25]

Exploitation. We assume that the elite is able to expropriate some part of the earnings of the rest of the population, that they are able to tax the rest of the population and keep the proceeds for themselves. In effect, we treat the prerevolutionary elite as an exploitative government. One effect of the revolution is to end this exploitation. There are other ways of modeling but in practice they would come to much the same thing. We might, for example, have viewed the elite as owning the land and getting their returns by letting peasants work it for, say, a certain fee. But whether you call it a fee or a tax it comes to the same thing: a transfer of money from peasants to the elite. In the one case we would say legalistically that the peasants "own" the land (but are subject to heavy taxes on it) while in the other they do not own the land but use it (subject to heavy fees); it amounts to much the same thing in different words.

A crucial question is how heavy the taxes are (for that largely determines how rich the elite is) and how much different members of the exploited population pay (for that has much to do with how the revolution will affect income among them). To begin with, we assume that the elite must leave the rest of the population enough to live on at a bare subsistence level. If taxes go above that level in the long run, the exploited population will rebel, flee, or die. In the normal run of things, we can assume that the exploited population lives at or above the subsistence level. Note that this assumption, although obvious and compelling, is not innocent for it means that taxes are almost always *progressive* in the sense of taking a higher percent of the income of the middle class and big peasants than of poor peasants.[26] There is no way to take very much from a peasant on the margin of subsistence; there simply is not anything there to take. It is the more prosperous peasants and the nonagricultural middle and working classes who have a surplus over subsistence that can be taxed. So if taxes come to some flat proportion of income above subsistence, they will take a much higher percent of the income of big peasants and the more prosperous segments of the middle and working classes. In our baseline model we assume just such a flat percentage tax, set at 50 percent. With the other assumptions this amounts to a tax of 11 percent on a typical, mid-career poor peasant's income, 25 percent of a big peasant's income, and 27 percent of a nonagricultural middle or working-class income. The elite pay no taxes but receive, and divide equally among themselves, all the taxes collected from the rest of society. The amount the elite receive will vary noticeably from model to model, being more when the exploited population is large and prosperous or the elite small, and less when the exploited population is poor and small, or the elite large. In our baseline model the elite gets an income over ten times the subsistence level from these taxes. Counting all sources of income and tax, a typical elite member at mid-career would have an income eighteen times that of a poor peasant and over eight times that for the simulated society as a whole. These are typical figures for preindustrial societies (Kuznets 1966: 423–426).

Establishing the Baseline. We establish our prerevolutionary baseline by simulating a society subject to the assumptions just described. We begin with an initial population divided into the four classes in appropriate proportions, divided up equally over the thirty years of the working lifetime, with the resources of property and human capital we have described. We then simulate a single year, which gives everyone a year's savings and the elite a year's receipts from their exploitation of the rest of society. We then simulate another year, like the first except that people now have incomes from savings as well as other resources, and then another and yet another, until we have simulated a generation, thirty years in all. At that point the society is stable in the sense that the average levels of income, wealth, and inequality remain the same from year to year even though people continue to be born and to die. That is our prerevolutionary baseline. We treat the simulated population just as we would treat survey data from people in a real society. Thus income inequality, for example, is simply measured by the standard deviation of income for our simulated population.

We simulate a revolution by changing the rules of the game in this stable society and observing the effects. We will make these changes a few at a time so we can observe the consequences of each of a revolution's many aspects. We begin with the most fundamental one.

REDISTRIBUTION AND THE END OF EXPLOITATION

One of the defining characteristics of a radical revolution is that it redistributes income, land, and wealth, taking from the old rich and giving to the poor; it ends the traditional exploitation of the prerevolutionary elite. We model this straightforwardly, by eliminating the taxes the old elite was able to extract from the rest of the population. This mimics the elimination of all forms of economic exploitation at the very beginning of a revolution—land reform, the end of traditional privileges and taxation, the end of all the economic advantages that flow from political power, and the like. Of course in reality these reforms will be spread over several years but for simplicity, we introduce them simultaneously at the beginning of the revolution. As we model it, the new revolutionary society is born full fledged at year 1.

Effects on Income. According to our theory, the end of exploitation has profound effects. The first change, obvious but important, is that peasants and the rest of the previously exploited are much better off after the revolution, their incomes rising by the amount they had previously been taxed. Just how large the rise is of course depends on how heavy the taxes were before. By way of illustration, in our baseline model their incomes rise by about a quarter immediately following the end of exploitation. Then in the generation following the revolution their incomes rise slowly but steadily as they accumulate savings and investments, and eventually stabilize at a level about 40 percent higher than in prerevolutionary times.

Inequality in the Society as a Whole.   What peasants and the rest of the exploited gain the elite loses. Hence inequality in the society as a whole, the gap between rich and poor, declines immediately after exploitation is ended. This is, of course, what radical revolutions are all about. How sharp these changes are depends on how exploitive the society was to begin with, how rich or poor, and other things (which we take up later). But by way of illustration, let us look at the effects in our baseline model. In that model, inequality drops by roughly half in the first year after the revolution (see C in fig. 1.1). Inequality then continues to decline after the revolution, as the previously exploited population invest some of their newly found income and in time reap the benefits of these investments, and as the older members of the traditional elite die or retire, dissipating the wealth hoarded over a lifetime of exploitation. It takes a generation for these effects to work their way through the population. After that the revolutionary society stabilizes, with inequality remaining at about a quarter of its prerevolutionary level in our baseline model.

Inequality among the Previously Exploited.   But ending exploitation has another effect, one not quite so expected: it *increases* inequality among peasants and the rest of the previously exploited population, that is to say, it increases inequality among the great majority of the society. This is shown as A in figure 1.1. In our baseline model, inequality among the previously exploited grows (from its previously low level, of course) by about half in the first year of the revolution and then increases steadily thereafter as the previously exploited gradually accumulate additional savings and investments from their new income.[27] Inequality continues to grow for a generation after the revolution, eventually stabilizing at roughly twice its previous level.

This increase comes about not only when inequality is measured by the standard deviation, our preferred definition, but also when it is measured by the traditional Gini coefficient (B in fig. 1.1). Here and elsewhere, we will see that inequality measured in these two ways follows very much the same patterns so that much the same conclusions would follow no matter which definition of inequality is used.[28] In general, changes in the Gini coefficient are smaller with, for example, revolution reducing inequality in the society as a whole by less in Gini

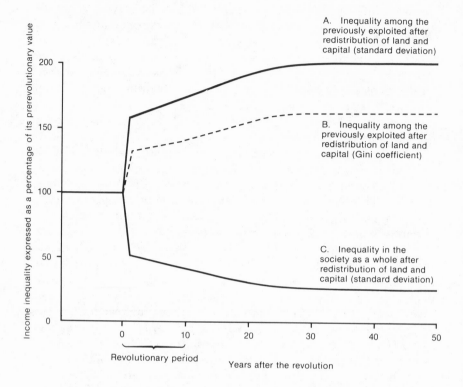

Figure 1.1   Predicted effects of redistribution and the end of exploitation on inequality. Inequality among the previously exploited is measured alternatively by (A) the standard deviation of income or (B) the Gini coefficient. Inequality in the society as a whole (C) is measured by the standard deviation. *Source*: Computer simulation described in the text.

terms but also increasing inequality among the previously exploited less in these terms than with the standard deviation.

According to our model, this increase in inequality among the previously exploited population comes about for several reasons. First, the end of exploitation leads to an across-the-board increase in income for the previously exploited population but by the same token, to an equivalent increase in differences among them. For example, if a big peasant earned a thousand dollars more than a poor peasant in prerevolutionary times, he was not a thousand dollars richer because a large part of that thousand went in taxes to the elite; he could not invest a thousand dollars in a tractor or in schooling for his children, but only a fraction of that. But after the revolution, he has the full thousand, and he can invest in a full thousand dollars worth of tractor or education. In that simple and important way inequality among peasants is directly increased by the elimination of exploitation.[29]

Second, the end of exploitation was of greater benefit to big peasants and to the more educated and prosperous members of the previously exploited population generally. Because of their human capital and property, they had more income above the subsistence level and paid more in taxes to the old elite. Hence big peasants and the nonagricultural middle and working classes gain more than poor peasants, while the old (with a lifetime of accumulation behind them) gain more than the young from the end of exploitation. This further increases inequality.[30] Indeed it seems likely that our model underestimates the rise in inequality that comes about in this way because it posits that prerevolutionary taxes were a constant proportion of income above subsistence while in reality the taxes were more often graduated, extracting a higher percentage of large incomes than of small. They were graduated for much the same reasons that taxes in modern societies are often graduated: the diminishing marginal utility of money. Peasants just at the margin of subsistence will be desperate to avoid taxes since each dollar means a great deal to them.[31] But peasants well above subsistence will not be as desperate since their more urgent needs are already satisfied and taxes are coming out of their (modest) luxuries rather than out of their necessities. So the old elite would have found it easier (not to mention safer, since the threat of peasant revolt was rarely far away) to tax prosperous peasants much more heavily than poor ones. And that is what they seem generally to have done (for example, Wright 1966:50–51).[32] As a consequence, the end of exploitation will almost always be of more benefit to the already more prosperous segments of the exploited population than to the poorest, and hence increases inequality between them.

A third reason that the end of exploitation increases inequality among the previously exploited population is that it makes more money available for savings and investment. As incomes rise well above subsistence, there is more opportunity to save and invest in the future. But the benefits of this will go mainly to the more prosperous peasants and the more educated and prosperous elements of the nonagricultural middle and working classes, and more to the old rather than the young, and hence will increase inequality.

In short, our theory implies that radical revolutions increase inequality among the previously exploited population as a direct consequence of their simplest and most fundamental characteristic: redistribution of land, wealth, and income from the old elite to the poor. Inequality increases as a consequence of redistribution alone, quite apart from the effects of any other changes revolution brings in its train. Thus, the growth of inequality among the previously exploited is, we believe, a fundamental feature of radical revolutions (Hypothesis 5). But that is not the only feature of revolution that leads to changes in inequality and we now turn to the others.

DISRUPTION AND DESTRUCTION

Radical revolutions typically destroy or disperse much of the wealth accumulated in the old society. They do this in a variety of ways, from outright destruction of the old elite's property (not to mention the old elite itself), to the more pervasive dissipation of savings, pensions, and investments through inflation and expropriation. In the course of changing the old society, they also disrupt it, leading to confusion, disorganization, and disturbances that lower productivity, disrupt the market, paralyze the financial system, and generally reduce earnings, especially in commercial agriculture, manufacturing, and commerce. This in effect reduces the returns to investments in land and physical capital. We model these changes in two ways. First, we assume that the value of accumulated savings, pensions, and investments declines in the revolutionary period, in our baseline model by 10 percent a year. Inflation alone could do this and outright expropriation (for example, repudiation of the old government's bonds or the expropriation of rental property) would have similar effects.[33] We assume that this loss continues throughout the revolutionary period, say for a decade fol-lowing the revolution, before stability returns in the postrevolutionary era. This reduces the value of prerevolutionary savings and the like by roughly two-thirds over the course of the revolutionary period; a modest figure by the standards of some revolutions (the Bolivian among them). The second way we simulate disruption is to reduce the returns to land, physical capital, and other kinds of property on the argument that merchants and big peasants, for example, would get less of a return on their property in the midst of the disturbances of revolution. In our model, we reduce these returns to half what they were before the revolution and return them to their original level after the revolutionary period ends a decade later.

Short-Run Effects.   Our model implies that income drops in the revolutionary period, because of the losses entailed by the destruction and disruption. For the society as a whole, the amount of the decline depends on the amount of savings and investments lost and the extent that the disruption lowers the returns to property. For peasants and the rest of the previously exploited population, the effects depend both on these losses and on the offsetting gains from the end of exploitation; in our baseline model they lose something less than 10 percent of their income in all (see B in fig. 1.2). The general pattern seems to be that poor peasants lose less than they gained from redistribution, since their savings and investments were small, while big peasants and the more prosperous of the nonagricultural middle classes lose more than they gain, since they had more savings and property. The net effect is a substantial reduction in inequality among the previously exploited population in the revolutionary period. In our baseline model this

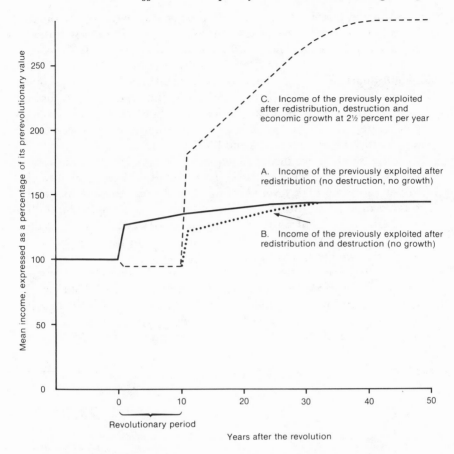

Figure 1.2   Predicted effects of redistribution, destruction, and the emergence of new opportunities on the income of previously exploited groups. Mean income of the previously exploited after (A) a revolution that redistributes property and so ends exploitation but does nothing else; or (B) a revolution that redistributes but in addition destroys some property and disrupts production in the postrevolutionary period; or (C) a revolution that redistributes, destroys, and in addition leads to economic growth beginning a decade after the revolution. *Source*: Computer simulations described in the text.

amounts to roughly a 30 percent reduction (A in fig. 1.3). But inequality never disappears, as differences in human capital, and to a lesser extent in property, remain. So if the model is correct, the destruction and disruption accompanying revolution seem to account for a short-run decline, but not disappearance, of inequality.

Long-Run Effects.   After the revolutionary period, we assume that things return to normal—that the disruption and confusion accompanying the reorganization of society have run their course, and that it is once again possible to save, build up pensions, invest, and so on. At that point the dynamics of postrevolutionary society are precisely those we have already seen. The only difference is that the society starts at a rather lower beginning point economically, because of the losses of the revolutionary period, but that matters not at all in the long run. Income among the previously exploited population increases abruptly just at the end of the revolutionary period and then more gradually for another generation, but in the end it returns to where it was because of the redistribution (compare A and B in fig. 1.2).

At the same time, income inequality rises swiftly, for the same reasons it rose following redistribution, and after a generation stabilizes at the same high level (A in fig. 1.3). In our baseline model, it roughly doubles in the end. And measuring inequality by the traditional Gini coefficient rather than the standard deviation leads to the same pattern: a short-term drop in inequality in the revolutionary period followed by a larger long-term increase (B in fig. 1.3).

Thus two of the basic features of radical revolutions—the ending of exploitation and the destruction and disruption of the revolutionary period—lead to what we believe is a characteristic pattern of changes in inequality among the previously exploited population. Inequality first drops because of the destruction and disruption but never vanishes

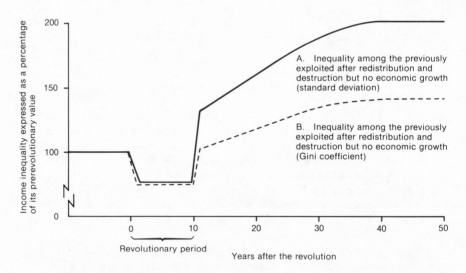

Figure 1.3   Predicted effects of redistribution and destruction on inequality among previously exploited groups. Income inequality following a revolution that redistributes property and so ends exploitation (as in fig. 1.1) but in addition destroys some property and disrupts production in the postrevolutionary period. Inequality is measured alternatively by (A) the standard deviation of income or (B) the Gini coefficient. *Source*: Computer simulation described in the text.

(Hypothesis 2). Then it grows apace as peasants and the rest of the previously exploited population are able to retain for themselves the fruits of their labor, land, and human capital (Hypothesis 5). But there are yet further changes introduced by revolution, changes that amplify this trend.

New Opportunities and Economic Growth

In the long run, revolution provides, we believe, a variety of new opportunities. By ending the old elite's monopolies, by destroying the rigidities and institutionalized inefficiencies of the old society, by opening up new markets for commercial agriculture, by freeing transportation and commerce from traditional constraints, and as a result of deliberate government policy, a radical revolution usually opens up new opportunities for previously exploited groups. These new opportunities allow them to make fuller use of their human capital, property and other resources and we model them by increasing the returns to human capital, property, and unskilled labor in the postrevolutionary period, leaving the rest of the model unchanged.[34]

These new opportunities have great consequences. Suppose, for example, there was sufficient economic growth to double the gross national product in the generation following the revolution. That would be a marked improvement and enormously important to the people in the society, but by no means an exceptional growth rate as these things go, amounting to a little less than 2½ percent a year for the first thirty years of the postrevolutionary period. In our baseline model, it corresponds to an increase of about half in the returns to human capital, property, and unskilled labor.[35] Let us simulate this change by the rough but simple expedient of increasing the returns by half at the beginning of the postrevolutionary period. This almost triples the income of peasants and the rest of the previously exploited (C in fig. 1.2). But it also dramatically increases inequality. In the first postrevolutionary generation, inequality among the previously exploited population rises, eventually reaching a level over four times as high as it was before the revolution (A in fig. 1.4). If economic growth is more rapid, inequality in our model grows more rapidly as well. For example, if the society increases its income by some four times in the postrevolutionary generation, a growth rate of a shade under 5 percent per year and enough to raise a typical preindustrial society's living standards to roughly half those attained in industrial societies (Kuznets 1966:chap. 7), income inequality would increase to roughly ten times its prerevolutionary level. Conversely, where economic growth is slow, income inequality grows much more slowly as well. For example, if the economy grows only by a third in the postrevolutionary generation, a growth rate of about 1 percent per year, income inequal-

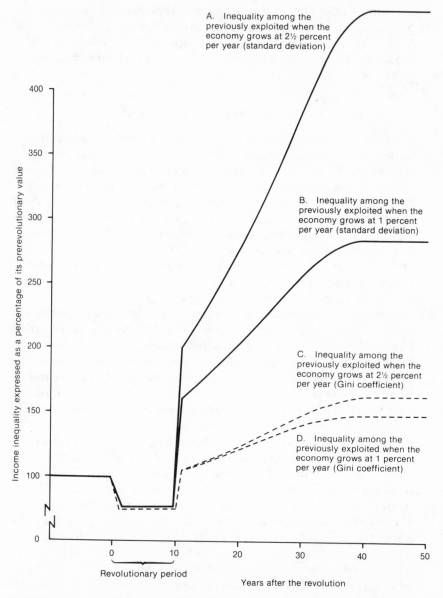

Figure 1.4   Predicted effects of new opportunities and economic growth on inequality among previously exploited groups. Income inequality following a revolution that redistributes property and so ends exploitation, destroys property and disrupts production in the postrevolutionary period (as in fig. 1.3), and in addition leads to economic growth beginning a decade after the revolution. Economic growth is assumed to be alternatively at 2½ percent a year or at 1 percent a year, and income inequality is measured alternatively by the standard deviation of income or the Gini coefficient. *Source*: Computer simulations described in the text.

ity among the previously exploited population would almost triple (B in fig. 1.4). And, as we have seen, if there is no economic growth our theory implies only a doubling of income inequality among the previously exploited (A in fig. 1.3). Measuring inequality by the Gini coefficient leads to similar conclusions except that the changes in these terms are, as usual, much more muted (C and D in fig. 1.4). In short, our theory implies that rapid economic development leads to rapid growth in income inequality among the previously exploited.

COMMUNIST REVOLUTIONS

In the models we have considered so far, some of the inequality that appears after a revolution comes from the property of big peasants and the nonagricultural middle and working classes and one might well wonder what happens if a revolutionary government expropriates even this modest capital. We argued earlier that doing so would be difficult. But it can be done, and a number of communist revolutions have done so, so it is worth looking at what this implies according to our theory.

We modeled a communist revolution of this sort simply by eliminating all property in the revolutionary and postrevolutionary periods. We assume that economic growth follows the revolution at the rate of about 2.5 percent per year, which is probably low for the USSR and many other communist societies. A higher rate would, as we have just seen, imply a more rapid growth of inequality. For the rest of the model, we use our standard baseline assumptions; the model is thus identical to model A in figure 1.4 except that private property is abolished.

This model implies that inequality among the previously exploited population will grow steadily even after a revolution of this kind, one that entirely eliminates private property (see A in fig. 1.5). The pattern is in fact just like that seen in earlier models except that the changes are slower and the final level of inequality lower. But inequality is still higher than in prerevolutionary times, about 70 percent higher in the model we are considering. The culprit is, of course, human capital. Even a communist revolution cannot redistribute human capital and it creates inequality. Thus, even communist revolutions lead, we believe, to the rebirth of inequality.

INEQUALITY IN THE SOCIETY AS A WHOLE

So far we have argued that a radical revolution, by its very nature, inevitably leads to growing inequality among the previously exploited. But that does not imply, nor is it in general true, that inequality grows in the society as a whole. Indeed, on one hand, we have already seen

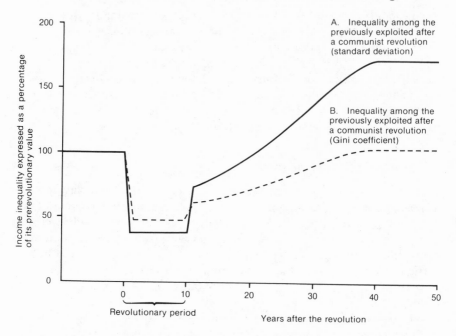

Figure 1.5   Predicted effect of a communist revolution on inequality among previously exploited groups. Income inequality following a revolution that redistributes property and so ends exploitation, destroys property and disrupts production in the postrevolutionary period, leads to economic growth at 2½ percent per year beginning a decade after the revolution (as in A and C of fig. 1.4), and in addition eliminates all private property throughout the revolutionary and postrevolutionary periods. Income inequality is measured alternatively by the standard deviation of income and the Gini coefficient. *Source*: Computer simulation described in the text.

that the effect of redistribution is to decrease inequality for the society as a whole (C in fig. 1.1); on the other hand, economic growth will increase inequality in the society as a whole just as it did among the previously exploited. It is not, therefore, obvious whether the forces tending to increase inequality will be stronger or weaker than those tending to decrease it. But there is a further complication as well: the level of inequality in the society as a whole depends heavily on what happens to the elite and to the urban industrial work force, if there is one. What happens to them depends on forces beyond the scope of our theory, for reasons set out earlier. But let us at least consider the consequences of some of the obvious possibilities, concentrating on the elite, since many preindustrial societies have no urban industrial labor force large enough to worry about.

A New Elite?   It is by no means obvious whether a new elite emerges after a radical revolution. The ideology of most revolutionary parties is against it, but the links between ideology and reality are sometimes tenuous. And there are strong theoretical reasons for thinking that a new elite will emerge (Djilas 1957; Dahrendorf 1959). So let us envision three possibilities. First, a new elite might emerge which was as exploitative as the old elite. Some revolutions that lead eventually to moderate socialist or to state capitalist regimes might be used as an example, as well as more than a few recent anticolonial revolutions. Second, let us envision a new elite only half as exploitative as the old. Some of the communist elites of Eastern Europe might serve as illustrations, at least on some accounts of the privileges of rank in them. Finally, let us envision a society where there is no new elite at all, an unlikely possibility. China during the Cultural Revolution period might be an example, although even that is far from clear. We model such societies by a straightforward extension of our baseline model (that of fig. 1.4) in the variant with economic growth at 2½ percent a year in the postrevolutionary generation.

In all of these simulations, inequality in the society as a whole follows the same general pattern: a sharp drop just after the revolution, with inequality remaining low throughout the revolutionary period, followed by a sharp increase in the first years of the postrevolutionary period and then a slow, steady increase for a generation thereafter before stability is reached once again (A, B, and C, fig. 1.6). Whether inequality in the end is higher or lower than before the revolution depends crucially on the new elite. If it is very exploitative the society may stabilize with two or three times as much inequality as before (A in fig. 1.6) and if the new elite takes little or nothing for itself, inequality will be less than before (although still much greater than in the revolutionary period or at the beginning of the postrevolutionary period (see B and C, fig. 1.6). The nature of the new elite is thus crucial to the final level of inequality reached, although not to the basic pattern of revolutionary decline and postrevolutionary growth in inequality.

Economic Growth and Other Considerations.   Economic growth also matters a great deal in determining the level of inequality in postrevolutionary society. If economic growth is rapid, especially in a society where the nonagricultural middle and working classes were not especially prosperous to begin with, then inequality in the society as a whole can grow rapidly and stabilize at a level far above that in prerevolutionary times (see A in fig. 1.7).[36] If economic growth is slow, however, especially when the peasantry was much poorer than the nonagricultural classes to begin with, then inequality in the society as a whole will grow only slowly and stabilize at a level well below that in prerevolutionary society (B in fig. 1.7).[37] These are the claims underlying Hypothesis 7.

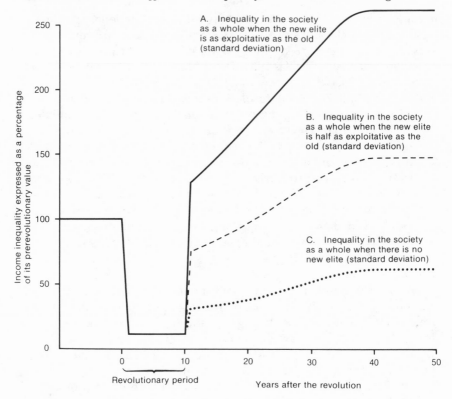

Figure 1.6   Predicted effects of the nature of the new postrevolutionary elite on inequality in the society as a whole. Income inequality following a revolution that redistributes property and so ends exploitation, destroys property and disrupts production in the postrevolutionary period, and leads to economic growth at 2½ percent per year beginning a decade after the revolution (as in A of fig. 1.4). The new postrevolutionary elite is taken alternatively to be (A) as exploitative as the old prerevolutionary elite, (B) half so exploitative as the old elite, or (C) not at all exploitative (i.e., there is no new elite). Inequality is measured by the standard deviation of income in the population as a whole. *Source*: Computer simulations described in the text.

INHERITED PRIVILEGE

According to our theory, revolution's effects on inherited privilege will closely parallel its effects on inequality. Revolution will lead to a decline in inherited privilege in the short run because it leads to a decline in inequality (Hypothesis 8). But inherited privilege will not disappear because inequality does not disappear and also because human capital is impervious to revolution and itself confers great advantages on children born into high ranking families. In the longer

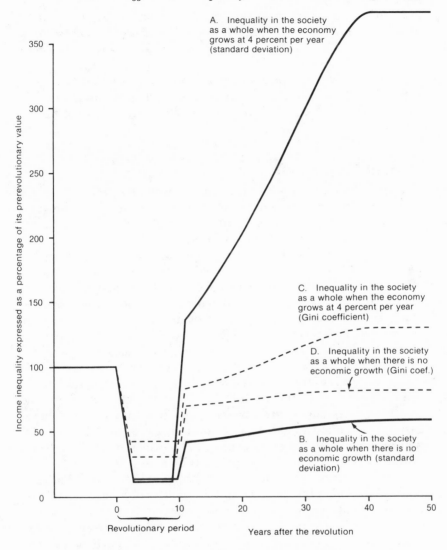

Figure 1.7   Predicted effects of economic growth on inequality in the society as a whole. Income inequality following a revolution that redistributes property and so ends exploitation, destroys property and disrupts production in the postrevolutionary period, and has a new elite half as exploitative as the old. In (A) economic growth is taken to be rapid (4 percent a year) and the nonagricultural middle and working classes to be initially poor. Alternatively, in (B) economic growth does not occur and the nonagricultural middle and working classes are initially prosperous. Inequality is measured alternatively by the standard deviation of income or the Gini coefficient. *Source*: Computer simulations described in the text.

run, inherited privilege among the previously exploited will grow again as a consequence of the growth of inequality (Hypothesis 9). If inequality in the society as a whole remains below its prerevolutionary levels, so will inherited privilege in the society as a whole, and if inequality rises above prerevolutionary levels, so will inherited privilege (Hypothesis 10). The model underlying these claims is set out in detail in Appendix 1, section 2, so we will not repeat the argument here.

CONCLUSION

These, then, are the patterns we predict will follow a radical revolution. We argue that a violent social revolution that frees peasants and other exploited groups from their traditional exploitation will in the short run improve their standard of living, reduce inequality in the society as a whole, and reduce inherited privilege. At this stage the peasants and the radical revolutionary intelligentsia have the same goal, the overthrow of the traditional elite and the end of exploitation, but that does not last. Peasants with more land, human capital, or other resources are able to exploit their advantages more fully after the revolution. Furthermore, revolution inadvertently sets loose forces that, if unchecked, will in the long run allow inequality and inherited privilege to grow steadily and, in some circumstances, to exceed their prerevolutionary levels. The result will be a relatively rigid rural stratification system of a familiar capitalist type with rich peasants playing the role of capitalist entrepreneur. Thwarting these forces is never easy and often impossible. Liberal policies, or even moderate socialist policies that allow a mixed economy, will hardly repress these deeply rooted forces. They involve the property of modest family farmers and the opportunities for skilled workers, small traders, small businessmen, government bureaucrats, and the holders of human capital who will accumulate wealth and pass it on to their children. By giving in to these forces, accepting the new status quo and abandoning any further redistribution in the countryside, a revolution can maintain the allegiance of the new elites, leaving a peaceful, prosperous, and highly stratified countryside. The only viable alternative is a radical attempt to root out even the smallest vestiges of private property, as in China or Cuba. Among other things, this requires extensive economic planning, a large and effective bureaucracy with unusual commitment and incorruptibility, the power to overcome strong opposition in the countryside, and the willingness to bear the substantial human costs involved. But even this does not solve the whole problem. If differences in education, skills, language, ability, or other kinds of human capital remain they will eventually (albeit more slowly) lead to inequality and, unless children are raised apart from their parents, to inherited advantage. That is much harder to control. Confiscating land and machines is easy compared to controlling human capital, and even in simple societies it is at least as important to the economy. To date, only China during a brief period of its history has been willing to bear the costs of a determined assault on human capital and even there both the outcome and the will to continue the assault are far from clear.

In short, we have argued that revolution inevitably leads to the rebirth of inequality. And it does so for reasons inherent in its very nature: redistribution itself increases inequality among the previously exploited. The destruction and disruption of the revolutionary period can, we argue, only slow but never halt the inevitable growth of inequality. And if the revolution leads to new opportunities and to economic growth, as will often be the case, the growth in inequality and inherited privilege will be much more rapid.

We hold that our model is applicable to any revolution where a dominant traditional elite has previously been able to expropriate a large fraction of the surplus produced by the exploited masses and where the revolution liberated the masses from their exploitation. But a theory, however plausible, can hardly be believed until it has been subjected to an empirical test and it is to that that we must now turn. To test the theory, we will analyze data from a modern society transformed by a radical revolution, the Bolivian National Revolution of 1952. These are probably the best data available on the consequences of a violent and fundamental social revolution on inequality and status inheritance among the population at large. In the next chapter we will therefore describe the nature of these data and then, in the following chapters, we will attempt to show how this profoundly traditional and rigidly stratified society was dramatically and irrevocably changed as a result of revolution.

2
Bolivia: The Setting, Data, and Methods

We have two complementary aims in this book, first, to develop and test a theory about the effects of a radical revolution on inequality and social mobility and, second, to provide a rigorous, empirical description of the actual effects of a radical revolution on the lives of ordinary people, a matter of great interest and about which little is known. These aims are complementary since no theory is complete without a rigorous test and any empirical analysis benefits from the focus supplied by theory. We have already presented the theory in the previous chapter and in this one we describe the data and methods we use in our empirical analysis.

Our analysis focuses on the Bolivian National Revolution of 1952. At least for our purposes, it provides the best quantitative data available for any radical revolution; indeed for some important topics, the Bolivian survey data are the only data available. To have extensive quantitative and qualitative data on a society which has just had a social revolution of the magnitude of Bolivia's 1952 revolution is exceedingly uncommon. Given the violence and the antiforeign bias of most major social revolutions, there is generally no possibility of obtaining extensive survey data. But because the Bolivian revolution received massive U.S. aid, it has been unusually receptive to North American and other researchers who have been able to study Bolivian society to a degree unusual in underdeveloped nations and unique in those in the midst of violent social revolutions. And of all these studies, without doubt the most complete social survey ever undertaken was that by the Research Institute for the Study of Man (RISM) which was kindly made available to us by Vera Rubin and Lambros Comitas. It includes ethnographic fieldwork in six representative rural areas, a census of all inhabitants of the areas, and an extensive social survey of 1,130 heads of households. The social survey includes detailed information, both current and retrospective, on stratification, politics, and related topics and is our main source of quantitative data.

The data available in this study allow us to test many but not all of our theoretical predictions. The heart of the theory deals with the effects of a radical revolution on inequality in one generation and the inheritance of status from one generation to the next, and we have appropriate retrospective survey data to measure status inheritance before, during, and after the revolution.[1] The data include detailed information on father's occupation and education (the appropriate measures of family background) and on respondent's education and first job (the comparable information for the next generation); we can thus measure status inheritance before, during, and after the revolution and in that way test our predictions about revolution's effects on it. But we have no such retrospective information on income, standard of living, or wealth; retrospective information on such things is unreliable under the best and simplest of conditions and in a suspicious peasant society with few written accounts and great fear of tax collectors, it is out of the question. So, unfortunately, we cannot test the predictions about changes in inequality within a single generation directly from our survey data, although we will be able to bring some other, less direct materials to bear on this question, both from our respondents and from other sources. We will also be able to test some of our less central predictions about revolution's effects on education. In all, while we cannot test all our predictions, those we can test pertain to key aspects of the theory, and so provide indirect tests of the rest of the argument.

In analyzing the effect of a radical revolution on the lives of its people, we address three basic sets of issues. First, we describe how the general population perceived the revolution—what they thought it did, who they thought gained from the revolution and how, who they thought lost from the revolution and how they lost. Looking back over the fourteen years since the revolution, we will see who, in retrospect, favors the revolution and who opposes it. Second, we review a wide variety of data on the revolution's effects on agriculture, industry, standard of living, and income inequality, seeing how these changed in the immediate aftermath and what happened in the longer run. Finally, we take a very detailed look at revolution's consequences for social mobility, disentangling its short-run effects from the quite different consequences that come about in the longer run.

To understand the Bolivian revolution, we must first know something about Bolivia, about the data we have on the Bolivian revolution, and about the methods we use in analyzing those data. It is to these topics that we now turn.

THE SETTING

GEOGRAPHY

The historical development of Bolivian society has been significantly influenced by its geographical setting. Situated on the western side of South America, Bolivia is dominated by the Andes, a range of enormous, snowcapped volcanic mountains sweeping from the Straits of Magellan at the southern tip of South America along the Pacific coast to the isthmus of Panama, in many places towering over twenty thousand feet. For the most part, the Andes run in two or sometimes three parallel folds leaving broad valleys between. It is in these high valleys that, for millennia, men have lived in settled agricultural villages, and civilizations have developed, shaped by their spectacular geography.

The Altiplano. The largest of the high Andean valleys and one of the highest permanently settled areas in the world, the altiplano is Bolivia's heartland. It was the traditional population center throughout history and still is the home of almost half of the population. The altiplano is a cool, windy, barren, treeless, relatively flat plateau in the Andes between 11,500 and 13,000 feet above sea level, flanked on the east and west by vast ranges rising to 23,000 feet. The Bolivian altiplano is the widest and most level plain within the Andes, roughly 120 miles wide (see map 1). The altiplano is defined by two major mountain ranges running north and south and internally divided by lower hills and mountain ranges cutting largely east to west. The western range, the Cordillera Occidental facing the Pacific coast, is the leading edge of the South American plate. It is a narrow but rugged volcanic range, rising abruptly from the Atacama desert on the Pacific coast, reaching heights of 21,000 feet, and then descending steeply to a mostly arid region of the altiplano marked by a series of enormous salt flats. Thus the mountains form an effective block to extensive Bolivian contact with the Pacific. North of Bolivia the mountains are much less defined, breaking up into numerous plains and wide river valleys giving easy access to the Pacific from the altiplano in what is now Peru; in earlier times highland Bolivia's contact with the Pacific was mainly by that route.

The altiplano has not been uniformly settled, for it is not uniformly hospitable to man. Although only a few degrees south of the equator in the tropical zone, the concentration of Bolivia's population on the high plains has meant that Bolivia was primarily developed within a cold and relatively hostile physical environment. The heartland is the area around Lake Titicaca in the north. This enormous lake, 138 miles long and 70 miles wide at its widest, moderates the normally cold and dry altiplano climate and makes agriculture possible along with the usual altiplano herding economy. From La Paz to the lake a series of open plains have been the center of Bolivia's population throughout history. Potatoes are the main crop, followed by grains and beans; herding is important, originally the traditional llamas with sheep becoming widespread after the Spanish conquest.

The altiplano is dotted with small villages of dirt-floored, thatch-roofed, adobe houses, without electricity, running water, or the most rudimentary sanitary facilities and inhabited by poor, illiterate,

Map 1   Geographic profile of Bolivia. Source: Wennergren and Whitaker 1975. Study communities are indicated by letters: (a, Reyes; b, Sorata; c, Compi; d, Coroico; e, San Miguel; f, Villa Abecia)

Aymara-speaking peasant farmers. We have data on two of these communities. One, San Miguel, is an isolated village of some 1,200 persons situated at 13,000 feet in the province of Oruro. Even now, it is inaccessible during the wet season, although during the dry period trucks driving cross-country stop twice a week. There are no telephones or newspapers. Mainly subsistence farmers, the villagers plow the barren land with oxen (or harness themselves to the plows when working small fields), planting mainly potatoes, quinoa (a highland grain), beans, and oca; every family has a few chickens and guinea pigs in the house and herds of llamas and sheep. Land is privately owned and a few prosperous peasants rent land for cash or a half share in the harvest, although most are dirt poor. It has always been a free community, never part of a hacienda. A second altiplano village in our study, Compi, has a population of about 1,400 and is less isolated, with an all-weather dirt road to the outside world. There are no telephones, no regular supply of periodicals, and fewer than ten percent of the men speak Spanish but many have transistor radios and some go into the capital, La Paz, once or twice a month on business. Compi is situated at 12,500 feet on the shores of Lake Titicaca, which gives the village a mild climate and less barren aspect than the rest of the altiplano. The soil is more fertile but farming, by far the predominant occupation, is much the same as elsewhere on the altiplano except that cash crops are more important, with onions and some pigs grown for sale in the capital. Standards of living are no higher than elsewhere on the altiplano because landholdings are very small, few peasants having more than two and a half acres. Prior to the Revolution it was a hacienda.

   The Valleys.   Defining the altiplano to the east and west is the much wider and more complex series of mountain ranges generically called the Cordillera Real (or sometimes Cordillera Central or Oriental). They have numerous plains and valley systems at all altitudes and allow access (easy by Bolivia's harsh standards) to the eastern foothills and then to the Amazonian floodplains in the north and dry plains known as the Gran Chaco in the south, from which Buenos Aires and the Atlantic are an easy trek of about a thousand miles of level ground. The Cordillera Real valleys, important population centers since pre-Columbian times, are of two basic kinds. The higher subpuna valleys, averaging 6,000 to 8,000 feet above sea level, have a largely temperate environment and, though the climate is dry, ground water is plentiful. They are long open plains, lower and more fertile than the altiplano; potatoes, grains, and other temperate climate crops grow well. More humid are a series of pleasant, verdant, and highly productive valleys in the central part of the Cordillera Real known as the Yungas. These steep river valleys at 3,000 to 7,000 feet, separated from the altiplano by some of the most rugged terrain in the world, are humid and warm and allow intensive cultivation of tropical and semitropical crops.

   The valleys of the Cordillera Real have been populated by settled village agriculturalists from pre-Columbian times to present and about forty percent of the population live there now, mainly in Cochabamba, Chuquisaca, the western part of Potosí province, Tarija, and the Yungas valleys near La Paz (see map 1). The Yungas valleys farther south in the provinces of Cochabamba and Santa Cruz remained largely inaccessible and lightly settled until the twentieth century. To supplement the deficiencies of the highlands, the altiplano populations have long had recourse to these extensive and varied valleys, obtaining all the traditional crops available to pre-Columbian and postcontact

Amerindian populations and providing a crucial addition to the main diet on the altiplano. Together, these subpuna valleys, the Yungas valleys, and altiplano comprise only 40 percent of the national territory yet, after years of out-migration and colonization, still contain 80 percent of the population. Thus Bolivia through most of its recorded history can be defined as a core heartland of high plateau and associated valleys, intimately tied to similar systems north of Lake Titicaca, and only loosely connected to the vast lowland and coastal territories over which it claimed sovereignty.

In appearance the Yungas towns are colonial Spanish, laid out in a grid pattern, typically with two plazas and narrow, often cobblestoned, streets; the buildings are plastered adobe or brick, with tiled roofs and iron-railed balconies. The culture of the towns is predominantly Spanish, although the peasants and the poor are mainly Aymara. The towns were established in the sixteenth and early seventeenth centuries but were accessible only by foot or horseback until the 1920s or 1930s. They are now connected to the altiplano by dirt roads, bulldozed out of the side of vertical mountains. Newspapers from the capital are now regularly available and there are radio broadcasts and a telegraph. The area has always been important agriculturally, growing coffee, bananas, fruit, and coca, long chewed on the altiplano (and the source of cocaine). The occupational structure is diversified with subsistence farmers, many cash crop farmers (some prosperous), unskilled laborers, skilled craftsmen (who have difficulty competing with machine-made goods), merchants and prosperous traders, and the usual complement of clerks, officials, and professionals. There are sharp differences between educated and illiterate, rich and poor, Spanish and Aymara speaking—categories that generally coincide. We have data from two such towns. One, Coroico, is located at about 6,000 feet, has a population of 2,200, and is mainly agricultural with coffee and bananas the main crops. It was long a trade center as well but that, and the town itself, is now in decline. We also have data on Sorata, a town at 5,000 feet with some 1,800 inhabitants, which is mainly a commercial gateway to the tropical region below. It has had recurrent booms and busts depending on gold finds and the vagaries of the international market for rubber and cinchona bark and is now in decline. Beginning in the late 1940s, many prosperous Spanish families left town and a slight majority of the population is now Aymara; peasant and worker "unions" (*sindicatos*) dominated by Aymara are now influential, controlling the municipal government, transport, and gold mining.

In the far south is a lightly settled area of barren mountains interspersed with fertile river valleys with a sunny and dry Mediterranean climate, populated entirely by Spanish monolinguals. Socially this is a quiet, almost Mediterranean backwater. We have data from one town in this traditional region, Villa Abecia, situated in a small valley at 6,500 feet with a population of 600. The town, built around a small plaza, has cobblestoned streets and mostly single-story adobe houses with cane roofs. It is on a relatively busy all-weather dirt road connecting the altiplano and Argentina; mail and newspapers come once a week and a few people have radios. Although sheep and goats are raised on neighboring hills and some fruit is grown, the economy depends primarily on 270 acres of irrigated vineyards. Both the land and the crucial water rights are privately owned by small and medium landowners who generally work their own land with help from skilled farmhands, who are long-term employees living on the land. The wine is sold in distant markets but fruit is often bartered in neighboring villages. Some farmhands spend the off-season cutting cane in Argentina at relatively high wages and invest their savings in Villa Abecia, so there is more money in town than might be expected.

The Lowlands. The third major ecological zone is the lowlands, a vast tropical plain at some 700 feet above sea level, extending endlessly eastward from the edge of the Andes toward the distant Atlantic Ocean. These are divided into two quite distinct zones. Toward the north the lowlands are humid, covered with alternating patches of grassland, tropical forest, and marsh. The area is usually flooded in the rainy season from December to April. Although long settled, by nomadic Amerindians before the conquest and ranchers afterward, this remains a sparsely populated frontier. To the south is the Chaco, dry, sandy plains with scattered scrub forest, extending to the borders of Brazil, Paraguay, and Argentina and virtually unpopulated. Altogether the lowlands make up over half of Bolivia's surface area but contain only a minor part of its population.

We have data from one town in the northern lowlands, Reyes, which is connected with the rest of Bolivia only by air and radio, and then only in good weather. The town has some 2,100 inhabitants and is laid out in standard Spanish grid pattern with two plazas. The houses are generally one story, made of adobe, wooden poles, or even palm leaves, and set in large plots with a garden and fruit trees. Reyes was founded by Jesuit missionaries around 1705 as a communal, utopian community. But it ended half a century later as a result of the Jesuit expulsion. The Indians were soon despoiled, and a system of debt peonage was established, remnants of which persist to the present. The town, now entirely Spanish speakers, has gone through periods of boom and bust depending on the international market for rubber and cinchona bark and is now dominated by cattle ranching (meat being exported by air), with some trading, craft production, and cash crop farming for local markets. Land is plentiful and many people make their living, albeit a poor one, by subsistence farming and odd jobs.

Population.   Bolivia, with a total land area about the size of France and Spain combined, or of Texas alone if you like to calculate it that way, had a population of about 1,800,000 at the turn of the century, 3,000,000 at mid-century, and 4,600,000 in 1976 (Averango Mollinedo 1974; Republica de Bolivia 1977). The great bulk of the population has always been on the altiplano and associated valleys, although in recent years there has been important migration to the lowlands. Available land on the altiplano is, however, meager and the population density has been high.

The Aymara and Quechua Indian populations of Bolivia, despite their postconquest exploitation, survived as the most important element in Bolivian society, and unlike most of America's republics, the Amerindian population of Bolivia still predominates. Although estimates vary somewhat, as do definitions, there is consensus that something over 60 percent of the population still speak Amerindian languages (mainly Aymara and Quechua) as their sole or at least primary language. This is the highest figure in America, followed by Guatemala at 54 percent Amerindian, Peru at 47 percent, Ecuador at 30 percent, with all the rest under 10 percent (Wilkie and Reich 1977: table 610).

DATA

SELECTION OF TOWNS

On the basis of a three-month field reconnaissance by three senior researchers from the Research Institute for the Study of Man (RISM) team, the six communities mentioned above were chosen for the study (McEwen 1975). While a national survey might have been desirable, it would in practice have been impossible, and the actual design has the advantage that detailed ethnographic surveys of each of the six towns were possible and so provide an analytical base of unusual depth and quality. The six communities were chosen to represent the major types of rural communities in Bolivia; table 2.1 summarizes their main features and a detailed and excellent description is given by McEwen (1975). The main criteria involved social stratification and experiences in the revolution, while geography was an additional consideration.

Many Bolivian communities have been highly stratified since before the Inca conquest, and the degree of stratification increased further following the Spanish conquest in the sixteenth century. In ecologically favored areas with large Amerindian populations the Spanish imposed themselves as a ruling class but generally allowed the preconquest government and elite to continue as before, albeit in a subservient role. In the course of time an intermediate social and economic strata arose,

TABLE 2.1
The Communities in the RISM Study.

Community	Involvement in the revolution	Social stratification	Ecological zone	Dates of anthropological fieldwork[1]	Population (from RISM census)	Number in head of household survey
Compi	Great changes; ex-hacienda	Simple	Altiplano	Dec. 1964–Jan. 1966	1,120	137
Coroico	Substantial changes	Complex	Yungas	Dec. 1964–Oct. 1965	2,086	207
San Miguel	Few changes; free community	Simple	Altiplano	April–Dec. 1965 and July–Dec. 1966	982	159
Sorata	Great changes	Complex	Yungas	Nov. 1964–Feb. 1965 and July 1965–Sept. 1966	1,386	278
Reyes	Substantial changes	Complex	Lowland; isolated	Oct. 1964–Sept. 1965	1,887	257
Villa Abecia	Substantial changes	Complex	Southern valleys	Oct. 1965–June 1966	622	92

[1]Senior anthropologists were Hans Buechler in Compi, Dwight Heath in Coroico, Solomon Miller in San Miguel, William J. McEwen in Sorata, Victor Novick in Reyes and Villa Abecia.

the *cholos*, sharing culture, language, and often parentage with both the Spanish elite above them and the Indian masses below. The result was a complex stratification system marked by great inequalities between rich and poor, educated and illiterate, and between Spanish speakers and Indian speakers. In contrast to these communities with complex stratification systems, many small villages had neither Spanish nor Indian ruling elites and still have very simple stratification systems without distinct social strata. While there are differences in wealth, education, linguistic skills, and prestige, these are relatively modest and have not led to the formation of distinctive social classes. As we have seen, the RISM study includes two communities with simple stratification systems of this sort and four with complex stratification systems.

A second consideration was involvement in the 1952 revolution. Before the revolution the great mass of the rural population was effectively isolated from national politics, which was entirely the province of a small Spanish elite. In some towns the revolution led to radical changes, as we will see in subsequent chapters. Large estates were confiscated and title to the land given to peasants, quasifeudal labor obligations were abolished, active peasant unions formed, arms widely distributed, and universal suffrage instituted. Armed and politicized peasant unions soon became the bulwark of the revolutionary government and drove the prerevolutionary elite out of rural communities into exile in La Paz or abroad. Other communities were, in contrast, less changed. Some were free Indian communities which had never had Spanish elites. Others were so remote and isolated from the revolutionary centers on the altiplano and the adjacent valleys that the revolution's effects were slow in coming and perhaps somewhat attenuated. The study includes two communities which were dramatically transformed by the revolution, one where it had little effect, and three in between. At the time the study was designed, these differences seemed larger than they in fact turned out to be (McEwen 1975) and it now seems that in practice the revolution had a profound impact on almost all Bolivian communities, with the possible exception of the free communities (see chaps 4 and 5, especially fig. 4.1).

As a third but less salient consideration, there was an attempt to cover the three main ecological zones in Bolivia, the altiplano, the eastern valleys, and the tropical lowlands. As we have seen, two of our communities are from the altiplano, two from the adjacent Yungas valleys, one from a remote southern valley, and one from the lowlands.

The six communities chosen represent the major cultural patterns of Bolivia. They include towns primarily of whites, towns in which cholos predominate, and finally towns in which Indians are the dominant element. The prime criterion for measuring these "social races" (Wagley 1952) is language. As can be seen in table 2.2, the six communities cover the gamut of social race as defined in Bolivian society. Differ-

TABLE 2.2

SOCIAL CHARACTERISTICS OF RESPONDENTS IN THE RISM
HEAD OF HOUSEHOLD SURVEY.

Characteristic		Stratified communities			Indian villages	
	Reyes	Villa Abecia	Coroica	Sorata	San Miguel	Compi
1. Social race (percent)						
Spanish	82	77	58	17	0	0
Cholo	18	23	38	30	32	7
Indian	0	0	5	54	68	93
2. Mean years of education	3.1	2.4	4.3	2.2	1.8	0.8
3. Percent in agriculture	61	68	35	44	92	97
4. Mean occupational status[1]	34	29	44	29	7	5
5. Mean standard of living[2]	59	48	57	60	23	26
6. Mean Spanish diet score[3]	6	5	6	5	2	2
7. Percent belonging to a union	28	23	24	45	0	92
8. Inequality						
Standard deviation of education	3.9	4.2	4.1	3.8	2.0	1.8
Standard deviation of occupational status	28	29	25	26	14	7
Standard deviation of standard of living	21	23	25	23	18	17
Number of cases	(257)	(92)	(207)	(278)	(159)	(137)

Source: Head of household survey.

[1]Occupational status is defined so that the highest occupations get a score of 100 and the lowest zero and is measured in the ethnographic metric described in the text below.

[2]Defined so that the richest get a score of 100 and the poorest zero.

[3]There are characteristic differences between Spanish diets (meat, eggs, fruit) and Indian diets (potatoes, etc.) and the scale measures style of consumption. It has an arbitrary mean of 5 and a standard deviation of 1.

ences in education, occupational status, standard of living, and diet also run the gamut found in rural Bolivia, from the relatively advantaged Spanish-speaking and mixed towns (advantaged, that is, by the harsh standards of rural Bolivia) to the exceedingly poor, predominantly Indian highland villages. The differences among towns in degree of stratification are also large, with inequality much greater in the relatively prosperous stratified towns and less in the uniformly poor Indian villages.

Representativeness of the Communities. Our six communities thus reflect the economic and geographic regions of rural Bolivia and encompass most of the major ethnic and social groupings. The RISM study is, to our knowledge, the most complete study ever undertaken of the Aymara and cholo rural communities (see Omran, McEwen and Zaki 1967; Muratorio 1969; Heath 1969; McEwen 1975 and the papers cited there). Only the works of La Barre (1948), Vellard (1963), Carter (1964), and Burke (1967) have previously treated these groups even in passing. We have the most complete body of survey material ever gathered on this crucial sector of the Bolivian population.

Unfortunately, our data do not include the large urban centers, the mining communities, or the Cochabamba valley which is the heartland of the Quechua-speaking Indian population. The exclusion of the more complex urban society and the already highly organized and politicized mining encampments is unfortunate but they represented only a minority of the population (probably less than 30 percent). The mining communities are small enclaves of militant and unionized workers. The omission of the Cochabamba valley, however, is particularly unfortunate. This was a major zone of temperate agricultural production with an advanced peasantry and hacienda system before the revolution, and with the revolution, the syndicates in Cliza and Ucureña became among the most important peasant organizations in Bolivia. So in all, our data are representative of rural Bolivia and of the Aymara, Spanish, and cholo communities within it but not of the urban and industrial areas or the Cochabamba and similar southern Bolivian valleys which together make up an important part of the Bolivian population.

ANTHROPOLOGICAL DATA

There are excellent qualitative data from anthropological fieldwork in all six communities which form a useful background for our analysis. The data were collected by teams of anthropologists who stayed in their communities between seven and eleven months, with each team headed by a senior anthropologist. The approximately 104,000 field notes, classified according to topic, are available on microfilm. An excellent analysis of these data is available (McEwen 1975) and a number of specialized papers have been written from them (Comitas 1966; Muratoria 1969; Heath 1973).

THE RISM CENSUS

At the beginning of the fieldwork period, a complete house-to-house census was taken in each of the towns. For each person in the household information was obtained on name, age, sex, region of birth, relation to head of household, years of schooling, occupation, and languages spoken. This provides information on 8,946 people living in

1,760 households. The data and codes are, however, of lower quality than the head of household survey data, so we use the census only as a check on the representativeness of the survey data.

THE HEAD OF HOUSEHOLD SURVEY

Our main source of data is a survey of 1,130 heads of households in the six communities. This excellent survey was designed by Vera Rubin, Lambros Comitas, William J. McEwen, and Blanca Muratoria. The pretest and final data collection were directed by Blanca Muratoria, assisted byMichael Pettit, who headed the Aymara-speaking part of the survey team. The data were coded, punched, and cleaned at Berkeley under William J. McEwen's supervision. The amount of work involved in conducting a survey in isolated rural areas of a developing country, in two languages, and carefully coding and cleaning the data is enormous, and we are very grateful to Vera Rubin, Lambros Comitas, and William J. McEwen for permission to use them and assistance in doing so. The project was funded by the Peace Corps under contract Pc(W)-397 and by subsequent grants from the Research Institute for the Study of Man, directed by Vera Rubin. For various personal and financial reasons, these data have not heretofore been analyzed and this is the first report on them.

Study Design. The questionnaire was designed after the anthropological fieldwork was nearing completion by anthropologists intimately familiar with the population and problems to be studied. It benefited greatly from this familiarity. Preparation began in the fall of 1965, and the questionnaire was pretested the following May in Sorata and subsequently revised. Final interviewing began in the summer of 1966 in Villa Abecia and ended that September in Sorata. Interviews averaged well over two hours in length. There were two interviewing teams, one working in Aymara and one in Spanish, who worked together throughout the project, moving from community to community with the supervisory personnel. The core of the two teams were fieldwork assistants who had earlier been working with the project anthropologists. They were thoroughly trained and obtained 81 percent of the interviews, the remainder coming from assistants recruited locally and trained by the survey team. Access was no problem since the project's anthropologists were either still in the community or had only recently left it. Most people in each community were familiar with the project, aware that it wasn't in league with the tax collectors, and accustomed to having strangers nosing about asking questions. We are confident that the questions were answered frankly and completely, something which is not always true for surveys conducted in societies unused to this type of research.

Head of Household Sample. At the beginning of the fieldwork a complete house-to-house census was taken of each town and the sample was drawn from it. Only adult male heads of household were sampled.[2] The completion rate was a quite satisfactory 83 percent, ranging from a low of 64 percent in one Indian village (San Miguel) to a high of 95 percent in the other, with the rest in the mid-eighties. The great majority of the losses were people who could not be located at home, primarily farmers who stayed on their land some hours away, returning to their village homes only erratically; refusals were only some 10 percent of the losses. The sample is large relative to the population; in all, over two-thirds of the male heads of household were interviewed. The restriction to heads of household is not particularly serious as 40 percent of all males between ages twenty and twenty-four and 86 percent of males twenty-five and older are heads of household (República de Bolivia 1955: 66–67). The restriction to men is unfortunate.[3]

Representativeness of the Head of Household Sample. The sample appears to be representative of the towns and surrounding hamlets from which it was drawn, although illiterates and bilingual Indians are slightly underrepresented. Compared to household heads in the RISM census, the sample has 3 percent fewer illiterates, 32 percent to 35 percent (where we follow the Bolivian census's generous convention of considering only those with no schooling as illiterate). It appears to have 7 percent more monolingual Aymara speakers and 17 percent more monolingual Spanish speakers with bilinguals correspondingly underrepresented, partly because of the deliberate undersampling of the two large, heavily bilingual towns. The overrepresentation of Spanish speakers is probably a genuine bias but the underrepresentation of bilinguals is probably not—bilingualism has very high status among the Aymara and it is easy to claim facility in Spanish on the single census question (or have the family member providing the information claim it for you) but impossible to exaggerate it in the course of a two-hour personal interview in which true bilinguals would invariably use Spanish. There is no difference in age, which averages forty-five (with standard deviation of sixteen) in the survey and forty-four (with the same standard deviation) in the population. The occupational distributions also appear very similar.

More crucial for present purposes, the regression estimates obtained with the sample appear to be essentially the same as those that would be obtained for the whole population of the six towns in our study. Using the RISM town census, we are able to compare the regressions of education and language on occupation separately for the entire census population and for those also in the survey. The comparison, presented in Appendix 3, section 1, suggests that there is no appreciable bias.

It is more difficult to say whether the sample is representative of rural Bolivia as a whole but in our judgment it is probably representative of the Aymara, bilingual, and Spanish-speaking populations, the main weakness being the omission of the large Quechua Indian community. Nationwide data from the 1950 census show that the age distribution in the sample is virtually identical to the national figures and the proportion Indian is very close (57 percent in the sample, 61 percent nationwide; República de Bolivia 1955: 59, 100). Illiteracy is more problematic since it has been rapidly declining but we estimate that it is approximately 47 percent in the nation, 15 percent higher in the sample;[4] however, for those who have attended school, the educational distributions are very close (78 percent primary only, 16 percent secondary and 6 percent university for the sample compared to 81 percent, 14 percent, and 6 percent in the population).

Weighting. To make the sample more representative we have weighted it to match the proportion Indian and the age-specific illiteracy rates for the nation, an adjustment which makes no difference to the correlations or regressions[5] but makes the significance tests only approximate.[6]

NATIONAL ACCOUNTS AND RELATED DATA ON BOLIVIA

In a number of contexts, we use findings based directly or indirectly on Bolivia's national accounts data. Unfortunately these data are less reliable than corresponding data from other Latin American countries and so must be used with some reservations (Whitehead 1969; Zuvekas 1977: 1–6). These reservations are particularly applicable to data on income and gross national product but are real even for such basic facts as population size and migration patterns. But despite their uncertainties, these data are nonetheless the best available for many purposes and we will use them, noting the relevant qualifications at appropriate points in the text.

Other published statistics for Bolivia are meager and of decidedly variable quality. Many are based on the national accounts data and so subject to those uncertainties and a few are wholly untrustworthy (e.g., on income inequality).[7] There are some good surveys on limited topics (as on land tenure by the University of Wisconsin's Land Tenure Center) and a number of good studies of single communities. But on the whole reliable data are very rare, particularly for the country as a whole. We will therefore have to be content with somewhat more fragmentary and problematic data than would be available in many other societies.

CROSS-CULTURAL DATA

To give a wider perspective on Bolivia, in a few places we compare Bolivian results with those for thirteen diverse societies from throughout the world (Australia, Denmark, Finland, Great Britain, Malaysia,

Netherlands, Northern Ireland, Norway, the Philippines, Sweden, Taiwan, the United States, and West Germany). These results are from a larger project in collaboration with Donald J. Treiman and are described in detail elsewhere (Treiman and Kelley 1974; Kelley, Treiman, Robinson, Roos, and Thompson 1980). The data are all from representative samples of the general population. The results presented here are for men, 20 and older with labor force experience. The number of cases ranges from a low of something over 300 (for Finland) to a high of some 20,000, with the median around 700. The total number of cases is 35,233.

MEASUREMENT AND METHODS

For our quantitative analysis we need measures of occupational status, education, standard of living, and a few other variables. Most of these pose no real problem but occupational status is more difficult, and we leave it to last.

EDUCATION

We measure education in years of schooling. This implicitly assumes that a year at any level provides the same benefits in occupational status. This assumption would not be reasonable in many societies, but it is in Bolivia (as it is in the United States). An effect proportional weighting scheme which does not make this assumption (Treiman and Terrell 1975a) gives equivalent results; it is correlated .98 with years of schooling in Bolivia and has virtually identical correlations with other variables. We therefore report the conventional and more easily interpreted years of schooling.

LANGUAGE AND SOCIAL RACE

In Bolivia there is a clear and universally recognized distinction between peasants of Indian origin (*indios* as they were derogatively called before the revolution, *campesinos* now) on the one hand and Spanish-speaking, Western-oriented groups on the other. There are marked differences in culture, dress, diet, and, most importantly, in language spoken (McEwen 1975). Aymara and other campesinos are monolingual speakers of Amerindian languages while facility in Spanish is a key distinguishing feature of the other group. We counted anyone whose parents were essentially monolingual Spanish speakers as coming from Spanish background[8] and those from monolingual Aymara families as of Indian family background. A tiny handful of people whose parents spoke other European languages were counted as Spanish and a few whose parents spoke other Indian languages were counted with the Aymara. Only 3 percent of the sample came from families with mixed or unknown linguistic patterns; they are treated as missing data. Respondents had no difficulty or uncertainty in reporting their parents' language and, for so salient a matter, errors in recall are surely small.

Social Race. Among respondents themselves things are more complicated since between the two extremes there is an intermediate group of cholos, almost all people of Amerindian background who have acquired some Spanish, and some of the cultural, dress, and dietary characteristics of the Spanish elite. This group is clearly recognized by both locals and anthropologists throughout Bolivia and neighboring societies (McEwen 1975) although the label "cholo" is not one that the group itself uses. For some purposes it is useful to distinguish cholos from the other groups. Given the fundamental role played by language in the society and culture, we decided to use it as our criterion and classified as Indian anyone whose parents spoke primarily Aymara (or other Amerindian languages) and who themselves answered the two-hour interview in Aymara. We defined those who came from the same family background but themselves answered the interview in Spanish as cholos. Those whose parents spoke mainly Spanish and themselves spoke Spanish in the interview were classified as Spanish.[9] Only 3 percent of the respondents could not be classified by these criteria. By this definition, 38 percent of the heads of household are Spanish, 25 percent cholo, and 37 percent Indian. Following Wagley (1952), we call this "social race."

STANDARD OF LIVING

In highly developed societies like that of the United States, income clearly provides a satisfactory measure of standard of living. But for Bolivia and other peasant societies the matter is not so simple since there is a large subsistence sector where cash income has little to do with standard of living, because most people are self-employed and have incomes that vary unpredictably from week to week, month to month, and year to year, and because many people do not accurately know, or would be fearful of revealing, their incomes. Consumption measures are therefore generally preferred in such societies (Van Ginneken 1976; Zuvekas 1977: 62), since they tend to be more stable over time, more accurately reported, and more reliable indicators of standard of living over the long term. We have rough but adequate data on a variety of aspects of consumption including characteristics of housing, servants, food consumption, and the like and have factor analyzed these items, choosing for our final scale five items measuring quality of housing and number of domestic servants;[10] correlations among the items average a satisfactory .36. Under Bolivian conditions, this scale provides a rough but nonetheless adequate measure of standard of living. Since the scale has no natural metric, for the regression analyses we transformed it so that each score represents the *cumulative* percentage of respondents with a standard of living at that level or lower; thus the poorest person receives a zero (no one is lower), someone in the middle fifty (half the population lives worse), and the person with the highest standard of living is one hundred (everyone else is worse off). This transformation has no appreciable effect on our conclusions, but makes the results easier to follow intuitively.[11]

Age

Age is measured in individual years. There is no difficulty here except for the well-known tendency, of no consequence for our purposes, for older respondents to report their ages in multiples of 5 rather than by year.

Occupational status

In Bolivia, as throughout the world, a man's occupation is the crucial determinant of his status in society, largely determining how he lives and how he is regarded by others (see table 2.4 below). It is difficult in practice, however, to measure occupational standing and we have devoted considerable effort to the question. To begin with, in a society like Bolivia there is a difficulty in deciding just what occupation to code since people may have one occupation during the growing season, one or more secondary occupations at the same time, and sometimes a different full-time occupation in the off-season. Fortunately we have the extensive data necessary to deal with this and it turns out not to be a major problem. Half of our respondents pursued secondary occupations, mostly for brief periods during the same days in which they worked their main occupation, and 16 percent had different full-time occupations at different (albeit brief) periods in the year. But on the average men worked at their main occupations 7.7 hours a day, 5.9 days a week, and 11.0 months a year, so it is clear that this one occupation is central to their position in society.

Retrospective Data. We have information not only on current main occupation but on the respondent's main occupation in the past and on his father's occupation. This information seems reasonably reliable since in Bolivian conditions the information is clear, salient, and relatively simple. The occupational structure is relatively simple, many people stay in the same jobs throughout their lives, and much work is done in and around the house so that even the father's occupation is often a routine aspect of a child's life. Respondents showed no hesitation or apparent difficulty in recalling their previous jobs, or their father's occupation, or in giving quite detailed information about them. Nonresponse was minor, 1 percent for own occupation and 4 percent for father's occupation (including vague and unclassifiable answers, coding and punching errors, and all other sources of lost information). These are lower rates than typically found in careful studies elsewhere in the world.

We used the information on main occupation in the past to define *first job*. The definition is imperfect since we unfortunately do not have information on the men who had a third (or fourth) different occupation at some point earlier than that they reported as their past occupation. There are however good reasons to believe that this difficulty is not of much practical importance. In the first place, the number of people involved is probably small. Almost half the population (44 percent) had the same occupation throughout their lives,[12] so the number who had a third or fourth occupation in the remote past is presumably small, probably well under a fifth, judging from what we know of Bolivia. Furthermore, the occupations people held in the past tended to be very similar in status to their present jobs, the correlation between the two being .72; so it is likely that the status of their third or fourth previous job was quite similar to the status of their past occupation. What we lack is information on a small fraction of the population holding jobs presumably very similar to ones we do know about. Unless their experiences in the revolution were very unusual, it is unlikely that we have erred very much by estimating the status of their job in the way we have.

Coding. Our information on father's occupation, respondent's first job, and respondent's current occupation is extensive, including land-ownership, number of paid employees, number of family employees, and whether or not self-employed. It was coded into an expansion of the International Labor Office's (1958) four-digit International Standard Classification of Occupations with, among others, additional distinctions among farmers (see Appendix 3, section 2). We used information on landownership to make further distinctions beween farmers who owned their own land, tenant farmers, and landless laborers. We also further distinguished large from small farmers, defining as large those who had paid employees, a reasonable and important distinction in the Bolivian context (see table 2.4 below which shows sharp differences in education and standard of living between large and small farmers).

A Local Classification of Occupational Groups. Even with as large a survey as ours, there are too few people in most individual occupations to permit any meaningful analysis of them. We therefore developed a scheme for classifying individual occupations into broader groups, guided by theory, ethnographic knowledge, and our data.[13] After some consideration, we settled on the fourteen categories described in table 2.3. Note that this table does not list all occupations but only illustrative ones; the full classification is given in Appendix 3, section 2. Those familiar with rural Latin America will, we suspect, find the categories familiar and reasonable.

As a way of clarifying the classification some selected characteristics of people in each group are shown in table 2.4. Of course, by far the

TABLE 2.3

AN OCCUPATIONAL CLASSIFICATION FOR RURAL BOLIVIA:
(THE "ETHNOGRAPHIC" CLASSIFICATION). NOTE THAT THESE ARE ONLY
EXAMPLES OF TITLES INCLUDED; FULL DETAILS ARE IN APPENDIX 3, SECTION 2.

Occupational group	Examples of titles included
Elite white-collar	Accountant, medical doctor, clergyman, lawyer, mayor, school principal, chief of Criminal Bureau of Investigation
Large farmer	Farm owner with *paid* employees (those with only family members working for them are small farmers)
Cattle rancher	Cattle rancher, dealer in cattle
High white-collar	Schoolteacher, nurse, contractor, administrator of a cooperative, first undersecretary of the mayor
Skilled modern blue-collar	Mechanic, truck driver, plumber, telegraph operator, movie projectionist
Clerical and sales	Secretary, office worker, cashier, salesman
Small business	Retail merchant, merchant middleman, wholesale merchant
Specialized farm[1]	Coffee, coca, or fruit planter; horticulturist
Skilled traditional blue-collar	Carpenter, mason, brick maker, tailor, hat maker, shoe maker, leather worker, blacksmith, baker, faith healer, lasso maker for cattle, tinker
Unskilled nonfarm	Day laborer, transporter of wares, doorman, domestic gardener, muleteer
Tenant farmer	Farmer who rents rather than owns land
Farm laborer (peon)	Unspecialized peon, peon working in a vineyard
Small farmer	Farm owner with no paid employees (whether or not he has family members working for him)
Small livestock owner	Farmer without land who herds llamas, goats, pigs, etc.

[1] In the RISM head of household survey, about 80 percent are owners. The few workers were, however, very similar in education and standard of living and so were combined with the owners.

TABLE 2.4

CHARACTERISTICS OF MEN IN VARIOUS OCCUPATIONAL
GROUPS IN RURAL BOLIVIA.

| | | Distribution | | Son's characteristics | |
| | | Father | Son | Mean education | Mean standard of living[1] |
Occupational group	Status	(percent)	(percent)	(years)	(0 to 100)
Elite white-collar	100	2	3	11.6	85
Large farmer	75	2	2	4.0	77
Cattle rancher	72	4	2	4.1	72
High white-collar	71	2	3	8.2	77
Skilled modern blue-collar	66	1	3	4.9	72
Clerical and sales	62	2	1	7.0	70
Small business	57	7	6	4.3	70
Specialized farm	33	6	7	4.4	55
Skilled traditional blue-collar	31	10	18	2.6	55
Unskilled nonfarm	31	2	3	1.5	48
Tenant farmer	12	4	3	0.5	46
Farm laborer (peon)	9	24	6	0.7	39
Small farmer	4	32	38	1.0	35
Small livestock owner (landless)	0	2	5	1.2	30
Total[2]		100	100	2.5	50
Number of cases[3]		(1,085)	(1,116)	(1,124)	(1,130)

Source: Head of household survey.

[1]Defined so that the richest get a score of 100 and the poorest zero.
[2]Detail may not add to total because of rounding.
[3]Excluding missing data.

largest category is small farmers who make up over a third of the total. Skilled traditional blue-collar occupations are next with 18 percent of the population and no other group exceeds 10 percent. The fathers of men in our sample followed a similar set of occupations except that there were more farm laborers, since the fathers had for the most part not benefited from land reform. There were also fewer fathers in skilled traditional blue-collar jobs and, of course, in skilled modern blue-collar ones. Educational differences are very marked, ranging from almost twelve years for the average man in elite white-collar occupations to a year or even less for small farmers, farm laborers, and tenant farmers. Differences in standard of living are also marked, elite white-collar men living on the average better than 85 percent of the population while small farmers and small livestock owners brought up the rear over 50 points behind.

We decided to measure occupational status quite simply by the average standard of living incumbents of each of our fourteen occupational groups.[14] These scores were then transformed to a convenient and conventional metric with the highest occupational group (elite white-collar) getting 100 points and the lowest (small livestock owners) getting zero; this linear transformation does not, of course, affect correlations and was done simply to express occupational status into more familiar and intuitively understandable metric. The results are shown in table 2.4 and graphically in figure 2.1. We also scored status in an alternative way, by the mean education of incumbents, a procedure which focuses on human capital rather than income. This, as can be inferred from the great similarity in the rankings of occupation by education and by standard of living in table 2.4, produced scores that were for all practical purposes identical.[15]

Adequacy of Our Measure. Although perhaps plausible, it remains to be shown that our measure of occupational status adequately captures

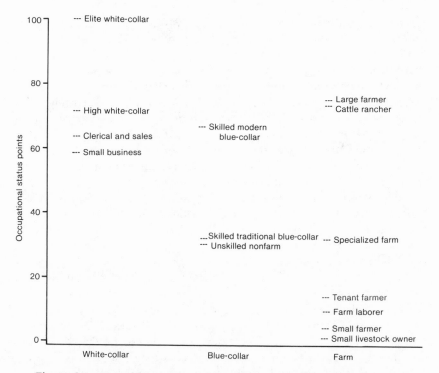

Figure 2.1 Occupational status hierarchy used in the analysis: The "ethnographic" measure of status. See the text and Appendix 3, sections 2 and 3, for details.

what is important about occupations. This is a very real issue since measuring occupational status is difficult, with different procedures often giving different results which easily can lead, and have, to inaccurate substantive conclusions (Treiman 1975, especially in table 3). For our purposes the problem is eased since we are not especially concerned with the absolute size of coefficients but with the changes in them over time; any bias that affects people in all periods equally will therefore have no effect on our conclusions. But the problem is still substantial and we therefore scored occupations by two additional procedures, on the argument that if several different but seemingly reasonable procedures give essentially interchangeable results, much more confidence can be placed in the conclusions.[16]

As it turns out, our fears were groundless. Any one of several very different measures, based on different underlying schemes for classifying occupations and very different ways of assigning status scores to the classification, lead to virtually identical conclusions. The procedures and results are described in detail in Appendix 3, section 3.

METHODS OF ANALYSIS

Cohorts and Time Periods. Our analysis is based on the assumption that the changes we observe in rural Bolivia in the decade and a half following the 1952 revolution can reasonably be attributed to the revolution. We shall see that that is a reasonable assumption since rural Bolivia (and especially the areas we study which exclude the mines and the more politicized Cochabamba valley) was a stagnant, largely unchanging society before 1952; the revolution was not an outgrowth of a long period of politicization and conflict but a sudden change introduced from outside rural society. But we can take up these matters more usefully in later chapters after describing the history of the revolution and so do not discuss them further here.

We also defer to a more appropriate time any discussion of just what is the "short term" (the time period to which some predictions apply) and what is "long term" (to which other predictions apply). We will be able to discuss these more sensibly in chapters 6 and 7 after we learn a good deal more about the revolution.

Regression Analysis. We rely primarily on regression analysis (of which path analysis is a special case) and on related techniques. These are powerful and efficient methods which are now standard in modern work on stratification (Blau and Duncan 1967; Duncan, Featherman, and Duncan 1972; Haller, Otto, Meier, and Ohlendorf 1974; Treiman and Terrell 1975a). For readers unfamiliar with these methods, Appendix 2 gives a brief guide to their use and meaning. We also use an extension of regression analysis, the analysis of covariance, which provides a powerful way of testing our hypothesis that the pattern of relationships is different in different cohorts. Adding a dummy variable for cohort and appropriate interaction terms to an ordinary regression equation gives an analysis of covariance in convenient form (Goldberger 1968: chap. 8).

In their simplest form, these techniques assume that relations are, to a reasonable approximation, linear and additive (Johnston 1963: chap. 4). But when it is theoretically or empirically reasonable to suspect nonlinear relations or interactions, there are well-developed techniques for dealing with them using dummy variables, various nonlinear functional forms, and interaction terms. We have spent considerable time looking for interactions and nonlinearities but have found none of consequence for the questions at hand. Furthermore, a rather large body of experience in stratification research suggests that the assumptions implicit in regression analysis are reasonable (Jackson and Curtis 1972) and, in any event, regression techniques are famously robust in the sense that even quite appreciable violations of the assumptions tend to have little effect on the results (Bohrnstedt and Carter 1971).

Log Linear Analysis. There is, however, a very different procedure introduced by Goodman which seems to offer a valuable way of dealing with some of the issues at hand (see Goodman 1979 and the papers cited there). But when we used it in some early analyses on a related project (Kelley, Robinson and Klein, 1980), we found what appear to be fundamental weaknesses in the technique when it is applied to the type of question of interest here. A computer simulation seems to have confirmed our suspicions (Pescosolido and Kelley 1979) and we have therefore not used these procedures.

CONCLUSION

In this chapter we have described the data and methods we use to test our theory and on which we base our analysis of the effects of the Bolivian revolution. Our primary source is a large and excellent survey of heads of household conducted fourteen years after the revolution in six diverse and representative areas of rural Bolivia. We have described in some detail the geographical and social setting of the six communities and the nature and representativeness of the sample drawn from them. The survey provides extensive data on respondents' subjective perceptions of the revolution and detailed objective data on their family background and occupational history with which to test our predictions about revolution's effects on education and status inheritance. We described our measurement procedures in detail, focusing particularly on the most difficult among them, the measurement of occupational status. We showed that various reasonable alternative measures of status are essentially equivalent to ours, so that our results are not atypical but instead seem to reflect the true status of occupations in rural Bolivia. Our measurement and analytic procedures are, we believe, appropriate and effective for the issues at hand; they are also those which have become customary in modern studies of stratification and social mobility. With these methods and considering the excellent quality of the original survey—and survey data on revolutionary societies are exceedingly rare—we will thus be able to provide what is probably the most rigorous and detailed analysis yet available on the effects of a radical revolution on the lives of ordinary people. But in order to see how revolution changed Bolivian society, we must first find out what that society was like before the revolution. We need, that is, a baseline against which to measure the changes.

3
Prerevolutionary Economy and Society

Revolution changed Bolivia profoundly, but to understand the changes we need to know what it was like before the revolution, we need to have some idea of the context in which revolution appeared and some baseline against which to measure change. The main purpose of this chapter is to provide that baseline. We first describe the Bolivian economy on the eve of revolution, and then describe the conditions under which most Bolivians lived, focusing particularly on inequality and inherited privilege, the issues that will be our main concern throughout the book. A second aim of this chapter is to put Bolivia itself into a wider context, to show the ways in which it is like, and those in which it is unlike, other societies throughout the world. Of course every society is unique in many and important ways, but we will see that, in the broad sweep of things, Bolivia is much like many other poor, highly stratified, mainly agricultural societies found throughout the preindustrial world, and more than a little reminiscent of the agrarian predecessors of many modern European societies. Such societies held the great majority of the world's population from Classical times to the beginning of this century and even today hold a large fraction of it, so what we learn from the Bolivian revolution may not speak to Bolivia alone, or only to the present.

ECONOMY

At the time of the 1952 revolution, the most conspicuous features of the Bolivian economy were two: agriculture and poverty. Roughly two-thirds of the labor force was in agriculture, leaving only a third in mining, manufacturing, commerce, construction, government, and all other industries combined.[1] That is a large agricultural sector, but many Asian and African societies were even more heavily agricultural (see fig. 3.1). So were many industrial societies in the not too distant past; for example, as late as 1750 over two-thirds of the populations of France, Sweden, and the Republic of Venice were agricultural, and they were by no means atypical (Cipolla 1976:73–74; Kuznets 1966: 105–108). Bolivia was also poor, much poorer than the industrial societies of Europe and North America, with a gross national product

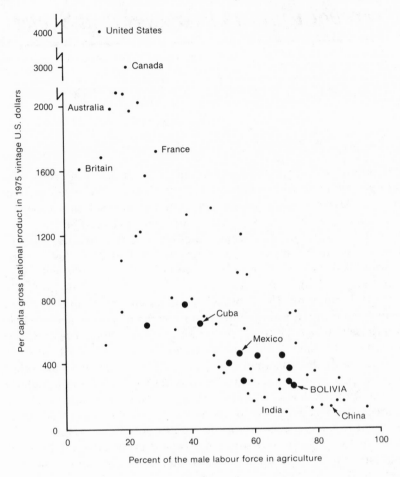

Figure 3.1   Percent of the male labor force in agriculture and per capita gross national product for various countries, circa 1950. Latin American countries are shown by bold dots. *Source*: International Labor Office 1971 and International Bank for Reconstruction and Development 1971.

of only $270 per capita (in 1975 vintage U.S. dollars).[2] That put it below most other countries, as can be seen in figure 3.1, but still above a good many others, mostly in Asia and Africa. Because of the great poverty, food consumption was low, about two-thirds of estimated needs (Wilkie and Reich 1977, tables 106–109). Mortality was high, with a life expectancy of only forty-one years (Celade 1974:54–55), a normal figure for societies at Bolivia's level of development but one nonetheless in sharp contrast with a life expectancy of around seventy years in industrial societies (Kuznets 1966:388). Crude birth rates (47.1 per thousand) were very high but the overall rate of population growth, 2.3 percent, was modest by Latin American standards (República de Bolivia, PDES, vol. 1, table 2).

AGRICULTURE

The main reason Bolivia was so poor was that agricultural productivity was abysmally low, coming to less than $200 a year for each worker (table 3.1). Such low levels of productivity are, of course, common in agrarian societies. In contrast, productivity among traditional artisans was over twice as high, in industrial manufacturing over four times as high, and in mining, Bolivia's premier industry, over sixteen times as high. One reason for agriculture's low productivity was low investment, estimated at less than $400 per worker (table 3.1), but even so other sectors were roughly twice as productive, with mining perhaps ten times as productive. This low productivity was in part a consequence of high population densities on the poor and limited arable land of the Altiplano, together with the appalling costs of transporting goods from more fertile areas to urban markets through some of the world's most rugged mountains. It also reflects the scarcity of attractive opportunities for investment in agriculture, the limited demand and low prices for agricultural goods beyond subsistence crops, and the modest capital resources and limited entrepreneurial skills of most large landowners. Large landowners were basically unwilling to invest in agriculture, preferring to put their surplus

TABLE 3.1

THE STRUCTURE OF THE BOLIVIAN ECONOMY IN 1950:
DISTRIBUTION OF THE LABOR FORCE, GROSS NATIONAL PRODUCT, INVESTMENT,
AND PRODUCTIVITY BY INDUSTRY.

Industry	Labor force (percent)	GNP (percent)	Investment per worker (1975 U.S. $)	Production per worker (1975 U.S. $)
Agriculture and animal husbandry	72	33	382	188
Mining and extractive industries	3	26	9184	3139
Manufacturing:				
Industrial	4	9	4522	885
Artisanal	4	4		447
Other (construction, government, commerce, transport, services etc.)	17	29	2960	731
Total[1]	100	100	$1339	$411
N = 1,350,782		$554,000,000		

Source: CEPAL 1958:tables 19 and 72. The labor force includes both sexes. Converted to 1975 U.S. dollars using the consumer price index.

[1]Detail may not add to total because of rounding.

earnings into urban property, commerce, education for their children, and the like.

Bolivia also suffered from one of the world's more unequal distributions of land. Fully 48 percent of the cultivated land was owned by only 7 percent of the landowners (table 3.2). In sharp contrast, 60 percent of the landowners subsisted on just 6 percent of the cultivated land with an average of barely .8 hectares (2 acres) per family.

INDUSTRY

The industrial sector of the economy presented an equally depressing picture. The vital tin industry was traditionally the most productive sector of the economy. It alone accounted for a quarter of the GNP and was the only major source of foreign exchange, but it had stagnated since the Great Depression despite short cycles of prosperity. From the late 1930s onward there was little new capital investment and aging plants and declining quality ores eventually forced the costs of production up to levels that rapidly became noncompetitive except during wartime shortages. In fact, neither in terms of tonnage nor value has Bolivian mining ever achieved the peak reached in 1929.

The only major advance in the economy since 1930 was in the small sector of manufacturing and then almost exclusively in light industry. During the 1930s and early 1940s there had been an important expansion in this sector, though by 1950 it still employed only 4 percent of the economically active population and accounted for only 9 percent of the GNP (table 3.1).

HUMAN CAPITAL

Just as prerevolutionary Bolivia was very badly off in terms of physical capital and economic productivity, its stock of human capital was low; that, indeed, was one cause of its very low level of productivity. Adult males averaged only a little over two years of schooling.[3] It is useful to have some perspective on how this compares to other countries. While data on years of schooling are not widely available, figures on literacy are available for a variety of countries and are shown in figure 3.2. Bolivia's literacy rate was low in any absolute sense, but that was typical of countries at its level of development.[4] And the consequences of these low levels of education were fateful, since education is intimately linked to income, breadth of knowledge, and "modern" attitudes on a variety of subjects in Bolivia, as throughout the world (Inkeles and Smith 1974).

In Bolivia there were also marked linguistic differences. Spanish was the sole language of education and government and by far the

TABLE 3.2
OWNERSHIP OF AGRICULTURAL LAND BY SIZE OF HOLDING, BOLIVIA, 1950.

Size of property (hectares)

	Under 5–5	5–49	50–199	20–999	1000–4999	5000–9999	10000 & up	Total (N)
Percent of all owners	60	23	6	5	5	1	0.7	101% (85,160 owners)
Cultivated land								
Average amount cultivated (hectares)	0.8	4.4	15	33	42	69	139	7.6
Total owned (%)	6	13	12	21	26	9	13	100% (645,506 ha)
All land								
Total owned (%)	0.3	0.9	1.5	5.5	27	16	50	101% (32,741,096 ha)
Percent of land owned that is under cultivation	54	31	16	7	1.9	1.0	0.5	1.9%

Source: República de Bolivia 1950.

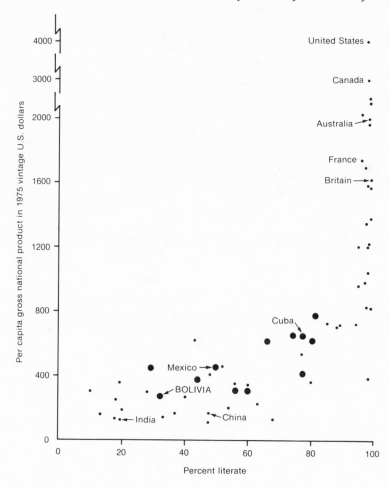

Figure 3.2   Illiteracy and per capita gross national product for various countries, circa 1950. Latin American countries are shown by bold dots. *Source*: United Nations 1961 and International Bank for Reconstruction and Development 1971.

dominant language of business and commerce. But not much more than a third of the male population spoke Spanish as their primary language (República de Bolivia 1955), most of the others being monolingual speakers of Aymara, Quechua, or other Amerindian languages. Lack of Spanish effectively isolated them from the powerful and economically advanced sectors of society. And without Spanish, acquiring education was extraordinarily difficult, since the language of instruction was Spanish and schools were ineffective in teaching the language to their Amerindian-speaking students.

OCCUPATIONAL STRUCTURE

Consistent with the low levels of investment in human and physical capital, the occupational distribution in prerevolutionary Bolivia was heavily skewed toward low status occupations, especially in agriculture. We have already seen the occupational distribution in the ethnographic classification in the last chapter (table 2.4) but can gain some comparative perspective on Bolivia's occupational distribution from table 3.3, which classifies Bolivian occupations into Treiman's classification (1977: 203–208), one for which data are available for a number of other countries in the cross-cultural data set described in chapter 2. For simplicity, we have averaged the occupational distributions for the three developing societies separately from the ten industrial societies in these data. Of course, the striking difference between Bolivia and the other developing societies on the one hand and the industrial societies on the other is that industrial societies have a much greater proportion of the labor force in agricultural occupations.[5] Except for this, however, the other differences are modest. In industrial societies, blue-collar workers are more numerous than white-collar workers and this is true in Bolivia as well, although in the other three developing societies blue- and white-collar workers are about equally numerous. Medium level production workers are consistently the largest group of blue-collar workers in all societies but the remaining blue-collar workers are disproportionately in the skilled, high prestige production jobs in industrial societies but more evenly split between those and unskilled, low prestige jobs in Bolivia and other developing societies. Bolivia seems to have had a rather small white-collar sector, small both absolutely and relative to the blue-collar sector. Within the white-collar group, high prestige sales workers are relatively more numerous in Bolivia and other developing societies than in industrial ones but low professional jobs are less common. High clerical jobs are rare in Bolivia compared both with other developing societies and with industrial ones. But in all we have a relatively simple picture: low-ranking agricultural occupations are much more numerous in Bolivia and other developing countries than in industrial ones, but other differences are relatively modest with much the same range of white- and blue-collar jobs as found throughout the world.

Consistent with the relatively low levels of income, physical capital, and human capital, occupational status in prerevolutionary Bolivia was low. But in comparative perspective, it was not unusually low, as may be seen in figure 3.3 which compares Bolivia with the other societies in the cross-cultural data. In this, as in so many other ways, prerevolutionary Bolivia seems to have been a relatively typical developing society, little different from other societies at the same low level of economic development.

Prerevolutionary Economy and Society

TABLE 3.3

The Occupational Distribution of Prerevolutionary Bolivia in
Comparative Perspective, Percentage Distribution of the
Economically Active Male Population, 10 or Older, in Bolivia in 1950
and Percentage Distribution of the Male Population, 20 or Over,
in Three Developing and Ten Industrial Societies.

Status	Occupations in Treiman's classification	Bolivia, 1950 census		Average, 3 developing societies		Average, 10 industrial societies	
		All	Nonfarm	All	Nonfarm	All	Nonfarm
White collar							
100	High professional	1	3	4	7	7	8
75	Administrative and managerial	0.3	1	3	5	6	7
70	Low professional	1	5	2	3	7	8
60	High clerical	1	2	4	7	5	6
51	High sales	3	9	7	13	5	6
38	Low clerical	2	6	2	4	4	5
32	Low sales	2	9	4	6	2	2
	(subtotal)[1]	(10)	(36)	(26)	(47)	(36)	(42)
Blue Collar							
37	High production	3	11	5	8	15	17
33	High service	1	4	3	5	3	4
24	Medium production	9	31	13	23	24	27
18	Low service	2	8	2	4	2	2
14	Low production	2	9	7	13	7	8
	(subtotal)[1]	(18)	(64)	(29)	(53)	(51)	(58)
Farm							
10	High and medium farm	16	--	26	--	10	--
0	Low farm	56	--	19	--	3	--
	(subtotal)[1]	(72)		(45)		(13)	
	Total[1]	100%	100%	100%	100%	100%	100%

Source: For Bolivia, República de Bolivia 1955. Other countries: Kelley, Treiman, Robinson, Roos, and Thompson 1980. The developing societies are Brazil, Malaysia, the Philippines, and Taiwan; the industrial countries are Australia, Denmark, Finland, Great Britain, the Netherlands, Northern Ireland, Norway, Sweden, the United States, and West Germany. The median number of cases is about 700 and the total N = 35,233. Figures shown are simple arithmetic averages with each country weighted equally.

[1]May not add to detail because of rounding.

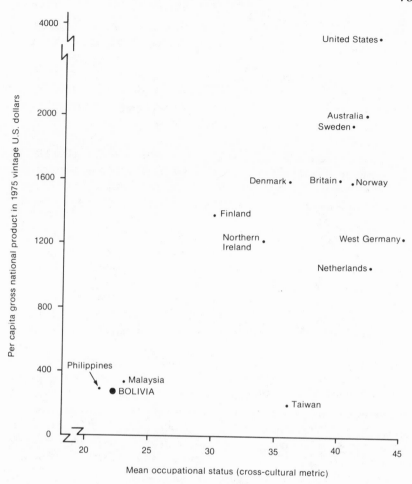

Figure 3.3 Occupational status and gross national product in various countries. Men, 20 years and over, in the experienced labor force. *Source*: Head of household survey and the cross-cultural data set described in chapter 2.

LIVING CONDITIONS

The Bolivian economy was so poor and unproductive that the majority of Bolivians were doomed to a hard life on the margins of subsistence. But the poverty was not equally shared. On the contrary, in Bolivia, as in so many poor, densely populated agrarian societies, there were great inequalities in wealth, power, and privilege. It is to these that we now turn.

LIFE IN RURAL AREAS[6]

Hacienda Peasants.   If Bolivians were on the average poor, the great majority of the rural population lived in truly desperate poverty. In the by no means atypical communities of our study, they lived for the most part in small, crowded, dirt-floored houses without running water, electricity, or sanitary facilities. Clothing was mainly homespun and most peasants went barefoot. Almost all were illiterate and newspapers, books (save for an occasional bible), and other means of contact with the outside world were virtually nonexistent. Nor was the lack of contact with the outside in any way something to be noted, much less regretted, for the great bulk of the rural population had been isolated for generations. This was not entirely by accident since it was in the interests of the rural elite to keep the masses ignorant. Even the now ubiquitous transistor radio did not exist before the revolution. Only Indians in the free communities like San Miguel had systematic contact with the outside world and that contact was restricted mainly to working for it in unskilled jobs.

Hacienda peasants were tied to the land and allowed to cultivate their home plots only on payment of three or four days *per week* of free labor on a regular basis by both the peasant and his wife. In addition to this free labor tax, known as *colonato*, hacienda peasants and their wives were subjected to a tax of personal service known as *ponqueaje*. Once or twice a year for a period of about a week they had to work as personal servants in the landlord's house, or trek to a distant town to deliver goods and provide services in the landlord's house. Except on the landowner's service, the peasant could not leave the land for more than a few days since his labor obligations had to be fulfilled each week. This effectively cut him off from trade and urban employment, even on a seasonal basis.

In addition to their labor, the hacienda peons owed their *hacendados* respect, deference, and obedience. They were expected to act as well-behaved, subservient children toward the hacendado and his family. Like children, they were physically punished if they did not. Even now, fourteen years after the revolution ended all this, many exhacendados look back with nostalgia on the time when "peasants showed us respect." A Sorata woman recounts, "The reform ruined Sorata . . . the peasants used to be humble, greet you when you passed, brought you stuff from their truck gardens—now none of that. They are uppity now." Nor have the peasants forgotten, or forgiven.[7] As we will see in chapter 5, their fondest memory of their revolution was that it made them free, it "made them men."

The relations between peasant and hacendado were paternalistic in other senses as well. The hacendado was an intermediary between the peasant and the outside world, marketing the crops, importing goods from the towns, and dealing with the police when the peasant got into trouble. The paternalism cut the peasant off from direct contact with the outside and prevented him from developing the contacts and skills needed to market his own produce or buy in urban markets. The hacendado handled all trade and not without looking to his self-interest; he was a monopoly supplier of goods and services and, like monopolists everywhere, charged more than the market price. In addition to these abuses, however, these paternalistic ties sometimes were of benefit to the peasant. Hacendados customarily supplied gifts or loans in times of need, hand-me-down clothing, and other modest but not unwelcome help. Through the long-established institution of godparent ties, *compadrazgo*, peasants were able to establish effective kinship ties with hacendados which, although not without some cost to the peasant, obligated the hacendado to provide additional assistance, particularly to the peasant's child. Nonetheless, while paternalism was not without its compensation for the peasant "children," it had a potential for abuse far beyond the more limited, contractual relations typical of exploitation in market societies. Hacendados could not only make a profit from the peasants, but had pervasive control over every aspect of the peasant's life, demanding obedience, respect, and deference from the peasant, his wife, and his children; settling disputes that arose in the peasant's family; using the peasant and his wife as personal servants; and enforcing his claims not just by economic sanctions but by corporal punishment.

Thus although there were strong and well-developed elements of exchange in the relation between peasant and hacendado, each providing some benefits to the other, the terms of this exchange were heavily tilted in the hacendado's favor. And peasants were perfectly well aware of this. They hated the system but were unable to do anything about it, or to express their resentment openly without taking the greatest risks. The system endured not because it was an equal exchange, or anything close to it, but because it was bulwarked by brute force. The police and government supported the hacendado almost without limit or exception; a peasant who disobeyed his hacendado, and sometimes even those who just tried to flee the land, would be promptly jailed, or worse. The army was the ultimate sanction. Throughout Bolivian history, peasants periodically rebelled and, armed with hoes and pitchforks, defied their masters. And throughout Bolivian history, the army shot them down, efficiently and without remorse. This almost feudal system, like its precursor in medieval Europe, was in the last analysis based on the force of arms and sustained by violence.

Even free Indians living on their own lands were effectively exploited by the elite through direct government taxation. Special discriminatory taxes on coca, head taxes on landowning Indians, and finally excessive corvée labor obligations were used to tax the resources of those Indians beyond the reach of the private landowner.

Life among the Elite.   While the peasants were desperately poor, hacendados and the educated elite of the towns lived in considerable comfort, if not luxury. They had large houses, with wooden floors, real furniture, at least a couple of books, and a radio. They had store-bought clothes in European styles, in plenty, kept clean and pressed by their servants. They had cooks and servants and someone to run their errands. They had money to spend entertaining, on parties, on drinking, and on imported goods. Particularly during the periodic times of boom in Coroico and Sorata, money was plentiful and imported goods abundant. For a while during Sorata's heyday, it had better shops than La Paz with goods imported directly from Europe and a substantial European community as well; people occasionally came by muleback from La Paz to shop there. Parties were innumerable, and champagne far from unknown. Children were educated and occasionally sent to foreign universities; leisurely visits to La Paz, and visits from friends and relatives living there, were common. The elite, although provincial by world standards, had horizons far beyond their small communities, and they had wealth, which though modest by world standards, far exceeded that of the poverty-stricken peasants who made up the bulk of the population.

The middle class also lived well, at least in comparison to peasants. Higher white-collar workers, clerical and sales workers, many small businessmen, and blue-collar workers with modern skills were common in the small towns. They far exceeded peasants in education and standard of living, living in modest but adequate housing, often (but not always) wearing store-bought clothes of European style, and with enough money to buy a few luxuries. Most were literate, many had radios, and almost all lived in towns; they were much less isolated and cut off from the outside world than peasants, although of course by no means as cosmopolitan as the elite.

INEQUALITY

In Rural Areas.   It is clear that in rural Bolivia there were great inequalities between elite and mass—great differences in wealth, in education, in culture, and in life-style. We can get some quantitative evidence on these wide differences from the head of household survey. As can be seen in table 3.4, educational differences between the classes are dramatic. Small farmers and the like, who made up the bulk of the population, were almost all functionally illiterate[8] averaging a year or less of education each. Skilled traditional workers had another year or two of education but most were illiterate. Toward the middle and

TABLE 3.4

CLASS DIFFERENCES IN SOCIAL RACE AND EDUCATION IN
PREREVOLUTIONARY BOLIVIA: SOCIAL RACE AND EDUCATION BY
RESPONDENT'S FIRST JOB FOR MEN 26 OR OLDER AT THE TIME OF
THE REVOLUTION.

Status	Respondent's first job in the ethnographic classification[1]	Percent of population	Social race (% Spanish)	Education (mean years)
100.	Elite white-collar	3	97	12
72.	Large farmers and cattle ranchers	4	92	3
66.	High white-collar, clerical and sales, and skilled modern blue-collar	7	82	6
57.	Small business	11	43	3
32.	Skilled traditional blue-collar, unskilled nonfarm, and specialized farm	37	37	2
9.	Farm laborer and tenant farmer	23	21	0.3
4.	Small farmer and small livestock owner	15	28	0.8
	Total	100%	40	2.2
	Number of cases[2]	(623)	(607)	(621)

Source: Head of household survey. Variables are defined in chapter 2.

[1]For this table the classification is collapsed to ensure a reasonable number of cases in each group.
[2]Excluding missing data.

upper parts of the class system, small businessmen were fairly evenly split between functionally literate and illiterate. High white-collar, clerical and sales, and skilled modern blue-collar workers were much more educated, almost all having had some schooling (save for a few of the skilled blue-collar workers), the majority being literate. In spite of their high status, large farmers and cattle owners were not particularly well educated, a situation by no means unique to Bolivia. Finally at the very top, the elite averaged almost twelve years of education, in dramatic contrast with the one year or less of the small farmers and farm laborers at the bottom. Given the profound implications of education for income, knowledge, breadth of vision, and life-style generally, these great differences are indicative of a highly stratified society with a vast gap between upper and lower classes.

This is a matter on which we can also get useful comparative perspective from the cross-cultural data described in chapter 2. As a

simple summary of the magnitude of the gap between the top and the
bottom of the status hierarchy, we take the difference in average
education between high prestige professionals on the one hand and on
the other hand farmers and farm workers.[9] In Bolivia, for example, the
high professional group averages twelve years of education, while
farmers and farm workers have a combined average of one year, for a
gap of eleven years. We computed similar figures for each of the
thirteen other societies in these data, obtaining differences shown in
figure 3.4. It is apparent that the amount of educational inequality
between the top and the bottom of the class system, the amount of
inequality in human capital between the elite and the masses if you like,
is relatively great in Bolivia. But it is not unique; one of the three
developing societies in these data has greater inequality and one of the
industrial societies is not all that far behind.

Differences between upper and lower classes are not confined to
education and income but include the fundamental and pervasive
differences of language, culture, history, style of life, and the complex

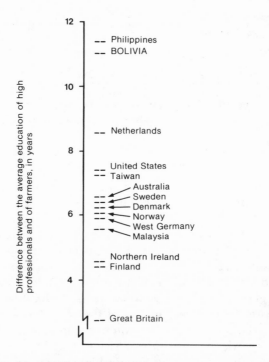

Figure 3.4   Class differences in education in various countries. Difference
between the average education of high professionals and the average education
of farmers and farm laborers for men, 20 years and over, in the experienced
labor force; education measured in years. *Source*: Head of household survey
and the cross-cultural data set described in chapter 2.

of ethnic differences that make up what has been with justice labeled "social race."[10] At one pole are monolingual Aymara Indians, heirs to an ancient Amerindian culture, and at the other pole are monolingual Spanish speakers, heirs to a cosmopolitan culture with an emphasis on literacy, business, and government, with long-standing connections to Europe and at least a passing acquaintance with science and technology. Even in the middle of the twentieth century, many Aymara lived in a style not far removed from that of their peasant ancestors in pre-Columbian times while Spanish speakers lived in a recognizably European style, albeit a generally poor and provincial one. There was also a somewhat smaller intermediate group, the cholos, in the process of moving from an Aymara past to a Spanish future.

These crucial differences in social race generally overlapped with social class, making differences among classes visible in dress, language, and life-style and reinforcing the already wide gulf between the top of society and the bottom. As can be seen in table 3.4, small farmers, small livestock owners, and tenant farmers at the bottom of the status hierarchy were overwhelmingly Aymara, while skilled traditional blue-collar workers and the like somewhat further up the hierarchy and small businessmen in the middle of the hierarchy were fairly evenly split between Aymara and Spanish.[11] The upper third of the hierarchy was overwhelmingly Spanish. But the relation between social race and occupational status was not entirely symmetrical. The elite was almost entirely Spanish with almost no Aymara among them, but there were many poor Spanish speakers so the lower classes were not as homogenously Aymara as the upper class was homogenously Spanish. Poor, Spanish-speaking peons (mainly from the monolingual Reyes and Villa Abecia areas) are a clear example. But for all these minor complexities, the link between class and social race was in the main simple: all of the upper classes were Spanish and most of the lower classes were Aymara. The high correlation between status and social race, .45, attested to a visible and familiar social fact.

Inequality in Bolivia as a Whole.   With these enormous differences between impoverished, illiterate peasants working barefoot on the land on the one hand and rich, literate, and cosmopolitan elites on the other, and with an appreciable middle class in between, prerevolutionary Bolivia was surely one of the more highly stratified societies in the world. While there are, to our knowledge, no systematic statistics on income available for prerevolutionary Bolivia—it was impoverished in statistics as well as in wealth—knowledgeable observers were in virtually unanimous agreement that the distribution of income was extraordinarily unequal, as was the distribution of land.[12] We turn now to a final difference between classes, one central to our concerns in this book: the extent to which the elites' advantages and the peasants' disadvantages are passed on to their children.

STATUS INHERITANCE

In a highly traditional and stratified society, how was status passed on from one generation to the next? How much of an advantage was it to be born into the comfortable home of a well-educated, high-status government functionary or large landowner, and how much of a disadvantage was it to be born into the home of a poor, illiterate, Aymara peasant? Since the differences in wealth and human capital between families at the top of the hierarchy and those at the bottom are very large, there are theoretical reasons to expect that the advantage of being born into a high status home, or the disadvantage of being born in a low status home, would be very large—when the differences between the fathers is large, the difference in the resources of physical and human capital that they have to give to their sons is correspondingly large, and the advantages of birth will be large (see chap. 1). We will see that prerevolutionary Bolivia clearly fits this general pattern, the advantages of birth being large both absolutely and in comparison to other countries.

A First Look at the Advantages of Birth

The head of household survey[13] gives us a good measure of the advantage of being born into a high status family in prerevolutionary Bolivia with respect to education and occupational status at the beginning of a career.[14] Let us begin by looking at the influence of father's occupation on son's education, shown in table 3.5. Sons from elite white-collar families are greatly advantaged, receiving on the average nine years of education, four times the usual figures for their generation.[15] Sons from high white-collar, clerical and sales, and skilled modern blue-collar families do almost equally well. Some from small business families lag behind, averaging five years.[16] Then there is another substantial gap, with sons from skilled traditional blue-collar and similar homes getting only three years of education. Finally sons of farmers and farm laborers, over half the population, are greatly disadvantaged, averaging only a year of education or less. The sons of large farmers and cattle ranchers do well, but not as well as would be expected from their fathers' high status and considerable wealth; in part this is because their fathers were less educated than fathers of comparable status in nonfarm occupations. With this exception, educational advantages decline quite consistently with status. What is really conspicuous is the large size of these advantages.

The occupational advantages of being born into a high status family are also very great, as shown in the last column of table 3.5. Sons from elite white-collar homes on the average wind up almost two-thirds of the way up the occupational hierarchy, in jobs around the high white-

TABLE 3.5

INFLUENCE OF FAMILY BACKGROUND ON EDUCATION AND OCCUPATION
IN PREREVOLUTIONARY BOLIVIA: EDUCATION AND STATUS OF FIRST JOB BY
FATHER'S OCCUPATION FOR MEN 26 OR OLDER AT THE TIME OF
THE REVOLUTION.

Status	Father's occupation in the ethnographic classification[1]	Percent of population	Son's education (mean years)	Son's first job (mean status on a scale of 0 to 100)
100.	Elite white-collar	3	9	61
72.	Large farmers and cattle ranchers	7	5	49
66.	High white-collar, clerical and sales, and skilled modern blue-collar	5	8	55
57.	Small business	8	5	56
32.	Skilled traditional blue-collar, unskilled nonfarm, and specialized farm	17	3	37
9.	Farm laborer and tenant farmer	29	0.5	18
4.	Small farmer and small livestock owner	32	0.6	24
	Total[2]	100	2.2	31 (595)
	Number of cases[3]	(597)	(596)	

Source: Head of household survey. Variables are defined in chapter 2.

[1]In this table the occupational classification for fathers is collapsed to ensure a reasonable number of cases in each group.
[2]Total may not add to detail because of rounding.
[3]Excluding missing data.

collar, clerical and sales, or skilled modern blue collar level. Sons of large farmers and cattle ranchers have a substantial advantage, but rather less than would be expected on the basis of their fathers' status. Sons from high white-collar, clerical and sales, skilled modern blue-collar, and small business homes tend to enter jobs only a little below elite white-collar sons (but six or seven points above large farmers). Sons from skilled traditional blue-collar and related families do noticeably worse, almost 20 points lower. Finally the great majority of the population who were born into the homes of small farmers, farm laborers, and the like have only meager prospects themselves. With the partial exception of the large farmers, the pattern is again quite regular with high status families providing consistently greater advantages than low status ones. And the size of that advantage is striking.

By way of summary, the correlation[17] between father's occupational status and son's education is .63, that single figure giving a compact summary of the relation we have just considered in detail.[18] Analogously, the correlation between the occupation of father and son is .53. Both of these figures are high in any absolute sense, as high as the correlation between the height of father and son, for example.

A Comparative Perspective. We can gain a useful perspective by comparing these correlations with those found in other societies. Data of this sort are rare but two useful collections exist. One, the cross-cultural study described in chapter 2, includes national sample data on ten industrial and three developing societies (Kelley, Treiman, Robinson, Roos, and Thompson 1980). The other, which we call the Latin American study, has data on nine Latin American cities, on the United States, and on the Toro, a tribal African society (Kelley 1978). Both collections have advantages and disadvantages for our purposes but together they provide useful comparative data for a wide range of societies from the relatively unstratified and equalitarian (Britain, Malaysia, Toro) to the highly stratified cities of Latin America.[19] Differences in method tend to make correlations systematically lower in the cross-cultural study than in the Latin American (something like .05 lower, judging from the results for Bolivia and the United States that appear in both collections), so a close comparison is not without risk.[20] Nonetheless, results for either study can be more closely compared with those for other countries in the same study.

The results, given in figure 3.5, show that prerevolutionary Bolivia was in no way atypical. The very close correlation between father's occupation and both his son's education and his son's first job in Bolivia is perhaps somewhat smaller than that typically found in large Latin American cities but somewhat larger than that typically found elsewhere. There is a great deal of variation from society to society, with both sets of correlations ranging from a bit under .3 to over .6, but Bolivia generally falls toward the upper end of the range.

MECHANISMS OF STATUS TRANSMISSION

We have seen that being born into a high status family conferred a substantial advantage in prerevolutionary Bolivia but have not yet seen how that came about—how much of the advantage is attributable to the father's occupational position and how much to the father's human capital? How much of the occupational advantage that a son acquires comes about indirectly because of the educational advantages of birth and how much from other, more direct reasons such as inheriting the family farm?

We can obtain good evidence on these questions by regression

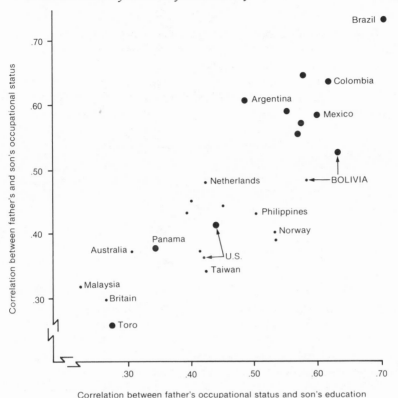

Figure 3.5 Influence of family background on education and occupation for men in various countries. Bold dots indicate societies, mainly Latin American cities, where occupation is first job measured by locally developed scales. Other dots indicate societies, mainly industrial, where occupation is current occupation measured by the cross-cultural scale. *Source*: Kelley 1978, and Kelley, Treiman, Robinson, Roos, and Thompson 1980.

techniques, robust, effective, and long-established procedures in this context (see chap. 2).[21] The results are shown in table 3.6 using both our usual "ethnographic" status score and the cross-cultural score for comparative purposes (see chap. 2). The partial regression (or path) coefficient in the upper left hand corner of the table, for example, shows the effect of father's occupation on son's education *deflated* to take account of the fact that some of the original relation (shown earlier in table 3.5) came about spuriously and should properly be attributed to father's education.[22] The metric regression coefficients present the relation in concrete units (e.g., years of education). The advantage of the standardized coefficients, and really it is their only advantage, is that they can be directly compared to each other, so in our example, we

Prerevolutionary Economy and Society

TABLE 3.6
INHERITED PRIVILEGE IN PREREVOLUTIONARY BOLIVIA IN COMPARATIVE
PERSPECTIVE: REGRESSION ANALYSES OF THE EFFECT OF FAMILY BACKGROUND ON
EDUCATION AND OCCUPATIONAL STATUS. STANDARDIZED (β) AND METRIC (b)
PARTIAL REGRESSION COEFFICIENTS FOR BOLIVIAN MEN, 26 OR OLDER AT THE
TIME OF THE REVOLUTION, AND MEN, 20 OR OLDER, IN VARIOUS OTHER
SOCIETIES. STATUS IS MEASURED EITHER BY THE ETHNOGRAPHIC METRIC
(COLUMNS 1 AND 2) OR BY THE CROSS-CULTURAL METRIC (COLUMNS 3 AND 4);
UNITS ARE SHOWN IN PARENTHESES.

| | Status in the ethno-graphic metric | | Status in the cross-cultural metric | |
| | Bolivia | | Bolivia | Mean, eight societies[1] |
Variable	β (1)	b (2)	b (3)	b (4)
Panel 1: Effects on son's education (years)				
1. Father's occupation (0 to 100)	.28	.039	.035	.035
2. Father's education (years)	.51	.503	.557	.424
3. (percent of variance explained, R^2)		(53)	(52)	(30)
4. (Constant)		(0.3)	(1)	(5)
Panel 2: Effects on son's occupation $(0-100)^2$				
5. Father's occupation (0 to 100)	.37	.346	.386	.337
6. Father's education (years)	.22	1.45	1.41	1.58
7. (percent of variance explained, R^2)		(30)	(29)	(19)
8. (Constant)		(20)	(9)	(18)
Panel 3: Effects on son's occupation $(0-100)^2$				
9. Father's occupation (0 to 100)	.27	.253	.273	.195
10. Father's education (years)	.04[a]	0.26[a]	−0.45[a]	−0.51[b]
11. Education (years)	.36	2.37	3.37	4.87
12. (percent of variance explained, R^2)		(36)	(42)	(42)
13. (Constant)		(19)	(6)	(6)

Source: Bolivian data from the head of household survey, N = 628. Other data from Kelley, Treiman, Robinson, Roos, and Thompson 1980; the median number of cases for the 8 societies is 550 and the total N = 27,340.

[1]Simple arithmetic average of separate analyses of Denmark, Finland, Norway, the Philippines, Sweden, Taiwan, the United States, and West Germany; other countries lacked data on father's education.

[2]First job in columns 1 and 2 and current occupation in columns 3 and 4.

   a. Coefficient not significantly different from zero at p<.05, two-tailed.

   b. Six of the 8 coefficients were not significantly different from zero at p<.05, two-tailed.

see that a son's education is shaped appreciably more by his father's education than by his father's occupation. We will, however, focus on the metric coefficients since they are more informative.

Our best estimate is that the *educational* advantage of being born into a high status home amounts, on the average and other things being equal, to about four hundredths of one year of education for each point of the father's occupational status (table 3.6, line 1). So, to take a concrete example, let us think of two fathers with the same education, one of whom has an elite white-collar job (100 status points) and the other of whom is a llama herder (zero status points). Our best estimate is that a son born into the first family will typically get 3.9 years of education more than a son born into the second, just because his father has a better job.[23] That is a substantial advantage, especially in a society where sons on the average get only two years of education.[24] It also helps to have a well-educated father, our best estimate being that each year of the father's education is worth half a year of education to his son (table 3.6, line 2). So, for example, if we compare two fathers with the same occupational status one of whom has ten years of education and the other of whom has none at all, the first's son will typically get five years more education than the second's.[25] That too is a very substantial advantage.

We have seen that being born into a privileged family in prerevolutionary Bolivia confers a substantial educational advantage and now ask what kind of an *occupational* advantage it provides. The simplest answers, given in Panel 2, show that the advantages are substantial. Other things being equal, every point of father's status is worth over a third of a status point to his son. For example, if we once again compare two fathers who have the same education but differ in occupation, one having an elite white-collar job and the second being a llama herder, the first will typically be able to help his son get a job thirty-five status points higher than the second's son. That is, for example, more than the difference between a landless llama herder and a skilled traditional craftsman, more than a third of the whole occupational hierarchy which runs from a low of zero to a high of one hundred. It also helps to have a well-educated father since each year of father's education confers an advantage worth one and a half status points to the son. So, for example, if two fathers have the same occupation but one has ten years of education and the other has none, the first's son will typically get a job fifteen status points higher than the second's, an advantage not to be scoffed at in a society where the average occupational status was only thirty points.

Some of these occupational advantages come about indirectly because family background influences how much education a son receives and that in turn affects his occupational status. We can see how much by introducing education explicitly into the analysis and that is done in Panel 3. In this analysis the effect of father's occupation is somewhat smaller than it was in the previous calculation, the difference between the two indicating the part of the advantage of having a high status father that comes about indirectly through education.[26] That comes to approximately a third of the total.[27] So most of the advantage of having a high status father comes about not through education but more directly; the inheritance of land and wealth is an obvious candidate.[28] Father's education, however, shows quite a different pattern (Panel 3, tenth line). If you compare the occupational status of two sons who themselves have the same amount of schooling and whose fathers have similar jobs, then it does not matter at all how much education their fathers had. This means that the substantial advantages of having a well-educated father come about entirely indirectly; well-educated fathers help their sons get extra schooling and that in turn helps their sons get better jobs, but that is the only way educated fathers can help their sons.[29]

We might ask if other aspects of family background, in addition to father's occupation and education, are important. In fact, social race does matter but not a lot, and we defer consideration of it to chapter 7.[30] But that seems to be all. Differences between farm and nonfarm families are insignificant,[31] and some considerable searching for other relevant factors turned up nothing of consequence.

A Comparative Perspective.   It is useful, once again, to put Bolivia in a wider perspective. To do this, we compare the advantages of family background in Bolivia to the corresponding advantages in eight societies for which we have comparable data.[32] We have averaged the coefficients for the eight and present the averages in table 3.6 (last column); this is a rough-and-ready summary procedure but serves to substantially simplify the presentation and focus it on Bolivia, advantages that more than make up for the loss of detail.

In prerevolutionary Bolivia these data suggest that family background conferred a greater educational advantage than in most other societies (Panel 1). The part of that advantage due to father's occupational status was the same in Bolivia as elsewhere but the advantage of coming from a highly educated home was much larger. So on the whole, family background explained more than half again the variance in son's education in Bolivia as in the eight other countries for which we have comparable data.

The effect of family background on occupational status was also at least as large in prerevolutionary Bolivia as elsewhere in the world (Panel 2).[33] In all, family background explained half again as much variance in son's occupation in Bolivia. Finally, education is the strongest single influence on occupational status in all societies but its impact was somewhat smaller in Bolivia than in the predominantly industrialized societies with which we are comparing it. So in all we have a by now familiar picture: the advantages of birth in prerevolutionary Bolivia were large but were by no means unusual. And the mechanisms by which these advantages were conveyed from one generation to the next were much like those found elsewhere (see Kelley, Robinson, and Klein 1980).

CONCLUSION

ECONOMY

Prerevolutionary Bolivia was predominantly agricultural. The land was very unequally distributed, the majority of farmers having less than one hectare while the top eight percent of landowners had almost half the cultivated land. With a large pool of free but unskilled labor and a small and uncertain market for farm products, most hacendados followed traditional, inefficient, labor-intensive forms of agriculture. They were unwilling to invest in agriculture or lacked the skills needed to do so, preferring to invest instead in urban property, various middlemen enterprises, and education. Agricultural investment was therefore low, under four hundred dollars per worker, and productivity appalling, less than two hundred dollars annually per worker.

Manufacturing industry was minimal, confined exclusively to light urban industries and semifinishing of local agricultural products. It absorbed only four percent of the economically active population. The heart of the national economy was the great tin mines but they employed only a small percentage of the labor force, had little impact on the rest of the economy, and were declining by 1950.

Consistent with the general poverty of the country, and one cause of it, was the low level of investment in human capital. The vast majority of the population was illiterate and adult males averaged only a little over two years of school. Good jobs were scarce and occupational status averaged a little over twenty points on a scale where industrial societies average about forty.

But in all this Bolivia was fairly typical of the less developed predominantly agricultural societies of the world. Other societies in Latin America, Asia, and Africa were as heavily agricultural and many had even larger agricultural sectors. Others were equally poor, and many more so. Others had as low levels of education and occupational status, and some had lower.

SOCIETY

Prerevolutionary Bolivia was thus a poor society. It was also highly stratified. A small, exploitative elite had for centuries ruled a large, impoverished peasant mass and a smaller middle class of traditional craftsmen, clerks, and the like. The hold of rural landowners over their peasants was essentially feudal; the hacendado was the lord and the peasants were serfs. In exchange for being allowed to cultivate a little land for subsistence, the peasants and their wives owed a crushing labor obligation of three days free labor on the hacendado's lands each week. In addition to this free labor tax, they were subject to a tax of personal service for extended periods several times per year. Deference and humility were also expected and disobedience often led to corporal punishment; the peasant was seen as a child. Brutal and exploitative as the system was, it was fully supported by the State. Peasant protests and rebellions were ruthlessly suppressed, Indians were denied access to arms, and garrisons of federal troops were located in all the rural areas to enforce the will of the local white and cholo elite.

The peasants lived in abject poverty, in dirt-floored homes, with minimal diets and homespun clothes. But the elite lived well, in large houses with servants and parties. They also lived in a different cultural world. In contrast to the illiterate and isolated peasants, unable even to speak the language of government and commerce, the elite were literate, fluent in Spanish, able to visit the capital, modestly cosmopolitan, and at least vaguely aware of modern science and technology. This was, then, a society of great inequality, with an enormous gulf between the top and the bottom.

In part because of this great inequality, the advantages of being born into a high status family were large and the disadvantage of being born into a poor family crippling. The elite lived well and were able to pass on land, wealth, and human capital to their children; the middle class did not live so well, albeit much better than the peasants, and were able to pass on a good deal to their children, while the peasants were mired in ignorance and poverty, and their children after them. These advantages were, however, not atypical in a wider perspective. They were greater than in most industrial societies but smaller than in many developing societies, particularly in Latin America. The advantages of birth came about in ways that were also common in other societies. Human capital was a crucial link; upper class fathers were much more successful than lower class fathers in getting education for their sons and that in turn gave their sons a great advantage in the job market. But that was not all; in addition to human capital there was a substantial advantage to having a high status father which probably reflected the advantages of money, land, and property.

The setting for the revolution was thus a poor and highly stratified society, but one like many other agrarian societies past and present. Having set the stage and provided a baseline against which to highlight the changes that were soon to occur, it is time now to introduce our protagonist, the revolution of 1952. We do that in the next chapter and then devote the rest of the book to describing the changes that flowed from this violent and dramatic transformation.

4
The Revolution

PRELUDE

The beginning of the end of traditional Bolivian society was marked by fundamental changes in the economy in the decade of the 1920s. The great tin mines were, as we have seen, the heart of the national economy but their brilliant postwar recovery masked a fundamental change for the worse. The progressive decline in the tin content of the ores led to the decline of foreign investment, to progressive decapitalization as the three giants of the tin industry invested their profits elsewhere, and thus to a substantial decline in productivity in the following decades. Aggravating this, the price of tin had begun a long-term decline in the middle 1920s and by the early 1930s the international tin market was in a state of near collapse as consumption dropped throughout the world because of the Great Depression. The impact on Bolivia was profound, with production declining and the mining industry reducing its work force and its contribution to the national economy.

THE GENERATION OF THE CHACO

The economic impact of the tin industry's decline and the Great Depression created severe political strains which the government was incapable of handling. In the 1920s, the Republican party had replaced the Liberals and in turn had split into several personalistic factions the most conservative of which, led by Daniel Salamanca, seized power in a coup de état in 1936. But the new government was unable to handle the political crisis created by the depression and, desperate for a distraction, seized an excuse to provoke a long-standing frontier dispute over some desolate and unpopulated areas in the southeastern lowlands into a full-scale war with Paraguay.

The Chaco War was a long and costly disaster for Bolivia. Three years of bitter fighting left 100,000 Bolivian men dead, wounded, deserted, or captured. It also lost far more territory than Paraguay had claimed even in its most extreme demands. The fact that Bolivia entered the war with a better equipped and supposedly far better trained army only aggravated the sense of frustration among the literate elite of the nation.

Previously wedded to the traditional elite and party system, the young veterans of the middle- and upper-class families now refused to support their rule. Suddenly the Bolivian political spectrum was filled with a host of small parties and groups that had not existed in the prewar period. Although some socialist and Communist groups had been formed in Bolivia in the 1920s, they had been destroyed by Salamanca during the war. Virtually no contact had existed between these extemely marginal groups (which were even poorly represented in the labor movement) and the traditional prewar parties. From 1935 on, however, this vacuum was filled by a host of competing groups, all of which sapped the strength of the traditional parties on the right and encouraged the expansion of the extreme parties on the left.

The Military Socialists. This new postwar political growth among literate whites and cholos prevented any one leader or party from gaining control of the government. Finally, in early 1936 the army seized power in a coup supported by a large number of the new moderate socialist groups. This was the army's first return to power since 1880. The newly politicized army reflected the new currents of what everyone was beginning to call the *generación del chaco*. The military regime was led by the junior officer veterans of the Chaco war who declared themselves socialist. The rule of the so-called military socialists led to fervent reformist activity, producing the first serious social legislation ever enacted in Bolivia and a major political restructuring. The radical military officers enacted Bolivia's first labor code, wrote a totally new national constitution which declared private property a right dependent upon social utility, and proposed the active intervention of the State in promoting welfare and social change. Standard Oil Company holdings in Bolivia were nationalized. Finally, the government promoted unionization of workers and supported the proliferation of a host of radical new parties to challenge the power of the old oligarchic entities.

But the radicalism of the union officers frightened the more traditional elements in the army, and when President Germán Busch committed suicide in 1939 the senior officers reasserted control and invited the traditional oligarchic parties back into power. Thus began the attempt, from 1939 to 1952, to reverse the political forces unleashed by the Chaco war and the radical regime of the military socialists. The traditional parties were forced to band together in a united front against the rising strength of the new political forces in that nation. At first committed to a traditional presidential and parliamentary system, by the late 1940s they abandoned all efforts to govern democratically, turning to the army as the sole guarantor of their political, economic, and social interests. But this return to conservative military rule was doomed to failure, given the political mobilization which had already begun, and which the traditional elite was incapable of stopping even through the use of force.

RISE OF THE MNR

Political Mobilization.   Bolivian politics had previously been the sole prerogative and concern of a small, literate elite of urban whites and cholos, political movements by other groups having been firmly suppressed, if necessary by force of arms. But beginning in the middle 1930s, new groups at all levels of Bolivian society were able to mobilize themselves politically. In the late 1930s and early 1940s tin miners were finally able to organize powerful unions. A series of bloody and violent strikes and government massacres ensued, the most famous being the Catavi massacre at the Patiño Company mines in December of 1942. Factory workers and other urban elements also unionized. Even among previously isolated peasants syndicalism efforts began, with some success among the Quechua peasants of the Cochabamba valley but little among the larger Aymara population.

During the early 1940s political opinion among the literate white and cholo population became steadily more radical. Radical Marxist parties of all types were organized, most of which demanded nationalization of the basic resources and other modifications of Bolivia's capitalist economy. Three radical parties eventually emerged: the Trotskyite Partido Obrero Revolucionario (POR), with close links to the unionized miners; the Marxist Partido de la Izquierda Revolucionario (PIR), with powerful support in the middle class; and the Movimiento Nacionalista Revolucionario (MNR), an amalgam socialist and fascist party which claimed both middle-class and union support. Though all three parties were prolabor, their respective international sympathies prevented a merger into a single revolutionary force; consequently, the traditional government was able to last for another decade, despite the basic weakness of the traditional parties and the continued division within the army between radical and conservative elements.

The First MNR Government.   The feud between radical and conservative elements in the army erupted again in 1946 when a fascist officer lodge seized the government and brought the MNR to power as its major civilian ally. The MNR succeeded in organizing the first national federation of mine workers and also held the first national Indian congress of peasant representatives. But its pro-Axis foreign policy and its support for internal violence alienated the powerful Marxist PIR as well as the traditional parties, all of whom—with powerful U.S. backing—formed an antifascist coalition and overthrew the MNR-military regime in July of 1946. In allying with the Marxist PIR, the traditional parties admitted their inability to control the electorate which, although limited to urban literates, had now become extremely radicalized. But in the six years of conservative rule that followed, the Marxist PIR's support eroded because of its alliance with a conservative government determined to depoliticize the working classes and remove all radical elements from the middle class.

The end result was the rise of the MNR once again to a preeminent position. Removing its more profascist elements and absorbing the most important labor supporters of the Trotskyite POR, the MNR became a powerful middle and working class movement of socialist reform and the leading opponent of the rule of the traditional elite. By mid-1949 it was able to lead a powerful revolt that almost succeeded in overthrowing the government. In the presidential elections of 1951 the party emerged victorious, only to have the military seize power to forestall an MNR government. Thus the stage was set for a full-scale assault on the national government on April 9, 1952.[1]

INSURRECTION

April 9, 1952

On Wednesday, the ninth of April, the MNR once again rose in rebellion against the government. Armed groups of civilians, municipal police, and tin miners seized La Paz in three days of heavy fighting during which they defeated the professional Army of Bolivia. Some 600 people were killed. MNR civilians seized the national armories and distributed the weapons to their supporters, an event which signaled the end of the traditional oligarchy. The national government collapsed and the army surrendered to the rebels.

The victorious rebels set out deliberately and systematically to destroy the old regime. They dismissed the entire officer corps, jailing or exiling most of them, and closed the military college. They continued to distribute arms to the civilian population and within five days had set up a national system of armed worker and civilian militias (Malloy 1970). The militias were turned into the nation's most powerful military organization and given the most modern arms. Making good on its pledge, the MNR created a state monopoly over mineral exports in July and then nationalized the big three tin producers in October, organizing them into a state company, the COMIBOL. This gave the government an overwhelmingly dominant role in the national economy. With the government oil monopoly (YPFB) and the state development corporation (CBF), both established before the revolution, the takeover of the mining industry made the State the single largest producer of goods and services in the nation and the largest single employer. Virtually the entire export sector and the bulk of such modern manufacturing industry as existed were in government hands.

Given the crucial role of organized labor in the revolt, the MNR permitted the steady growth of a powerful, armed, and independent labor movement that eventually rivaled the government in power. The miners were allowed to organize a national labor confederation, the COB (Bolivian Labor Center). Although nominally loyal to the MNR, the labor confederation encouraged members of the Communist and Trotskyite parties to participate and was dominated by no single party. The labor confederation was immediately granted the right to appoint three to five members in the national cabinet and, together with the miners' union, appointed two of the seven directors of the nationalized tin mining company. These directors were also given veto power over all decisions by the tin company, effectively giving the workers co-government of the mines. Every Bolivian was given the right to vote regardless of literacy or race, and the government granted both workers and peasants the right to organize and to bear arms.

REVOLUTION IN THE COUNTRYSIDE

Although it originated in the capital and in the mines, with only minimal support from the countryside where the vast majority of Bolivians dwelled, and triumphed in the capital, the revolution caused changes in the countryside which were even more fundamental than the sweeping changes in the mines and cities. Fearful for the conservative middle-class element in the MNR, the various Marxist radicals and the organized labor movement pushed hard for a thoroughgoing revolution in the previously quiescent rural areas. They began by distributing arms to the peasants, giving them effective weapons for the first time since the Spanish conquest four centuries earlier. Together with the collapse of the national army, previously the ultimate source of oppression, and the arrival of revolutionary organizers from the urban areas, this led to a violent revolution in the countryside.

With an uneasy government reluctantly keeping to the sidelines, the peasants used their traditional community organizations as the basis of formal union (*sindicato*) organizations and were able to mobilize rapidly, after centuries of impotence and oppression, quickly becoming the dominant military force in the countryside. Their immediate targets were the haciendas, their owners and families and retainers, and the exploitative small town marketing structures developed by whites and cholos. From April 1952 to the middle of 1953, armed peasants systematically terrorized their opponents and destroyed the old hacienda system. As in the "Great Fear" period of the French Revolution, the Bolivian peasants burned work records, killed or harassed landowners, and in short order forced the old elite into exile in the capital or abroad.[2]

So powerful did the peasants become that a reluctant MNR government was forced to accept the inevitable and move toward a radical agrarian reform. In January of 1953 a study commission was established to deal with the problem. But this only further strengthened the hand of the armed peasant unions. So powerful had these become, especially around the Lake Titicaca area of the altiplano (see Albo 1979) and in the Cochabamba valley (Dandler 1969), that they were able to stop urban-rural trade and to create systematic strikes against the government. In February of 1953 armed peasants even succeeded in invading and temporarily taking over Cochabamba, the second largest city in the nation, in protest over government attempts to stop the unionization movement. By the time agrarian reform was finally decreed in August of 1953 de facto land redistribution had already occurred in most areas of Bolivia. Moreover, fearing the cumbersome nature of the legalization process, and wisely so, the now organized unions encouraged their members to continue with land seizures until all were satisfied. So effective was this that by the mid-1950s there were no longer any traditional landlords and hacendados in most of the major Indian peasant areas and most rural violence then concerned traditional feuds between neighboring communities and leadership conflicts. Dispossessed landlords received no effective compensation from the peasants or the government.

Of course not all peasants benefited, since some already owned their land before the revolution and others lived in remote areas where the old elite was able to subvert or wholly evade land reform. Some very rough calculations suggest that a little less than one-half of the agricultural population benefited.[3] This makes the Bolivian reform one of the most extensive in the history of Latin America, trailing only the great Mexican reform of 1916 (and probably the Cuban reform, although firm data are lacking), and far ahead of any others (see table 4.1).

Not only was the hold of the hacendados broken and land redistributed but at the same time all the traditional feudal work obligations were destroyed. These were onerous burdens, generally involving three or four days of free work each and every week and effectively tying peasants to the land, preventing them from taking advantage of opportunities for seasonal work elsewhere and forcing them to rely on exploitative middlemen to market their produce and supply manufactured goods from the cities. The end of these work obligations enabled peasants to take advantage of employment opportunities elsewhere, to market their own goods, and to buy in the less expensive urban markets.

Political Participation. Our survey data also document the enormous increase in political participation ushered in by the revolution. Before 1952 virtually no one had joined a peasant union but a good number joined in that year and many more in the following year, when

TABLE 4.1

LAND REFORM IN FOURTEEN LATIN AMERICAN SOCIETIES.[1]

Country[3]	Date program began	Number of families benefited	Number of hectares distributed or confirmed	Approximate percent of all farm families benefited[2]
Bolivia	1955	208,181	9,740,681	45
Brazil	1964	46,457	957,106	1
Chile	1965	15,800	2,093,300	4
Colombia	1961	91,937	2,832,312	6
Costa Rica	1963	3,889	60,055	3
Dominican Republic	1963	9,717	46,082	3
Ecuador	1964	27,857	152,115	6
Guatemala	1955	26,500	166,734	5
Honduras	1963	5,843	90,642	2
Mexico	1916	2,525,811	59,413,656	67
Nicaragua	1964	8,117	357,989	5
Panama	1963	2,594	37,339	3
Peru	1961	31,600	850,522	3
Venezuela	1959	117,286	4,605,594	25

Source: Wilkie 1974: 3 for the first three columns.

[1]To 1969. Figures are, of course, approximate.

[2]A very rough estimate. The number of farm families is estimated as the percent of the 1960 labor force in agriculture times the 1960 population, divided by average family size, estimated as 5. See text for cautions.

[3]Data for Cuba are not available.

the revolution finally reached these rural areas (see fig. 4.1). The change in Compi, the ex-hacienda community near Lake Titicaca in the center of Aymara revolutionary ferment, was dramatic. Before the revolution there were no union members on the hacienda but a fifth joined in the earliest stages of the revolution and a year later four-fifths were members and the union controlled the now liberated hacienda. Membership soon stabilized at 90 percent and remained there until the time of our survey in 1966 and presumably thereafter. Control over land was, of course, the crucial issue and in the otherwise similar Aymara community of San Miguel, a free community that had always owned its land, there was no union at all, even a decade after the revolution. In the two ethnically mixed and highly stratified towns of the nearby Yungas, Sorata, and Coroico, fewer than 3 percent of the heads of household had been union members before the revolution but that increased noticeably in 1952 and dramatically a year later. Within a few years of the revolution it stabilized at about 20 percent for Coroico and 40 percent for the more politicized Sorata, where the unions dominated much of the local economy. It then increased very slowly for the next decade and a half. The two geographically isolated

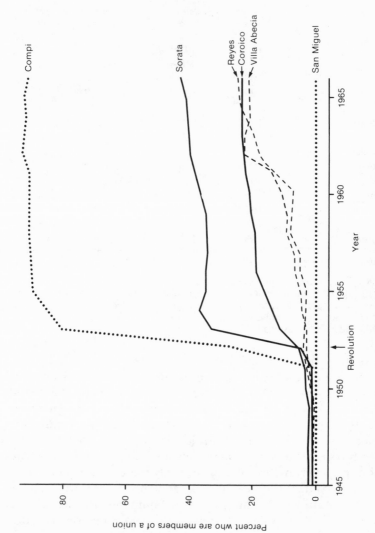

Figure 4.1 Proportion of the population of each town, 20 years or older, who were members of a union, 1945–1966. *Source:* Head of household survey.

Spanish towns, Reyes and Villa Abecia, did not feel the first blast of the revolution and changed only a little in the first few years. But in the years that followed the revolution gradually changed them and union membership slowly but steadily increased, finally reaching 25 percent, the same level as Coroico, a decade later. So the effects of the revolution on political participation were both swift and dramatic for the majority of the population living in the traditional center of Bolivian society, the altiplano and the nearby valleys; gradual but still important for the geographically isolated and socially traditional areas far removed from the center; and nonexistent for the already free peasant communities.

Support for the revolutionary party also showed an equally dramatic increase just following the revolution. Our retrospective data refer to formal party membership rather than simple support and so understate the level of popular support by about half,[4] but the pattern of change is again clear. Before the revolution very few people were members of a political party, even the governing party, but in 1952 and the couple of years immediately following, support blossomed, as can be seen in figure 4.2. This was almost all support for the MNR; not until it fell from power a dozen years later did its support wane, or substantial support for another party grow.

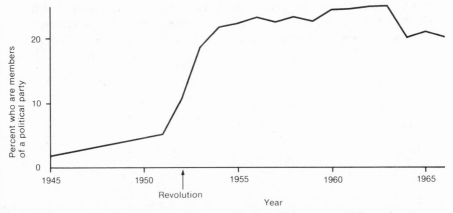

Figure 4.2 Proportion of the population, 20 years or older, who were members of a political party, 1945–1966. *Source*: Head of household survey.

ECONOMIC POLICIES

A severe economic crisis followed the revolution, as we will see in the next chapter. Agricultural production for the domestic market declined because peasants consumed much of the surplus the elite previously extracted from them, and the revolution disrupted production in industry and the mines. With ever increasing wages and other benefits extracted by the powerful miners' union, and with low world prices for tin as well, the government mining company, the mainstay of the nonagricultural economy, lost enormous sums. At the same time the MNR, genuinely committed to social reform, seriously tried to compensate for the years of exploitation and deprivation prior to the revolution. Investments in education were increased several fold and the number of children in school increased dramatically. Hospitals were built and the delivery of health care to the urban and rural poor improved. But these and other social services were expensive and the government had few resources to satisfy the many pressing claims put to it. Taxes on exports and imports were traditionally the main sources of government income, income and sales taxes being beyond its ability to enforce; with the decline of tin production and the general economic disruption, government revenues declined just as its needs grew dramatically. With no other politically or administratively feasible way to raise funds, the government resorted to the printing presses, issuing vast quantities of paper currency. This was effectively a tax on savings, pensions, rents, debts, and other obligations measured in currency since it inevitably fueled inflation and so reduced their value. In fact the inflation was astronomic, averaging over 100 percent per year between 1952 and 1956 (see fig. 4.3). This wiped out savings and debts—one hundred bolivianos in 1952 were worth only a shade over two bolivianos by 1956—and decimated the middle class. Pensions and annuities were denominated in bolivianos and they too became worthless. Even urban property, the traditional hedge against inflation

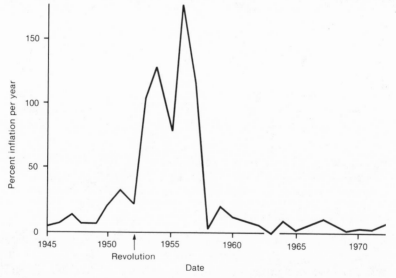

Figure 4.3   Inflation in Bolivia, 1945–1972. *Source*: Wilkie and Reich 1977:216.

and store of value in Latin America, lost its value because the revolutionary government outlawed rent increases and gave renters security of tenure at what soon became a purely nominal rent.

Thus while the MNR pledged itself to the maintenance of a capitalist system in both urban and rural areas, the often unintended consequences of its policies were to socialize a large share of the economy and destroy traditional sources of capital, even the modest capital of its middle-class supporters. The MNR fully intended to destroy the power of the traditional Bolivian government and successfully did so. It had long planned to undermine the power of the dominant mining elite and, by nationalizing the mines, was fully successful in that as well. The more radical elements in the MNR wanted to destroy many of the traditional institutions of rural Bolivia and, in spite of powerful opposition by more conservative elements in the government, the radicals achieved their aims, mainly by distributing arms to peasants. But in addition to these deliberate actions, the unintended effects of the policies the MNR chose to adopt—or was forced to adopt to satisfy the armed and increasingly powerful labor confederation and peasant syndicates—were equally profound. They destroyed the savings and capital of the middle classes, a large and powerful part of the disparate coalition that made up the MNR. The middle class increasingly turned hostile to the MNR and joined the Falange and other rightist parties in protest to the profound social and economic transformations which had been taking place.

POLITICAL DEVELOPMENTS

Conflict between the MNR government and the autonomous labor movement increased steadily and inevitably. The labor confederation and particularly the militant miners won concessions on wages, subsidized stores for miners, and grossly inflated levels of employment which, together with the low quality of the remaining ores, decapitalization of the mines, and weak world market for tin, produced enormous losses for the government mining company. The government had no practical way to pay for these losses and faced pressing demands for its limited resources from many other groups. In the late 1950s it tried systematically to reduce the labor confederation's power, a difficult and dangerous task since the workers' and peasants' militias were the most powerful armed forces in the country. Of necessity, the government formed an alliance with the peasants. With the rural elite destroyed, peasant syndicates favored no further fundamental changes and soon degenerated into personalistic and localistic factions; as long as no one threatened their ownership of the land, the peasantry basically wanted to be left to their own devices with the exception of some traditional public works concerns centering on new schools and roads. By offering these to the peasants and bribes to their leaders, the government was able to use the peasants' armed power to curb the labor confederation, calling peasant syndicates into urban areas to curb strikes and stage massive demonstrations for the government. In La Paz, for example, when faced with opposition or attempted coups, the government thought nothing of inviting thousands of armed Indian peasants from the altiplano into the city on a few hours notice. And the well-organized Lake Titicaca syndicates were able to truck several thousand armed supporters into La Paz with great ease, born of long practice. In the end, with the aid of the peasant syndicates and the newly reinvigorated national army and with the strong support of the United States and other international groups who insisted on it as a precondition for much needed foreign aid, the government suppressed the miners' union in a series of bloody clashes. Other unions were also repressed, albeit less drastically.

POLITICS AFTER THE REVOLUTION

By the early 1960s the MNR had finally disintegrated into bitter ideological and personalistic factions but the social and economic transformations it carried out remained intact and unchallenged even after the overthrow of the party in 1964. Thus by the time of our survey in 1966, although Bolivia was ruled by a military officer, René Barrientos, the situation in the countryside was little affected by changes in regime. Barrientos fully supported peasant unionization and arms. He also totally accepted land reform and made no moves to denationalize the mining sector or other elements of the economy although there was a severe repression of miners and urban workers. Thus at the time of our survey, Bolivia had passed through the first period of active revolutionary restructuring in the social and economic spheres and had entered a more conservative—but still relatively open—political period. The MNR had been destroyed, but the men who followed its rule claimed to follow its ideals and accepted the social and economic transformations which had already occurred.

POLITICAL PARTICIPATION

Perhaps the most fundamental political change introduced by the revolution was to bring the mass of ordinary people into active politics. This was a dramatic change, particularly in the countryside where a small white and cholo elite had monopolized politics for centuries, consciously and systematically excluding the peasant masses from all political involvement. After the revolution mobilized peasants for the first time in Bolivian history, their strong commitment to defending their newly established ownership of the land, and their use by the government as a counterweight to the miners and urban workers, kept them active and committed politically. And when the MNR fell from power in 1964, the peasants easily passed their allegiance to the new military rulers, who were more than willing to guarantee peasant unions, arms, and land in exchange for military and political support. As a result, levels of participation among peasants remained high long after the revolution, as can be seen for our communities in figure 4.1. The very sparse survey data available from other geographical areas suggest that our communities are by no means atypical. Surveys of peasants in the important Quechua community in the Cochabamba valley in the early 1960s show that over 90 percent had voted in the last election and the great majority were members of unions, 77 percent in one area and 92 percent in another; these figures are quite similar to ours for Compi, a comparable community.[5] By the mid-1960s there were some 7,600 unions in Bolivia, with no district unrepresented. Rural Bolivians remained politically mobilized on a vast scale, closely linked to the national political system through their syndicates, and active in defense of their new position.

Urban Bolivians, while probably more politically sophisticated and more strongly linked to political parties, seem to have taken a less active part in unions and other formal organizations by the mid-1960s. In Lavaud's 1969 survey of a working-class district of La Paz, only a third were members of a union.[6] This was not because they were unaware of politics as, when asked a complex question about the nationalization of foreign companies then in progress, over 90 percent had a clear opinion on the matter. Equally, in the Cochabamba valley district of Punata, small-town dwellers were more politically informed than local peasants but were less likely to be members of a union (29 percent were members compared to 77 percent of the peasants; Oropeza and Romero 1972). The reason seems to be that peasant unions were actively supported by the national governments of both generals Barrientos and Ovando, and by the MNR governments before them, since they were key allies in the conflict with miners and organized urban workers. As the government and their peasant allies triumphed over organized labor, urban unions came under increasingly severe repression and membership declined.

SUMMARY

In the course of some two years of violence, confusion, and organization of the rural masses, the MNR fundamentally and permanently transformed Bolivian society in one of the more sweeping and profound revolutions to occur in the twentieth century. The army was temporarily destroyed. Peasants were armed and their militias became the dominant force in rural areas. Land, the crucial resource in this predominantly agrarian society, was effectively redistributed, ending in one stroke a system of feudal exploitation that had endured for the four centuries following the Spanish conquest of the Inca empire. The mining industry, by far the dominant modern industry in Bolivia and virtually the sole source of foreign exchange, was nationalized. Miners and workers were armed and their militias became the dominant military force in urban areas, rivaled in the national arena only by the armed might of the newly aroused peasantry. Education and welfare were massively supported.

But the revolution was only partial. While the dominant export industry was nationalized and the state accounts for the bulk of economic investment, capitalism itself has been left to thrive in other sectors of the economy. Thus the Bolivian National Revolution can be considered a partial socialist revolution, in which private property and to some extent the class structure have been preserved, even as the state has become the largest source of investment and salaried income. Also, as in Mexico, while the law of the land decrees a type of modified socialist agriculture with inalienable communal landowning, the reality has been private control and the revolution actually moved Bolivian agriculture from the feudal pre-1952 pattern into a pattern more approximating modern capitalist agriculture.

Thus while Bolivia is not a Cuba or a China, it definitely has much in common with both. In many ways it can be considered either an arrested socialist revolution, or a modified capitalist revolution in a feudal society, at least as far as the rural economy and social order are concerned. In either case, Bolivia clearly experienced a profound and violent social revolution which abruptly and permanently changed the entire society.

5
Popular Perceptions of the Revolution

Many of the revolution's changes, particularly for the prosperity and well-being of the mass of ordinary people in this largely peasant society, cannot easily be measured. Many of the changes were in things that do not show up in standard statistics (labor taxes, authority and deference, opportunities to market one's own produce) and for many others there are only fragmentary and local statistics available (e.g., on peasants' standards of living). One of the crucial changes, the abolition of the heavy labor taxes which were the raison d'être of the hacienda system, does not appear in occupational data since peasants continued to be peasants after the revolution, the difference being that they worked full time for their own benefit rather than having to share their production with the landlord. But our survey has valuable information on these and related issues from a series of questions asking peasants and others about their views of the impact of the revolution of 1952. In this chapter we will attempt to show how the people who lived through the revolution perceived it, whether and how they thought it led to radical changes in Bolivian society, who they thought benefited and who lost, and whether in retrospect they supported or opposed the revolution. Such subjective data, especially of a historical kind, do of course have limitations. People can be mistaken even about what has happened to them, forgetting some things, seeing others piecemeal, and crediting or blaming the revolution for things that would have happened anyway. But subjective data do provide crucial information on what has actually happened to ordinary people, in practice, as opposed to what the government claims to have done, or wanted to do, or thinks it has done.

Needless to say, data on what the mass of the population think about a revolution is exceedingly rare. It is a matter on which revolution's supporters have strong views, as do its opponents, and both are wont to hold forth with passion and conviction, albeit hardly with agreement. But neither are conspicuously eager to find out what people really think, much less put the matter to a vote. Because of this and the obvious practical difficulties, survey research on such questions is rarely either feasible or permitted in revolutionary societies. Fortunately, however, Bolivia was an exception, one that will allow us to obtain a rare and intriguing view of a revolution through the eyes of ordinary people who lived through it.

SOME TECHNICAL DETAILS

THE VALUE OF SUBJECTIVE DATA

We will be dealing with many questions that are traditionally studied through an analysis of the policies, circumstances, personnel, and resources of the revolutionary government. This is a valuable approach (and, indeed, one we adopted in the last chapter) but also one that leaves much to be desired. What has *actually* occurred to ordinary people in the society at large cannot safely be inferred only from this conventional information since there is many a slip between the policies adopted at the rarified heights of the central government and what actually happens to ordinary people. There are many reasons for this. To begin with, a certain deviousness is not unknown in government; politicians are not always open about their aims, either with the public or with each other. Nor can governments always do what they might like to do. Even in the best of times, bureaucracies are often inefficient and self-serving and, disrupted by the revolution, with conflicting loyalties, new personnel, and an uncertain future, the years just after the revolution are hardly the best of times. In a simple decentralized economy where most transactions are made by private people, at varied times, and in cash, it is difficult for even the most efficient bureaucracy to find out what is happening, much less control or tax it; even the relatively efficient bureaucracies of western Europe and the United States are by no means wholly successful in controlling and taxing the small farms and proprietary businesses that are the dominant economic forms in Bolivia. No matter what its desires, the MNR government simply did not have the ability, for example, effectively to collect income taxes. Given the many examples where land reform has been adopted by the central government but not successfully implemented (e.g., India), some evidence on that would not be out of order either.

Nor are governments, even revolutionary governments, always strong enough to overcome political opposition to some of their policies. For example, in geographically remote areas like Reyes and Villa Abecia the old elites were able to maintain some of their power and at times the central government's writ was worth less than the paper it was written on. More crucially, the government could not even control the central areas of the country in the face of the armed militancy of miners, workers, and peasant syndicates; for years these groups were militarily stronger than the central government and conducted their own affairs in blissful disregard of its wishes. The MNR's writ long ended at the city limits of La Paz and did not always run freely even within those narrow boundaries.

Furthermore, revolutions are often made by quite heterogenous alliances of groups which, although united in their opposition to the traditional powers, nonetheless have different and often conflicting interests in other respects. The MNR, as we have seen, was originally an alliance of elements of the urban middle class, the tin miners, and urban workers. After the revolution the miners and workers forced the new government greatly to increase their wages and benefits, and to finance this the government was forced to print money not backed by real resources, leading to a dramatic inflation which destroyed the savings, pensions, and capital of their middle-class supporters. Equally, the revolution helped peasants more than any other group, but once they had their land, they turned conservative and provided the armed spearhead of the attack on the very miners and workers who had been crucial in making the revolution in the first place. So even within a successful revolutionary movement there can be great potential for conflict and, depending on how these conflicts work themselves out, some of a revolution's supporters may benefit more than others while some may even be worse off than they were before the revolution.

Finally, a government's policies often have unintended consequences. Given the piecemeal and haphazard way policies are made in the real world, the rather uncertain state of economic knowledge, and the absence of reliable information in the confused years following a revolution, policies may have consequences their framers never intended. It is, for example, by no means certain that the MNR ever clearly understood that adopting the policies advocated by workers, miners, and urban renters would, because of limited real resources and an ineffective tax system, inevitably destroy everyone's savings and pensions.

Because of these various uncertainties, an analysis of government policy is at best an uncertain guide in determining just who eventually gains from a radical revolution and who loses, or what is gained and what is lost. One good way to find out is to ask people who actually lived through the revolution what happened, who gained and who lost. That will also tell a lot about who supports the revolution and who opposes it, a matter of some considerable interest in itself.

DATA

To answer these questions, we have survey data from a series of open-ended questions about the revolution asked of a representative sample of the rural and small-town areas where the majority of Bolivians live. This unfortunately excludes the crucial middle classes and organized labor in the capital and the politically powerful miners. But our data on the armed and powerful peasants and the middle- and working-class residents of the small towns nonetheless gives a valuable perspective on two of the three crucial groups in postrevolutionary Bolivia (miners and other elements in the labor confederation being the third) and a much broader and more representative perspective than is available for the vast majority of revolutions.

Accuracy and Bias.   We believe these data accurately reflect what people actually thought. The interviews were done under very satisfactory conditions, detailed in chapter 2, and project researchers had already lived in the community for a year or more so that people were familiar with the project and aware that it was not in league with the government. There was in any case little reason to distort one's true opinions since the central government was in alliance with, and favorably disposed toward, peasant unions and the rural heirs of the revolution generally. Furthermore, the revolution was ancient history, an accepted fact in Bolivia, fourteen years in the past, something on which a divergence of views were widely and openly expressed but no longer a matter of active political concern. Its basic policies were no longer challenged by any important political group of the right or the left. The discussion of the revolution came naturally in the middle of a long and unthreatening interview, from an often familiar interviewer, asked in the privacy of the respondent's home and in his preferred language. There was no reason to distort one's true feelings.

Technical Details.   The questions were open ended and interviewers recorded the answers at length, without any attempt to force them into precoded categories.[1] We subsequently developed a coding scheme for them and had them coded by Antonio Mitre, a Bolivian doctoral candidate in history at Columbia University who worked closely with us. He was intimately familiar with the local scene and local linguistic styles. The Spanish text of the questions and an English translation are given in Appendix 4.

We have information from 1,057 of the original 1,130 respondents, the remaining 73 cases being lost or damaged in transit between data collection in Bolivia, coding the closed-ended questions in California, and our open-ended coding in New York. Don't knows and no answers varied from question to question but on the average some 20 percent of the respondents did not answer in ways that indicated clear agreement or disagreement; this is somewhat higher than corresponding figures for industrial societies but normal in societies with educational levels as low as Bolivia's. In addition to simple agreement or disagreement, detailed comments were recorded and, excluding those who did not answer the question at all and those who simply repeated their agreement or disagreement, about two-thirds of the respondents gave additional clarification, qualification, or justification. We coded these comments in detail.

CONSEQUENCES OF THE REVOLUTION, AS SEEN BY THE MASSES

EXPROPRIATION OF THE RICH

Not all revolutions that set out to radically redistribute wealth were able to do so in practice, but the Bolivian revolution was not one of these. It radically and effectively redistributed the wealth and land accumulated over the years by the prerevolutionary elite. As evidence, in addition to the consistent reports of outside observers—partisan and disinterested, Bolivian and foreign—we have the clear testimony of the ordinary Bolivians who lived through the revolution themselves. After a noncontroversial question on land reform and one on the efficiency with which peasants now work their land, we asked: "Some say that after the revolution of 1952 the rich and the well born lost everything and can now expect nothing. What do you think?"[2] Answers were recorded in detail but let us begin with a simple summary of agreement and disagreement, shown in table 5.1.

TABLE 5.1

SUMMARY OF OPINION ON THE QUESTION "SOME SAY THAT AFTER THE REVOLUTION OF 1952 THE RICH AND THE WELL BORN LOST EVERYTHING AND NOW CAN EXPECT NOTHING. WHAT DO YOU THINK?" PERCENT AGREEING OR DISAGREEING.[1]

Answer	All respondents (percent)
Agree, without conditions or reservations	55
Agree but with some conditions or reservations	17
Undecided, both true and false, mixed views	11
Disagree but with some conditions or reservations	4
Disagree, without conditions or reservations	13
Total	100
Number of cases	(826)

Source: Head of household survey, unweighted.

[1]Excludes 105 don't knows, 126 no answers, and 73 interview schedules lost in transit.

There is widespread agreement that the revolution devastated the rich. Over 70 percent agree that the rich lost everything, the great majority seeing no need to attach qualifications or reservations to this sweeping claim. Fewer than one respondent in five disagreed.[3]

Some Details. We can get a more detailed picture from the comments shown in table 5.2. While a quarter of the respondents gave no answers beyond a bare agree or disagree, the rest gave an average of

TABLE 5.2

DETAILED ANSWERS TO THE QUESTION "SOME SAY THAT AFTER THE REVOLUTION
OF 1952 THE RICH AND WELL BORN LOST EVERYTHING AND CAN NOW EXPECT
NOTHING. WHAT DO YOU THINK?" PERCENT OF RESPONDENTS WITH AN OPINION
GIVING EACH ANSWER; MULTIPLE RESPONSES CODED SO TOTAL IS
GREATER THAN 100 PERCENT.[1]

A. THE RICH LOST, WITHOUT QUALIFICATION 82%
The rich lost everything, 16%. The rich lost all they had (16).

Landlords lost everything, 65%. The rich have nothing to expect anymore, they
will not regain the land (33); Landlords lost all their land (14); peasants won't
give up the land (12); former owners cannot take the land back as peasants have
title (2); landlords abandoned their land and fled to the city (1); other (3).

B. QUALIFICATIONS OR UNCERTAINTIES 63%
Only some have lost, 24%. There were no rich persons in this region (7);
landlords lost only in certain regions (6); some have lost nothing (3); the big
miners lost everything (2); only some have lost their land (2); medium-sized
property was not affected (1); those connected with the MNR were not affected,
the MNR ring benefited (1); only those opposed to the government lost (1);
some have not lost their money (1).

They lost only part of their property, 19%. Landlords lost only part of the land (9);
the rich lost their peasant servants (7); expropriation took place in unoccupied
lands (1); other (1).

The rich may regain their land, 22%. The rich may regain the land later (9); they
may regain the land, depending on what future governments decide (9);
former owners may buy the land back, or regain it by hard work (2); peasants do
not all have valid title (1); other (1).

C. THERE WAS NO REVOLUTION 5%
The rich did not lose, 5%. Peasants still work for old patrons (2); the rich are now
richer, have more land (2); rich still remain rich, landlords did not lose their
land (1).

D. OTHER AND UNCLASSIFIABLE ANSWERS[2] 30%
Favorable evaluations, 18%. The rich and well born's losses were just, they
remedied past injustices (18).

Unfavorable evaluations, 6%. Expropriation was unjust because there was no
compensation (2); they were demagogic measures to win peasant support (2);
small plots should not have been touched (1); other (2).

Other, 6%. The rich sold all their property (2); landlords feel threatened by
peasants now (1); the rich are poor because they do not work anymore (1); all
other (1).

Source: Head of household survey, unweighted.

[1]Percentages based on the 601 respondents giving at least one codeable answer
(excluding other and unclassifiable). Multiple responses were coded and there are 1,076
separate responses in all. Detail may not add to total because of rounding.

[2]N = 180 responses. Percentaged to the same base as the rest of the table.

almost two comments apiece.[4] Over three-quarters in essence merely reaffirmed their answer, saying that the rich lost everything without hope of redress, or at least that rich landlords lost everything—few made any distinction between rich people and rich landlords, nor was there much reason to make the distinction in prerevolutionary Bolivia (Panel A). A very few, one in twenty, reaffirmed their claim that the rich had not lost (Panel C).

Some qualifications, or at least uncertainties, were also expressed (Panel B). There were three main reservations. First, one respondent in four noted that only some of the rich lost—land reform did not extend to all regions, in some regions there were no rich to begin with, middle and small properties were not affected, and the like. Another fifth noted that landlords lost only part of their property, or kept property while losing the free labor taxes which were the key feature of the hacienda system.[5] Finally, a fifth mentioned the possibility that the rich might regain their lands, particularly if some future government supported them. Although not widespread, this fear was one basis for the crucial alliance between peasants and the government against the miners and urban workers, the peasants supporting the government in exchange for its full legitimization of their title to land.

Support for Land Reform. Although some worried about the possibility of land reform being overturned, in fact virtually no one in rural Bolivia would have favored that.[6] Since land reform was fundamental to the revolution's restructuring of rural society, there was an explicit question on it: "They say that those who work the land should own it. What do you think?" In all, well over eight out of ten respondents thought that the peasants should own the land they worked, one in ten agreed but with some reservations or qualifications, and barely one in twenty disagreed outright.[7]

Since this is something that benefits peasants rather than larger farmers or the numerous rural Bolivians who are not farmers, it is useful to separate peasants from nonpeasants. We classified people as Indian peasants (*campesinos*) on the basis of their own self-identification as shown in the answers to all nine open-ended questions. Several of these explicitly asked about peasants and peasants would naturally be mentioned in the answers to many others. Some people identified as peasants explicitly, including phrases like "we peasants" in their answers, and others showed their identification by referring to peasants as "we" rather than "they" (*nosotros* rather than *ellos*). We counted anyone who so identified on any of the open-ended questions as an Indian peasant and everyone else as a nonpeasant. In all, 44 percent identified as peasants. Note that the key term in this definition, campesino, is a postrevolutionary euphemism for the derogatory prerevolutionary term *indio*, "Indian," defining what we call Indian peasants. In our sample these will almost all be from Aymara-speaking families, most themselves Aymara speaking. Equally poor non-Aymara-speaking small farmers, not to mention the large number of nonfarm rural poor, would not usually identify themselves as peasants in this way. This is therefore a narrow definition focusing on the group most crucially affected by the revolution. To avoid confusion, we will refer to it as "Indian peasant" except where the context already makes it clear that the restrictive usage is intended.

Land reform is, in any event, supported almost as strongly by non-peasants as by Indian peasants themselves (table 5.3, first two columns). If any party tried to overturn the land reform they would have found overwhelming opposition in the countryside from peasant and non-peasant alike.It is no accident that in the quarter century since reform, there has been no real attempt to undo it; the revolution expropriated landlords once and for all.

TABLE 5.3

SUMMARY OF OPINION ON THE QUESTION "THEY SAY THAT THOSE WHO WORK THE LAND SHOULD OWN IT. WHAT DO YOU THINK?" PERCENT AGREEING OR DISAGREEING.[1]

Answer	Indian peasants (percent)	Others (percent)	All respondents (percent)
Agree, without qualifications	93	81	86
Agree, but with reservations or qualifications	4	12	9
Disagree	3	7	5
Total	100	100	100
Number of cases	(374)	(470)	(844)

Source: Head of household survey, unweighted.

[1]Excluding 213 don't knows or no answers and 73 interview schedules lost in transit. Indian peasants are those who identified themselves as *"campesinos."*

WHO GAINED FROM THE REVOLUTION?

We asked specifically about the consequences of the revolution: "Some say that everything was better before the revolution of 1952. What do you think?" The answers fell naturally into two groups, gains and losses. The gains are shown in table 5.4, which gives the percent mentioning each particular point expressed as a fraction of the number of respondents who answered this question by mentioning *either* a specific gain or a specific loss.[8] Two-thirds of the respondents mentioned some gain.

Table 5.4

FAVORABLE CHANGES ATTRIBUTED TO THE REVOLUTION: ANSWERS FAVORABLE
TO THE REVOLUTION TO THE QUESTION "SOME SAY THAT EVERYTHING WAS
BETTER BEFORE THE REVOLUTION OF 1952. WHAT DO YOU THINK?" PERCENT OF
RESPONDENTS WITH AN OPINION EITHER FAVORABLE *ORUNFAVORABLE*GIVING
EACH ANSWER; MULTIPLE RESPONSES ARE CODED SO THE TOTAL CAN BE MORE
THAN 100 PERCENT.[1]

A. *FREEDOM FROM SERFDOM* 28%
Freedom, end of slavery, 28%. Peasants enjoy freedom (15); slavery of peasants
has been abolished (12).

B. *EDUCATION FOR PEASANTS* 13%
More schooling, 13%. More education available for peasants (13).

C. *ECONOMIC IMPROVEMENTS FOR PEASANTS* 11%
Abolition of labor tax, 4%. No more free work for landlords (4); peasants'
children no longer servants of the landlord (½).
Land reform, 4%. Agrarian reform, (3); peasants are landowners now (1).
End of the landlord's commercial monopolies, 2%. Peasants can now sell their
produce directly (1); the old monopoly on food by the old landlords has been
abolished (½); other (½).
Higher standard of living, 2%. Peasants can buy things now (1); peasants live
better, enjoy better housing (1); peasants have health care centers, free food
from government (½).

D. *OTHER ECONOMIC IMPROVEMENTS* 10%
For miners, working class, 3%. Nationalization of the mines (1); mine workers
enjoy greater freedom (½); mines produce more (½). Working class better off
(1).
General economic progress, 6%. Salaries, incomes are higher (2); goods more
abundant (1); industrialization (1); better roads (1); other improvements (1).
Inflation reduced, ½%. Things are cheaper now (½).

E. *GOVERNMENT AND DEMOCRACY* 2%
Freedom, 2%. More freedom for all now (2); people can more freely elect their
government (½).

F. *OTHER AND UNCLASSIFIABLE ANSWERS*[2] 3%
Social progress, 3%. There has been social progress (2); people can feel safer
now (½).
Other, ½%. There are airplanes now (½).

Source: Head of household survey, unweighted.

[1]Percentages based on the 515 respondents giving at least one codeable answer for *or*
against the revolution, excluding other and unclassifiable. Multiple responses are coded
and there are 767 separate responses in all. Detail may not add to total because of
rounding.
[2]N = 14 responses percentaged to the same base, 515, as the rest of the table.

Peasants' Gains. Most of the revolution's benefits went to peasants, half of our respondents mentioning some benefit they received.[9] Over a quarter mentioned freedom, the end of serfdom, the end of slavery— it is indicative of the oppressive nature of prerevolutionary Bolivian society that more than one respondent in ten explicitly used the evocative, if technically inaccurate, term "slavery" (Panel A). As we have seen, hacienda peasants were virtually serfs before 1952 and the abolition of that ancient and oppressive bondage was by far the most conspicuous benefit of the revolution in the eyes of ordinary Bolivians. In a deeply felt phrase that appears often in the anthropological materials, the revolution "made us men."

Educational advantages for peasants were also very salient, mentioned about half as often as the end of serfdom (Panel B). In some societies the poor have not seen much advantage in education, but a deep concern with their children's education has long been characteristic of Bolivian peasants as well, of course, as of more advantaged groups. This shows up strikingly in language use. Since all education is in Spanish, children who can speak it have a great advantage and their parents go to great pains to teach them if they can: a quarter of the men in the head of household sample who are bilingual in Aymara and Spanish—almost all native Aymara speakers with only a sketchy command of Spanish—speak mainly Spanish with their children even though they speak only Aymara with their wives. It is also evident politically. After title to land, the most common demand peasants have made on the revolutionary government is for teachers (they are usually willing and able to build the schools themselves but paying teachers is beyond their financial means), and the government responded by greatly expanding the school system, as we will see in the next chapter.

In spite of peasants' tremendous economic burdens under the old regime, the revolution's economic benefits were not very salient (Panel C). About one respondent in twenty-five mentioned the abolition of labor taxes, the same number mentioned land reform, about half as many mentioned the abolition of the old landlord's commercial monopolies, and the same number mentioned a general improvement in peasants' standards of living. In a sense all of these are part and parcel of the old hacienda system—the labor taxes were enforced by control over the land, and free labor together with exploitation of the advantages of commercial monopoly were the means by which landlords derived their profits at the peasants' expense. So freedom from serfdom in a sense entails these advantages; they are not a separate set of issues. And in an important sense that was true of education as well; educational opportunities were limited because landlords were unwilling to pay for schools and peasants did not have the political power to force the government to provide them. Nonetheless, it is striking that respondents did not choose to single out the economic aspects of serfdom but instead focused on the more personal aspects, something that is also evident in the anthropological materials where peasants' deep resentment at being treated as children, as personal servants, and as creatures not fully adult or perhaps not fully human, is manifest. From the landlords' point of view the most salient aspect of serfdom was surely economic but that does not mean, nor was it true, that the most onerous aspect of the system for the exploited was economic. And not only were the economic gains less salient than the personal aspects of serfdom, they may well have been less salient even than the prosaic educational gains.

Gains by Other Groups. The revolution's benefits to groups other than Indian peasants were very much less salient than those for peasants. In contrast to the one respondent in two who mentioned gains for peasants, only one in ten mentioned advantages for nonpeasants. These gains were mainly economic (Panel D). Only a few mentioned gains for miners or the working class—groups which were bulwarks of the MNR and who gained in the first few years after the revolution only to be suppressed later. About twice as many mentioned higher standards of living in general, investments in industry and infrastructure, or the like.

Political benefits from the revolution were not at all salient. Political freedom and democracy were not what this revolution was about (Panel E). Nor was anything else mentioned with any frequency at all (Panel F).

In short, as seen in retrospect by ordinary people who lived through it, the revolution was very good for peasants and offered a few economic benefits for other groups, but had no other salient benefits. The economic improvements for the previously exploited peasants are, of course, what we predicted (Hypothesis 4) and the improvement in their educational opportunities a feature of our theoretical analysis (Hypotheses 1, 5, and 6).

Who Lost from the Revolution?

The peasants' gains in the revolution do not seem to have been offset by any real losses for the peasants themselves. Virtually no one regrets the passing of serfdom, the only complaint being that peasants no longer show what would in the prerevolutionary days be considered proper respect for their betters (table 5.5, Panel A). No one at all has any objection to peasants' new educational opportunities (Panel B), and virtually no one is under the impression that peasants were economically better off before the revolution (Panel C).

Other groups did, however, suffer. The landed rich lost everything, as we have already seen in chapter 4, but no one worries about that. The economic costs of the revolution for the population at large,

TABLE 5.5

<small>Unfavorable Changes Attributed to the Revolution: Answers
Unfavorable to the Revolution to the Question "Some Say that
Everything was Better Before the Revolution of 1952. What do you
Think?" Percent of Respondents with an Opinion Either Unfavorable *or*
Favorable Giving each Answer; Multiple Responses
are Coded so the Total can be More than 100 Percent.[1]</small>

A. *ABOLITION OF SERFDOM* 1%
No deference, 1%. Peasants no longer show respect (1).

B. *EDUCATION FOR PEASANTS* 0%
(There was no mention of opposition to this.)

C. *ECONOMIC DISADVANTAGES FOR PEASANTS* 1%
Peasants worse off, 1%. Landlords were benevolent and helped and cared for
peasants (½); other (½).

D. *OTHER ECONOMIC DISADVANTAGES* 67%
For miners, working class, 2%. The poor were able to get things easier before
(1). Things were better at the mines, miners better off (½).

General economic decline, 37%. More production before, products were more
abundant (11%); more jobs for everyone before (6); harvests were more
abundant before (5); people worked harder before (3); economy in general was
better (3); there was more money circulating (2); peasants worked harder
under landlords (2); everyone had enough to live on, less misery before (2);
poverty is still around (1). More capital investment before (½); private property
no longer respected (½); the rich have fled and that has damaged the town's
economy (½); there is more consumption than production today (½); other
(½).

Inflation, 28%. Things were cheaper before (18); money was worth more, had
greater buying power (5); exchange rate was more favorable to the peso before
(2); inflation (2); one made less money but could buy more (1).

E. *GOVERNMENT AND DEMOCRACY* 6%
Loss of freedom, 1%. More freedom before (1); democracy (½).

Weaknesses of the revolutionary government, 4%. Corruption: governmental
corruption has increased (½); authorities no longer work for the people but for
their own pocket (½); other (½). Bureaucracy: one needs *"cupones"* for everything (1). Other: there is more anarchy now (1); other (½).

F. *OTHER AND UNCLASSIFIABLE ANSWERS* 6%
Social decline, 3%. Morality has declined (1); more peaceful before (1); level of
crime was lower (½).
Other, 3%. Weather was better before (2); all other (½).

Source: Head of household survey, unweighted.

[1]Percentages based on the 515 respondents who gave at least one codeable answer
either for *or* against the revolution, excluding other and unclassifiable. Detail may not
add to total because of rounding.

however, are highly salient. No less than two out of every three respondents who have anything at all to say about the revolution claim that it was economically disadvantageous (table 5.5, Panel D). Only a tiny fraction see it as disadvantageous to miners or the working class but more than one in three specifically mentions that it led to a general economic decline, that there was more production before the revolution, more jobs, that people worked harder, that there was less poverty, that harvests were more abundant, that peasants worked harder under the old system, and the like. The virulent inflation that followed the revolution is also highly salient almost a dozen years later; more than one respondent in four mentioned it.

The economic costs of the revolution are ovewhelmingly its most salient disadvantages, not much more than one person in ten mentioning any others. Political costs were hardly any more salient than political gains (Panel E). Hardly anyone mentioned a loss of freedom or democracy and only one in twenty-five complained of corruption, bureaucracy, or other faults of the revolutionary government. Only a few other topics were raised (Panel F). As few mentioned the general social decline caused by the revolution as earlier mentioned general social progress.

We have some further information on what people think about the revolution's effect on agricultural production, a crucial matter in a largely agrarian society. We asked: "Some say that with agrarian reform peasants got the land, but they don't work it now that they have it. What do you think?" Opinion is fairly evenly split, a modest plurality agreeing, or agreeing with some qualifications (table 5.6). Indian peasants have very different views than nonpeasants, however, with only one peasant out of four agreeing while two nonpeasants out of three do so. We will see in the next chapter that the sketchy statistical evidence suggests that agricultural production, at least for the market, declined after the revolution, while expert opinion, albeit not based on fully satisfactory data, consistently holds that peasants consumed more of their own production after the revolution. It is therefore tempting to speculate that the majority of peasants, desperately poor even after the revolution, continued to work as hard as they could (although perhaps not always as efficiently as before) but consumed more and marketed less, since the old landlords were no longer around to forcibly expropriate and market part of their production. This speculation would be consistent with our data since most of the peasants would know that they continued to work hard while nonpeasants, judging only from the decline in supplies available in the market, could easily attribute that to their no longer working so hard. Nonetheless, the issue remains unclear among experts and ordinary Bolivians alike and it is perfectly possible that some peasants worked less after the revolution since, no

TABLE 5.6

SUMMARY OF OPINION ON THE QUESTION "THEY SAY THAT WITH AGRARIAN
REFORM PEASANTS GOT THE LAND BUT THEY DON'T WORK IT NOW THAT THEY
HAVE IT. WHAT DO YOU THINK?" PERCENT
AGREEING OR DISAGREEING.[1]

Answer	Indian peasants (percent)	Others (percent)	All respondents (percent)
Agree, without qualifications	10	47	32
Agree, but with reservations or qualifications	16	18	17
Both agree and disagree, undecided	11	10	11
Disagree, but with reservations or qualifications	7	7	7
Disagree, without qualifications	56	17	34
Total[2]	100	100	100
Number of cases	(397)	(544)	(941)

Source: Head of household survey, unweighted.

[1]Excludes 116 don't knows or no answers and 73 interview schedules lost in transit.
Indian peasants are those who identified themselves as "*campesinos.*"
[2]Detail may not add to 100 percent because of rounding.

longer having to support the old landlords, they could satisfy their
needs (albeit at a minimal level) with less work.

Be this as it may, it is clear that, in the minds of the ordinary people
who lived through the revolution, its most salient costs were economic,
paticularly inflation and a general decline in productivity. In the next
chapter we will see that there is good statistical evidence for these
perceptions.

POPULAR SUPPORT FOR THE REVOLUTION

Having lived through the revolution, what do ordinary Bolivians
think of it on balance? We have seen that they feel it had both good
points and bad points. Almost everyone agrees that the rich lost almost
everything and, in spite of some lingering apprehension, the great
majority see no chance of the old rich recovering their position, nor
would there be any support for such an attempt. The fate of the old
rich is settled but they are a tiny minority, most long since fled, and
their fate is no longer of much concern to the rest of the population.
The issues that now come to mind when ordinary Bolivians are asked
to evaluate the revolution are gains for peasants and economic losses
for everyone else. The gains were mainly noneconomic and went
overwhelmingly to Indian peasants. In sharp contrast, the losses were
mainly economic (chiefly inflation and a general decline in productiv-

ity) and affected the population at large. In short, the revolution ended an ancient, oppressive system of virtually feudal exploitation of the peasants, and that was a very good thing for them, but it also disrupted the economy at large, and that was not at all a good thing for the population at large.

How then do Bolivians weigh these gains and losses on balance? The answer, shown in table 5.7, is a modest vote in favor of the revolution. Almost half think that life was better afterward, at least for most people, but a third think the revolution made things worse and the rest see no difference.

But there is a sharp disagreement between Indian peasants and the rest of the population. Roughly speaking, four out of six peasants think the revolution was a good thing, one thinks it made no difference, and one thinks it made life worse. In sharp contrast, only two of every six nonpeasants think life is better now, one sees no change, and three think the revolution made things worse. This smacks strongly of self-interest, the peasants strongly favorable because they very clearly gained from it while nonpeasants are slightly opposed, some altruistically favoring the revolution even though it harmed them personally but more opposing it for that reason.

TABLE 5.7

OVERALL EVALUATION OF THE REVOLUTION. SUMMARY OF OPINION ON THE QUESTION "SOME SAY EVERYTHING WAS BETTER BEFORE THE REVOLUTION OF 1952. WHAT DO YOU THINK?" PERCENT AGREEING OR DISAGREEING.[1]

Answer	Indian peasants (percent)	Others (percent)	All respondents (percent)
The revolution made things better for most people[2]	64	34	46
It made no difference, made things better and worse equally, etc.	22	15	18
The revolution made things worse	14	51	35
Total[3]	100	100	100
Number of cases	(340)	(435)	(775)

Source: Head of household survey, unweighted.

[1]Excludes 282 don't knows or no answers and 73 interview schedules lost in transit. Indian peasants are those who identified themselves as "*campesinos*"

[2]This includes people who said the revolution made things better without qualification (23% of the population) and those who said that only the rich lost (20%) or that the poor gained (3%) on the assumption, reasonable in Bolivia, that the rich are a small minority and the poor a large majority.

[3]Detail may not add to 100 percent because of rounding.

CONCLUSION

PERSPECTIVES ON THE REVOLUTION

In this chapter we have looked at the Bolivian revolution through the eyes of the ordinary Bolivians in whose name it was proclaimed and whose benefit it claimed to serve. But there is often a conflict between good intentions and practical results among revolutionary governments no less, and perhaps more, than ordinary ones, and especially in societies as fragmented and backward as prerevolutionary Bolivia. The reports of the ordinary people who lived through the revolution provide invaluable evidence as to what actually happened, evidence about what the revolution actually achieved for good or ill, and for whom. What then were the results of Bolivia's 1952 revolution as they perceived it?

In the first place, it is clear that the revolution did in fact expropriate the rich, particularly rich landlords, and so was a radical revolution in the sense we specified in chapter 1. Land reform was not, as has so often been the case in other societies, thwarted by the rural elite, or by incompetence or corruption in the government. Rich landlords lost their land; in the face of the armed might of the peasants and virtually unanimous opposition from everyone else, they have long since fled. The vast majority of the population, peasants and nonpeasants alike, support peasants' right to the land and in the quarter century since the revolution no Bolivian government has ever attempted to reverse land reform, nor would they have the power to do so if they tried. A cruel and exploitative system which held the peasants in servitude for generations past was abruptly overthrown, never to return.

The Indian peasants were the main beneficiaries and their gains were primarily seen in terms of liberation. In the eyes of the people themselves the most salient benefit of the revolution was freedom, the end of slavery. The revolution freed peasants from a rigid and pervasive control over their lives, freed them from an obligation to show humility and deference, to give personal service, freed them from paternalism, in their evocative phrase the revolution "made us men." The more prosaic benefits of the revolution, while no doubt important to landlords and the most consequential for inequality and social mobility, were less salient than freedom. The prosaic gain most often mentioned was the provision of better educational opportunities for peasants' children. Economic gains were mentioned almost as often, particularly land reform, the abolition of labor taxes, the end of the old landlords' monopolies on trade and commerce, and a general improvement of peasants' standard of living. But freedom for the Indian peasants was clearly the main gain from the revolution, mentioned by over a quarter of our respondents; only half as many mentioned education for peasants' children, or economic benefits for the peasantry. Virtually no one mentioned gains for nonpeasants.

In contrast to the gains of the revolution—mainly noneconomic, specifically for Indian peasants, and clearly expected by the revolutionary government—the most salient costs were economic, affecting the whole population, and unintended. At least in the eyes of ordinary Bolivians, there was a general decline in the economy, in productivity, employment, and effort; over a third of our respondents mentioned this. Almost as salient was the dramatic inflation which wiped out most savings, rents, and pensions in the few years immediately following the revolution. These were, of course, not consequences that the revolutionary government desired or intended, but were no less painful for all that.

Reflecting these gains and losses, evaluation of the revolution was mixed. Having lived through it, not quite half of the population thought it had on balance made life better, a third thought it had made things worse, and the rest were undecided. But these views seemed to be shaped in good part by self-interest, since two-thirds of the Indian peasants, the main beneficiaries, favored it while most of the rest of the population, who bore the brunt of the costs, opposed.

THEORETICAL IMPLICATIONS

The most salient economic consequences of the revolution in the view of those who lived through it are also those which are central to our theoretical analysis. Control over land, control over labor via labor taxes, and various commercial monopolies are the classic means by which peasants are exploited economically. Much of our argument turned on the consequences of removing this exploitation, so increasing the returns peasants could expect from their efforts and their capital (Hypotheses 4 and 5). Apparently these aspects of exploitation were salient to ordinary Bolivians as well, as they should be if they are in fact important. We also argued for the importance of human capital and the consequences that might follow from its wider availability (Hypotheses 1 and 6). And in fact education also was salient to ordinary Bolivians, as it should be if it is as important as we claimed. We argued that a radical revolution could be expected to destroy much of the accumulated savings and capital of the middle as well as upper classes, so reducing inequality in the distribution of physical capital (and, we predicted in Hypothesis 8, therefore reducing inherited privilege). Such a dramatic loss would surely be salient to those who suffered it and, in the transparent guise of inflation, it apparently was.

Finally, these results provide more direct support for one of our hypotheses, the argument that a revolution could be expected to improve peasants' economic position (Hypothesis 4). This is hardly an unexpected result but it is nice to see it confirmed by the virtually unanimous opinion of those involved. So in all, these results lend considerable credence to our general analysis and strong support specifically for one of our predictions.

6
Revolution's Effects on Inequality and the Economy

As we have seen in the last two chapters, the Bolivian revolution of 1952 led to dramatic and permanent restructuring of Bolivian society. Power was wrenched from the hands of a small, exploitative elite which had held it for centuries; the army was destroyed and worker and peasant unions became the dominant armed power in the land; landlords were forcibly dispossessed, labor taxes abolished, and land turned over to the peasants who worked it; the crucial mining industry was nationalized, with control shared between government and the miners; the government took control of the export industry and most modern manufacturing, leaving over two-thirds of the nation's capital in its hands; inflation destroyed the savings and pensions of the middle classes; and even urban property, the traditional hedge against inflation, was effectively redistributed by laws giving renters security of tenure at fixed rents which soon became purely nominal. It was, in short, a radical revolution both objectively and in the eyes of those who lived through it. But what effects does such a radical change have on the economy and how does it affect the distribution of income and wealth?

In this chapter we will attempt to answer those questions. Focusing especially on the numerically predominant rural population, we will attempt to show how the revolution affected economic productivity, how it changed the organization of agriculture and industry, how it affected education, and, finally, its consequences for inequality in the distribution of income.[1]

REVOLUTION AND AGRICULTURE

The revolution had a profound effect on Bolivian agriculture and so on the two-thirds of the population who made their living from it. We will see that the fundamental changes were the land reform, the concomitant destruction of the old elite's commercial monopolies, and the subsequent expansion of the market economy into a previously almost feudal rural society. All of these had important consequences on levels of production and on the distribution of income.

LAND REFORM

Control over labor had been the key element in prerevolutionary hacienda agriculture. The hacendados who owned the land extracted from their peasants three or four days of labor each week throughout the year, plus assorted additional labor services at various times, in return giving peasants access to land for their own use. These were onerous burdens, not only because of the outright tax of half or more of the peasants' productive time but also because they effectively forced the peasants to live on the land, preventing them from taking advantage of opportunities to work outside of agriculture during the slack season and forcing them to rely on exploitative middlemen to market their produce and supply manufactured goods from the cities. The revolution ended all that, as we have seen. Within the year, the hacendados had been driven from the land, the work records burned, and peasants took effective ownership of the land.[2] Well armed and organized into peasant unions, they successfully defended these gains in the years that followed. No government, even the most conservative, has challenged peasant control in the quarter century since; indeed, all governments have made a point of publicly supporting the peasants in their ownership and control of the land.

As a result of these changes, after the revolution the peasants consumed much of what the landlords had previously extracted from them (R. Clarke 1968; Heath 1969; Heyduck 1971; Patch 1967; Simmons 1974). By the 1960s, for example, Clark (1968) found that peasants in one area had four times as many bicycles, radios, and sewing machines as before the revolution; he also found that many had begun constructing new houses within three or four years of the land reform. And we have seen in the last chapter that the peasants in our survey consistently report that the revolution improved their standard of living. This redistribution of consumption from mostly rich landlords to poor peasants of course reduced inequality in the society as a whole.

Effects of Productivity.   But that was probably not the only change. As we have seen, many nonpeasants believed that production fell after the revolution and, since some hacendados had provided managerial skills and capital before the revolution, it is not unreasonable to expect that the loss of these inputs did reduce production. It is quite clear that agricultural production did not increase and national accounts statistics strongly suggest that it declined, with a drop of some 13 percent in overall levels of production in the five years after the revolution and some 20 percent in production per worker (fig. 6.1). Total production rose steadily thereafter, reaching its prevolutionary levels about a decade after the revolution and exceeding it thereafter. Production per worker never recovered, however, stabilizing at about 80 percent

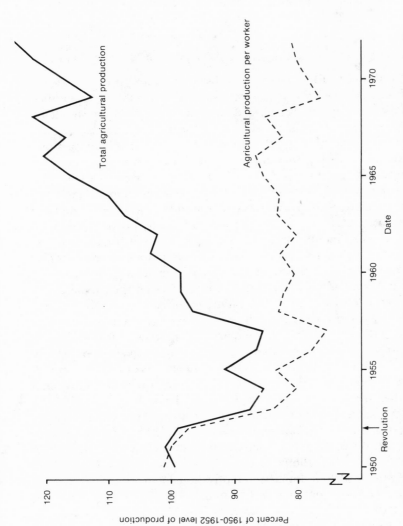

Figure 6.1 Agricultural production following the revolution. Total agricultural production and agricultural production per worker expressed as a proportion of their 1950–1952 values. *Source:* See Appendix 5, section 2.

of its prerevolutionary level as a growing population put increasing pressure on scarce resources in the altiplano. While there are necessarily some uncertainties in these statistics, the best guess is that there was *both* a genuine drop in production and an increase in what peasants consumed themselves.[3] This pattern is common in other revolutions; in the Mexican revolution, for example, agricultural production did not recover its prerevolutionary levels for 30 years.[4]

ECONOMIC REORGANIZATION AND EXPANSION OF MARKET FORCES

In addition to these changes in distribution and productivity, the revolution led to a thorough reorganization of Bolivian agriculture, with market forces extending their sway over a previously almost feudal economy. Prior to the revolution the bulk of farm products had moved to market through the hacendados, marketing both their own production as well as that of their region's dependent peasantry, but the agrarian reform wiped all this out. Most ex-haciendas and some free communities were organized into peasant unions (*sindicatos*), which began operating not only as community governments and labor representatives, but also as farm cooperatives and provided new marketing arrangements for their members. The old middleman monopoly of the hacendados was abolished and in their stead a complex system of trucking, diverse and competing middlemen, direct union sales, and individual peasant marketing, replaced the simple prereform arrangements. All this meant higher prices for peasant farmers, greater access to markets, and the exposure of a larger part of the rural world to direct contact with the market. A marketing survey done in 1967, for example, found that the overwhelming majority of peasant farmers had entered into cash sales arrangements during the preceding year, and that an important minority of them had purchased manufactured goods (Wennergren and Whitaker 1975:151, 158, 279, and 281). Many communities near urban markets, Compi among them, shifted their production toward cash rather than subsistence crops, with a concomitant increase in cash income (McEwen 1975: 331–333; Kornfeld 1969).

There also seem to have been motivational and attitudinal changes with a market orientation and rational economic decision making coming to strongly influence peasants. The Michigan State Marketing Survey found peasants' behavior to be consistently market oriented and economically rational (Wennergren and Whitaker 1975). And Clarke (1970), working in the lower Cochabamba valley, found that the accumulation of wealth and personal achievement, while frowned upon before the revolution, had become a valued route for upward mobility afterward.

With the abolition of the old landlords' control over their peasants' commerce and the reduction of the old elite's influence on government, new opportunities opened up in marketing and transport. Many former peasants and town Indians went into trucking, taking over much of the commerce between rural and urban areas. Aymara-speaking middlemen took over much of the lucrative trade in commercial crops, dealing directly with the Aymara-speaking peasants on the one hand and big urban buyers on the other, in the process cutting the old Spanish-speaking, small-town elite out of the profits and extending the sway of market influences over the countryside.[5] Equally, opportunities opened up for the peasantry in the new lands which were made available as a result of a major investment in new roads and colonization schemes. Areas such as the Alto Beni, Chapare, and Santa Cruz were now integrated into the national market and virgin lands were often given to landless or land-poor altiplano peasants. The development of new zones of large-scale commercial agriculture in Santa Cruz provided a new market for labor from the crowded altiplano. Improved transportation gave access to new markets for farm produce and was of substantial benefit to those peasants fortunate to live near new roads, or enterprising enough to settle on them, and accounts in large part for the sharp increases in income in Santa Cruz and other newly colonialized areas (Zuvekas 1977; Wennergren and Whitaker 1975:280).

CONSEQUENCES FOR ECONOMIC INEQUALITY

The land reform and concomitant changes were not of equal benefit to all peasants but were more valuable to those with the resources to exploit them effectively. Differences in skills, knowledge, motivation, and the like that separated one peasant from another became more important now that peasants were able to take full advantage of them and keep the benefits for themselves. There were also differences in landholdings that persisted from the past since the land reform did not redistribute land *among* peasants. Before reform hacienda peasants had private plots that they cultivated for their own use and in the course of time some had come to have more land, or better land, than others. After the landlords were driven away, each peasant kept his own customary plot (and perhaps got more) so that those who were advantaged before were advantaged afterward.[6] Substantial inequality in peasant landholdings, and consequently in income, have been noted repeatedly (Carter 1964, 1971; Heath, Erasmus, and Buechler 1969; and the many others cited in Zuvekas 1977:28). And with the end of the old labor taxes they had twice as much time to cultivate their land, so reaping even greater advantage than before.

Equally, the penetration of the market and the development of new commercial opportunities were often of greater benefit to farmers with more land and greater education and skills. All farmers benefited from commercialization and the general rise in food prices. And while benefits from the production of wool, coffee, and rice were widely distributed, those from milk, beef, cotton, and sugar went mainly to larger farmers (Wennergren and Whitaker 1975:67, 75). So inequality grew among farmers.

REVOLUTION IN MINING, INDUSTRY, AND COMMERCE

THE MINES

Like agriculture, mining was greatly changed by the revolution; these changes were especially important since mining was Bolivia's primary source of foreign exchange and the source of more than half of the government's revenues before the revolution (Thorn 1971:175). Miners had vast political power since they were crucial to the revolution's victory over the old regime and, armed and organized by their union, they were probably the strongest single military force in Bolivia for some years afterward. After the mines were nationalized in the first few days of the revolution and a joint union-government management took control of the nationalized company, COMIBOL, the miners forced management and the government to increase employment by more than a quarter over the next four years (see fig. 6.2). In addition,

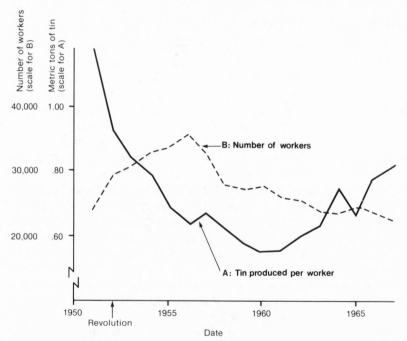

Figure 6.2   The tin mining industry, 1950–1967. Tons of tin produced per worker (A) and number of workers (B). *Source:* Thorne 1971–172.

the miners forced COMIBOL to grant wage increases, expand the commissaries run by the company at a heavy loss, and grant other compensation. As a result, benefits per worker increased by over 250 percent within a year of the revolution (Thorn 1971:173). Along with this there were problems because of the expulsion of foreign engineers and the continuing decline in the quality of the ores and in capital investment, all of which led to a substantial decline in production. Productivity per worker fell steadily for almost a decade following the revolution, dropping by about 40 percent (fig. 6.2). All of this was coupled with low international prices for tin and led to massive losses by COMIBOL. This was no small matter, as COMIBOL's revenues, and often its deficits, were substantially larger than the central government's (Malloy and Thorn 1971:380). Not until 1965 did COMIBOL finally make a profit and not until 1970 did the value of Bolivian mineral production again reach the levels achieved by the private sector before the revolution (Wennergren and Whitaker 1975:28). Until the mining sector finally stabilized and began to return a profit, the availability of government funds for the rest of the economy was limited.

INDUSTRY AND GOVERNMENT

Industrial production and productivity, like agriculture and mining, also went through the same pattern of postrevolutionary crisis and recovery (see table 6.1). In this particular case, however, the crisis period only lasted through the decade of the 1950s, and by the mid-1960s total production was exceeding prerevolutionary levels. While its contribution to the gross domestic product was significant, its relative importance in the labor force was small and it had much less of an impact on general living standards than did changes in agriculture and mining.

Commerce, transport, construction, and government were not so greatly affected by the revolution. As we have seen, there was some increase in marketing and transport to and from rural areas, largely because of the newly found purchasing power of the peasantry. Government employment also grew as a result of the increased delivery of goods and services, especially in education, health, and welfare. The small petroleum sector, geographically isolated, long owned by the government, and with ready access to foreign capital, was even more effectively isolated from the effects of revolution and grew rapidly.

Changes in local government in fact opened up new opportunities, particularly for peasant and worker unions. With government encouragement on the one hand, and the collapse of the old elite on the other, there was little to hinder the growth of unions and the opportunities

TABLE 6.1

GROWTH RATE OF GROSS DOMESTIC PRODUCT (GDP) BY SECTOR, 1950–1972.
AVERAGE ANNUAL PERCENTAGE GROWTH, ADJUSTED FOR INFLATION.[1]

Sector	Percent of 1950 labor force employed	Percent of 1950–1952 GDP contributed	Growth in GDP (percent per year)[1]		Growth in GDP per capita (percent per year)[1]	
			1951–56	1961–71	1951–61	1961–71
Agriculture	72	31	0.1	1.9	−2.2	−0.7
Mining	3	16	−6.3	6.6	−8.3	3.9
Industry	8	14	−0.5	6.6	−2.7	3.8
Petroleum	½	1	17.9	12.4	15.4	9.5
Commerce, construction, transport, government, and services	17	38	1.9	6.6	−0.5	3.9
Total, all sectors	100	100	0.1	5.4	−2.2	2.8

Source: The first column is from United Nations 1958:table 19 and the rest are from Wennergren and Whitaker 1975:tables 2.6 and 2.8.

[1]Growth rates are annual compound averages. They are based on the mean of the three years centering on the beginning date of the period indicated and the three years centering on the end.

for their leaders. Not only did peasant unions come to dominate rural politics but truckers' unions and various other workers' unions became important in many towns, in some cases dominating local politics, and not without benefit to their members or to their officials, as in Sorata (McEwen 1975:238–252). Leadership in the unions, however, went not so much to poor and monolingual peasants as to their more educated, generally bilingual brethren. So a new elite gradually began to emerge from the peasant masses.

OVERALL PERFORMANCE OF THE POSTREVOLUTIONARY ECONOMY

Overall then, the Bolivian economy clearly suffered for some years as a result of the revolution. Agricultural production declined markedly in the years just following the revolution but then began to increase steadily as the new forces unleashed by revolution developed their full impact, reaching its prerevolutionary level about a decade after the revolution and continuing to grow afterward. Agricultural productivity per capita, however, never recovered its prerevolutionary levels as an expanding population pressed on the scarce resources of the altiplano. Outside of agriculture, both total production and productivity per capita were stagnant or declining for almost a decade after the revolution (with a few exceptions) but then began a steady long-term growth (fig. 6.3). For the economy as a whole the effect was a decline in gross domestic product in the years following the revolution followed by a slow but lasting growth commencing something less than a decade after the revolution (fig. 6.3). Gross domestic product reached its prerevolutionary level about a decade after the revolution while per capita GDP did not reach that level for almost two decades. But in all we see a fairly consistent pattern of decline in the eight to ten years immediately following the revolution followed by a longer period of growth.

CHANGES IN EDUCATION

Along with the new opportunities in agriculture, commerce, and politics, there were major changes in education. Even before the revolution, peasants and the rural poor had shown a strong desire to educate their children. Pilot schools had been established in the rural areas as early as the 1940s, and some of the free communities had even paid for their own instructors (as in San Miguel), but the overwhelming majority of the rural population were without schools and teachers. This was to change dramatically after the revolution.

EXPANSION OF EDUCATIONAL OPPORTUNITIES

After the revolution, the peasants' newly found political power gave them great influence over the government. Having long desired schools for their children, they now militantly demanded them, and their demands were politically irresistible. As a consequence, the school system was expanded rapidly, at over six times the prerevolutionary rate (fig. 6.4). Since the population did not grow nearly as fast, this meant a substantial increase in educational opportunities.[7] That gain, prosaic as it might seem, was one of the most important benefits of the revolution according to rural Bolivians themselves, as we have seen (table 5.4).

We can get a more detailed picture of educational changes from the head-of-household survey. We do this by looking at differences between cohorts of men who came of age before, during, and after the revolution. The problems involved in defining cohorts and using them to infer what things were like in the past are taken up in the next chapter; suffice it to say here that using such information to infer changes in education is not especially problematic and any errors are likely to reduce rather than exaggerate the effects of the revolution.[8] If taken at face value, these data show a steady increase following the revolution. The cohort coming of age before the revolution averaged 2.2 years of schooling, the revolutionary cohort 2.5, and the cohort

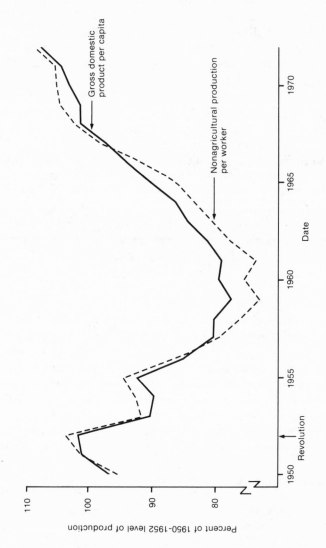

Figure 6.3 Productivity and gross domestic product for Bolivia, 1950–1972. Gross domestic product per capita and nonagricultural production per worker expressed as a percentage of their 1950–1952 values. *Source:* See Appendix 5, section 2.

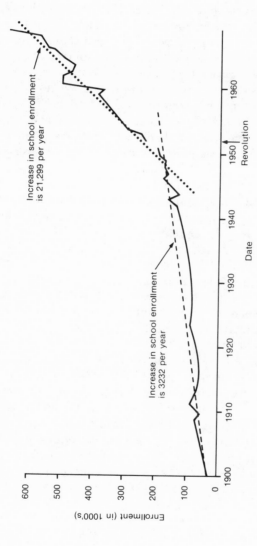

Figure 6.4 Primary school enrollment, 1900–1968. *Source*: Enrollment figures from Wilkie and Reich 1977:148, and Wilkie 1974*b*:191; trend lines estimated by ordinary least squares.

coming of age after the revolution 3.2 years, an increase of 40 percent over the prerevolutionary level. In the Bolivian context, the increase is substantial; it is also statistically significant.[9]

Revolution's Effects Net of Other Changes.   There is, however, a problem in attributing these changes to the revolution, the difficulty being that educational levels were also increasing (albeit slowly) before the revolution and that education depends very heavily on family background (as we saw in chap. 3), which was also changing slowly over time. What we need to do is to distinguish the long-term tendency for educational levels to rise, a trend found not only in rural Bolivia but throughout the world, from revolution's effects. We do this by projecting the prerevolutionary trends forward in time on the assumption that educational change would, in the absence of revolution, have continued in the same way, and at the same pace, as it had before the revolution. Specifically, we estimated trends from a regression equation predicting education on the basis of age (to measure the changes over time), father's education, and father's occupational status (to measure family background) for men in the prerevolutionary cohort. Since they followed significantly different patterns, we did this for the Spanish and the Indian populations separately. We then estimated what would have happened in the absence of revolution by applying this regression equation to the actual age and family background of men in postrevolutionary periods, obtaining an estimated level of education. We then infer that the revolution accounts for the difference, if any, between the actual and the estimated educational levels. Details on the estimate are given in Appendix 5, section 1, and the results are shown in figure 6.5.

For Indians, largely poor and uneducated, the results are straightforward. If prerevolutionary trends had continued after 1952, their educational level would have risen, but not nearly as quickly as it actually did. In the revolutionary period they obtained, on the average, about 40 percent more education than would have been expected on the basis of past trends and in the postrevolutionary period they obtained about 50 percent more (the first increase statistically significant at $p<.05$ and the second at $p<.01$). Especially in the Bolivian context where education had long been denied them, that was a substantial improvement, although their educational levels remained appallingly low in any absolute sense and the gains due to the revolution came to only some two-thirds of a year of schooling apiece. For the Spanish population, with much higher educational levels to begin with, revolution's effects were proportionally smaller, although roughly the same size in absolute terms. If prerevolutionary trends had continued, their educational level would in fact have declined somewhat, because the Spanish population in later periods came from somewhat less advantaged families than in earlier times.[10] But in fact, in the revolu-

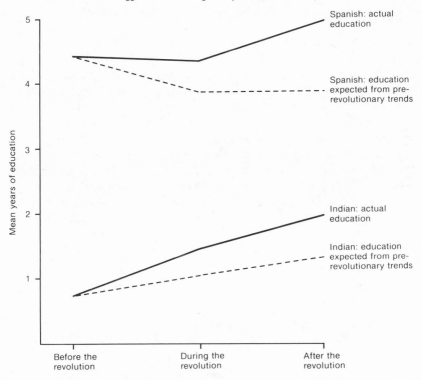

Figure 6.5 Revolution's effect on the amount of education obtained by Spanish and Indian men. Mean years of education actually attained by men, 24 years or older, coming of age before, during, or after the revolution (solid lines) and mean years of education expected if prerevolutionary trends had remained unchanged in later years (broken lines). Differences between actual and expected are significantly different from zero at $p < .05$ except for the Spanish in the revolutionary period. *Source*: Head of household survey; see Appendix 5, section 1, for details. N=245, 94, and 63 for the Spanish before, during, and after the revolution, respectively, and 368, 169, and 103 for Indians.

tionary period the Spanish averaged about 10 percent more education than would have been expected on the basis of prerevolutionary trends (not, however, a statistically significant gain) and after the revolution they averaged about 30 percent more (significant at $p<.05$). So in all the revolution seems to have increased educational opportunities, by about 20 percent for the population as a whole in the revolutionary period and by some 40 percent in the postrevolutionary period (the first significant at $p<.05$ and the second at $p<.01$). The gains were most dramatic for the predominantly peasant and largely uneducated Indian population who seem in this, as in other ways (see chaps. 4 and 5), to have been the main beneficiaries of the revolution.

EDUCATIONAL INEQUALITY

Revolution had effects not only on the amount of education people obtained but also on educational inequality. We can obtain evidence on this from the head of household survey, again by looking at differences between men who came of age before, during, and after the revolution. We measure inequality by the standard deviation, our usual measure of inequality for reasons set out in chapter 1. The relevant data are shown in figure 6.6 (and in more detail in Appendix table 5.1A).

There are once again sharp differences in the revolution's effects on Indians and on the Spanish. For Indians the substantial increase in educational opportunities we saw earlier was accompanied by an almost equally large increase in educational inequality. By the postrevolutionary period, inequality had grown by some 40 percent in compari-

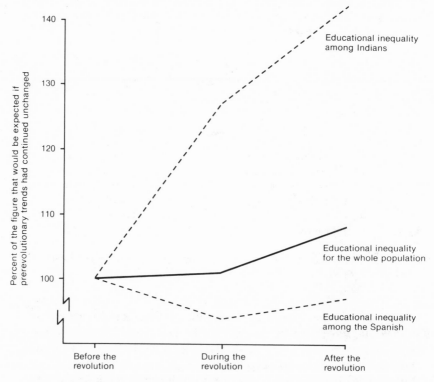

Figure 6.6 Revolution's effects on educational inequality. Inequality among Indians, Spanish, and the population as a whole, for men 24 years or older, coming of age before, during, or after the revolution. Inequality is measured by the standard deviation of years of education and expressed as a percentage of the value that would be expected if prerevolutionary trends had continued unchanged. *Source*: Head of household survey; see Appendix 5, section 1, for details.

son with prerevolutionary times, a quite substantial increase and one that is statistically significant (at p<.05). The pattern among the Spanish was very different. Together with the modest increase in educational levels in the revolutionary period there was if anything a slight decline in educational inequality (a decline of some 7 percent, a figure not significantly different from zero). And in the longer run, inequality remained at roughly its prerevolutionary level despite an appreciable increase in mean levels of education.

For the society as a whole, the picture is complicated by the fact that prerevolutionary trends implied a decline in educational inequality for reasons having nothing to do with the revolution. The magnitude of this decline can be estimated by much the same methods as those we used just above to estimate trends in educational levels (details are given in Appendix 5, section 1). We then can infer revolution's effects by comparing amount of inequality actually observed with the amount expected if prerevolutionary trends had continued. The results of this comparison are shown in figure 6.6 (and in more detail in Appendix table 5.1A). These results suggest a short-run decline in inequality followed by a clear, if not very large, long-run increase (the increase significant at p<.05). In all, it seems that the Bolivian revolution led to a clear and substantial increase in educational inequality among Indians; to no change, or perhaps even a short-run decrease among the Spanish; and, finally, to no change in the short run followed by a modest long-run increase in educational inequality for the population as a whole.

THEORETICAL IMPLICATIONS

We had argued on theoretical grounds that, in the long run, a radical revolution could be expected to lead previously exploited groups with little education to acquire more but also to create a more unequal distribution of education among them (Hypothesis 6). The Bolivian revolution's effects on the Indian population, the poorest and least educated group in prerevolutionary times and the main beneficiaries of the revolution, seem to have followed the predicted pattern fairly closely. But for the Spanish population, not so heavily exploited and including a few remnants of the old elite as well as many others who suffered from the revolution's economic effects, the pattern was not so clear. There was the predicted increase in the average level of education, but inequality did not follow the predicted pattern. For the society as a whole, the predicted pattern was followed reasonably closely, with an appreciable increase in educational levels and a modest long-run increase in educational inequality. So in all, these results give some support, albeit qualified support, for Hypothesis 6. We turn now to another form of inequality, one of central importance.

INCOME INEQUALITY

We have seen revolution's effects on the *average* level of production in agriculture, mining, and other industries and so by inference on the average income earned by Bolivians in each of these sectors. But we know little about the *distribution* of income and wealth. Yet inequality is a central concern of the society at large, of the revolutionary masses and their leadership, and of our theory, and we would very much like to know what effects the Bolivian revolution had on inequality. A definitive analysis of this requires data on the distribution of income and wealth before, during, and after the revolution. Unfortunately, adequate data simply do not exist. After a careful review of the fragmentary quantitative evidence available, however, Zuvekas (1977:20) tentatively speculates that income inequality declined in the years just following the revolution but began to increase in the late 1950s or early 1960s, and his extensive review of the qualitative evidence suggests a similar picture (1977:20−57).[11] In this section, we will add a new, more detailed estimate of income inequality, albeit a somewhat problematic one, by making use of macroeconomic data on productivity in different sectors of the Bolivian economy.

AN ESTIMATE OF INCOME INEQUALITY

Assumptions.   The basic data we use are annual reports of employment and productivity in different sectors of the labor force. These data are from the Ministry of Planning and are currently the most respected data available and are used by almost all analysts, but are nonetheless decidedly imperfect (see Whitehead 1969 and our discussion in chap. 2). The basic assumptions of our model are three. First, we assume that the income each worker earns has some constant relation to productivity, that is, that the income workers get has some simple relation to the value of goods and services they produce. There are of course strong economic arguments for such a link and clear evidence from other countries for a reasonably close correspondence. It does not matter for our purposes whether workers get the full value of their work or only some fraction of that, so long as the fraction does not change (or at least does not change in a way that mimics the theoretically crucial pattern).[12] For simplicity, we assume that workers get the full value of their product as income but if they really get only some fraction of that, it will not in any way affect the changes over time, the crucial question for present purposes, but only the absolute level of inequality. Second, we assume that the sharp differences between workers in different sectors is a key source, perhaps the key source, of income inequality in Bolivia. The sectors we can distinguish in the available data are agriculture, mining, petroleum, manufacturing industry, and services. As we saw in chapter 3, differences in productivity between these sectors were enormous (table 3.1), so it is not unreasonable to assume that they are a crucial source of income inequality. Finally, we assume that every worker's income is equal to the average for all other workers in this sector. This assumption is clearly false since we know perfectly well that different workers in the same sector earn different wages depending on their experience, training, ability, landholdings, and other factors. The effect is that we will consistently underestimate inequality in the society as a whole by ignoring this inequality within sectors. But so long as that underestimate is roughly constant from one year to the next it will not affect the crucial comparisons over time.

With these assumptions, it is then easy to estimate inequality in each year for which data are available, which means 1950 to 1972. We measure income inequality by the standard deviation (for reasons set out in chap. 1) and, for convenience, report inequality in each year as a percent of inequality in the three years just before the revolution. Further details on the data and procedures are given in Appendix 5, section 2, and the results are shown in figure 6.7 as estimate A.

Result. Our estimates suggest that inequality declined slowly and erratically in the first few years after the revolution and then dropped steadily for some years, reaching a minimum a little less than a decade after the revolution. Then there was a clear reversal and it began a slow but steady increase, reaching its prerevolutionary level about a decade and a half after the revolution and continuing to increase thereafter. If this can be taken at face value, it is a dramatic change.

However, a difficulty with estimates of this sort is that they could be affected by external economic factors as well as the internal changes we are interested in. In the Bolivian situation the most likely disturbances are two. First are changes in the international tin market which determine the price received by Bolivia's crucial tin industry. The second possible complication is the tiny but highly productive petroleum industry, which exhibited sustained and rapid growth in the decades following the revolution (see table 6.1). Since it had long been owned by the government and was geographically and politically isolated, it was virtually unaffected by the revolution, changes in its performance reflecting Bolivian geology rather than Bolivian politics. The other sectors (agriculture, manufacturing industry, and services) produced almost entirely for the domestic market and changes in them can, at least in a broad and approximate way, reasonably be attributed to the revolution. We have therefore made a second estimate of income inequality that is unaffected by changes in tin prices or in the petroleum industry. We do this by evaluating output in the mining sector on

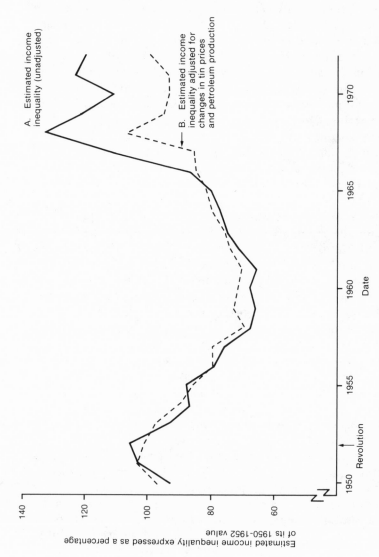

Figure 6.7   Estimated income inequality in Bolivia, 1950–1972. Inequality is measured by the standard deviation and expressed as a percentage of its 1950–1952 value. Alternative estimates with and without adjustments for changes in tin prices and petroleum production. *Source:* See the text and Appendix 5, section 2.

the basis of constant tin prices and by assuming a stable rather than growing petroleum industry. Details are given in Appendix 5, section 2.

The adjusted figures are shown as estimate B in figure 6.7. They show essentially the same pattern as the unadjusted figures (estimate A) and lead to the same conclusions. So we can be reasonably confident that the changes are not due to fluctuations in the international tin market or to changes in the petroleum industry.

Theoretical Implications. Although with some variation, and subject to the several and very genuine uncertainties involved in these estimates, these data do nonetheless seem to support our key theoretical prediction that, in the short run, a radical revolution produces a more equal distribution of income but at the same time sets loose forces which in the long run cause inequality to increase steadily once again (Hypotheses 2 and 5).[13]

CONCLUSION

SUMMARY

The social, economic, and political transformations carried out by the revolution had a profound impact on the economy. With the abolition of the heavy labor taxes, peasants improved their standard of living although overall levels of agricultural production declined seriously for some years after the revolution, probably because of the disorders resulting from land reorganization, the ending of what little private investment existed in agriculture, and the loss of managerial skills. But at the same time, market forces penetrated deeply into the rural economy; traditional marketing monopolies crumbled, enabling peasants to get better prices for their crops, buy manufactured goods more cheaply, and sell on the more profitable urban markets; and land reform freed peasants to take advantage of new opportunities outside agriculture. These gains were not, however, evenly spread throughout the rural population, but seem to have accrued disproportionately to those with the land, education, and skills to take advantage, so increasing inequality among peasants.

As for the mines, the politically and militarily powerful miners' union forced the government to greatly increase employment and along with problems of untrained management, declining ore contents, and poor world tin prices, this led to enormous losses for the government mining corporation. Only with the input of large amounts of government capital did production again begin to achieve prerevolutionary levels. Most other branches of industry showed similar albeit less severe declines, followed by recoveries beginning in the 1960s.

All of these factors meant that economic production in the economy as a whole declined sharply in the years following the revolution, gross domestic product per capita, for example, dropping 20 percent in a decade. But after that there was a clear recovery and production began to increase steadily, seemingly as a consequence of the expansion of market opportunities in agriculture and investments in transportation, industry, and rural development. This growth went on for more than a decade with the end not yet in sight.

Along with expanding opportunities in the economy, there were growing opportunities for rural Bolivians to educate their children. Within a little more than a decade, educational levels had increased by some 40 percent, with gains proportionately larger among the poor and mostly illiterate Indians. But in the long run educational inequality grew among the previously homogeneous Indians.

These changes were paralleled by changes in income inequality. As far as we are able to tell from the limited data available, income inequality seems to have declined for eight or ten years following the revolution, then grew steadily, surpassing its prerevolutionary level about two decades after the revolution.

THEORETICAL IMPLICATIONS

There seems to be considerable evidence for some of the basic mechanisms underlying our theoretical arguments about revolution's effects on income and income inequality. The revolution clearly created new opportunities for the great majority of rural Bolivians who had been exploited by the old elite. Instead of facing heavy and restrictive labor taxes, peasants became free to devote their time and energies entirely for their own benefit, and to accumulate wealth and land for themselves and for their children. The revolution also created new opportunities for cash crop farming as market forces penetrated a previously almost feudal society. Outside of agriculture new opportunities opened up as well, particularly in transport and marketing. These opportunities were of benefit to peasants but of equal, or greater, benefit to the largely cholo and Spanish residents of the small towns who had also been taxed and restricted, albeit less heavily, by the old elite. The abolition of old commercial monopolies and long-established commercial arrangements gave them a chance to establish themselves in trade and in lucrative middleman businesses. These new opportunities were of benefit to all save the old elite. But peasants with small plots or limited skills did not gain so much as those with larger holdings or greater skills. Equally, opportunities outside of agriculture went more often to those who already had the education and skills to exploit them effectively, than to the poorest and least educated. These are precisely the mechanisms underlying our argument for Hypotheses 2, 4, and 5, and so the evidence, although based on diverse and sometimes fragmentary data, on the whole offers considerable support for our theory.

We predicted that revolution would increase educational opportunities for previously exploited groups, but also that it would in the long run create greater educational inequality (Hypothesis 6). And it seems to have done so, although some qualifications are clearly in order for the Spanish population. Finally, a crucial implication of our theory is that revolution leads to a short-run decline in income inequality followed, however, by a long-run increase (Hypotheses 2 and 5). And, although the data on income inequality leave a great deal to be desired, the effect of the many and various changes introduced by the revolution does seem to have been much as we predicted.

On the whole, then, the data seem to offer substantial support for our theoretical claims about income and education, and about the long-term rebirth of inequality following a radical revolution—predictions made in advance, not ex post facto.[14] If our argument is correct, these changes have clear implications for inherited privilege. In the short run, the decline in income inequality implies a decline in inherited privilege but the existence or even expansion of opportunities to use education and skills in agriculture, commerce, and government implies that inherited privilege will not disappear. But in the long run, the growth of economic inequality implies a corresponding growth in inherited privilege in the decades following the revolution. These predictions can be tested with clear and definitive data from the head of household survey, and it is to this crucial test that we now turn.

7
Revolution and Inherited Privilege

In every society parents with education, wealth, and status are able to give their children an advantage in life, helping them to get more education, more money, and higher status jobs than children born into less privileged families. These privileges are a source of deep resentment to the vast majority, and the destruction of inherited privilege is almost always a central goal of radical revolutions. In prerevolutionary Bolivia, the advantages were among the largest in the world, as we saw in chapter 3. The abolition of such advantages was a major point on the Bolivian revolution's agenda, perhaps second only to redistribution of wealth; indeed we have seen in chapter 5 that Bolivians were more concerned with revolution's effects on their children's education than with its effect on their own standard of living. But was the Bolivian revolution in fact able to destroy inherited privilege? Is it reasonable to think that radical revolutions can in general do so?

Revolutionaries certainly believe they can, and their opponents fear they can. The rhetoric of revolution and of counterrevolution is full of images of society turned upside down, of the elite brought down to the level of the masses or below. Marx and his successors thought inherited privilege would end after the communist revolution, as did the Chinese revolutionaries. But while radical revolutions attempt to uproot inherited privilege, good intentions do not necessarily change the world, and the persistence of anxieties about the class background of students and the elite in eastern Europe and China decades after the communists came to power suggests that they did not do so (Khrushchev 1970; Lipset and Dobson 1973).

On theoretical grounds, we argued in chapter 1 that revolutions cannot be expected to overturn the whole stratification order; inequality and inherited privilege will necessarily remain, though diminished. Revolutions can redistribute income, wealth, and other kinds of property and so eliminate the inherited privilege that flows from them (although even that is often difficult and sometimes impossible). But even revolution cannot, we argued, eliminate human capital and the privileges that flow from it (Hypothesis 8). High status families are generally well educated, fluent in the dominant language, skilled in dealing with schools and bureaucracies, knowledgeable, and informed, and that gives their children an advantage quite apart from the money that revolution can devalue, the capital that revolution can confiscate, the contacts and connections that revolution renders useless, and the prestige that revolution can undermine. Culture is, we argued, a great advantage and poverty does not erase it. Once their children get education and human capital, that should give them a great advantage both during revolutionary times and afterward. Even a revolutionary society needs engineers, accountants, literate clerks, machinists who can follow written instructions, and shopkeepers who can keep at least rudimentary records; human capital is vital and, indeed, may in some ways become even more important, as the revolution opens up new opportunities and wider prospects. Thus elite children are still able to convert their educational advantages into status and into income as well (although perhaps not as much income as before).[1] So we argued that a radical revolution cannot be expected to overturn the stratification order nor to eliminate inherited privilege but that it can only reduce inequality and status inheritance, and that only to the rather limited extent that they depend on physical rather than human capital.

And, we argued, as time goes on inequality and status inheritance reemerge. New opportunities for using human capital lead to an expansion of education but also to a more unequal distribution of human capital among disadvantaged groups, to more status inheritance, and to the accumulation of new wealth. Unless there is a thoroughgoing expropriation down to the modest peasant farmer and tiny village entrepreneur, small-scale capitalism creates new inequalities where none existed before, or greater inequalities where some existed before. So differences in property reemerge over the years and children born into privileged families once again benefit from their parents' money. They also benefit from their parents' human capital. So inherited privilege is, we argued, born again from the ashes of revolution (Hypothesis 9).

But this is all theory and we must find out what actually happens in practice. Do revolutions really overturn the stratification order—do children of the poor inherit the earth—or does inherited privilege survive the fires of revolution and appear again in the aftermath?

In this chapter we will find out what happened after the Bolivian revolution of 1952, using data from the head of household survey. We will consider revolution's effects on both property and human capital and its effects on the Spanish- and Aymara-speaking populations as well as on the society as a whole. Finally, to test our hypotheses further we compare the Bolivian experience with that of a very different revolution in a very different setting, the communist revolution in Poland.

SOME TECHNICAL PRELIMINARIES

The primary source of data for this chapter is the head-of-household survey. The data, definitions of variables, and other technical issues were described in detail in chapter 2. There are, however, a few further technical issues that require brief consideration before we go on.

DEFINITIONS

Cohorts from Before, During, and After the Revolution.   Our basic strategy in this chapter is to divide the 1,130 heads of households in the survey into cohorts who came of age before, during, and after the revolution and measure the effects of the revolution by noting the differences in the experiences of those three cohorts. As a rough but serviceable approximation, we assume that rural Bolivians became adults in the sense of finishing their education, taking up their first jobs, and marrying (and hence becoming eligible for our head of household sample) sometime between their mid-teens and mid-twenties. So we can fairly safely define those who were twenty-six or older at the time of the revolution as having come of age *before* it. The boundary between those who came of age during the revolutionary period (for whom our predictions about short-term effects apply) and those who came of age after the revolution (to whom the long-range predictions apply) is a little more difficult. As we have seen in earlier chapters, the economic changes, the establishment of mass parties and pressure groups, the legal and administrative processes involved in transferring land to the peasants, the formation of peasant unions and similar cooperative and union style organizations, the exploration of new occupational and economic options by the peasantry, and similar major adjustments took many years, particularly in the rural areas with which we are concerned. Things were still unsettled and in the midst of change six or seven years after the revolution but had clearly settled down ten or twelve years later; we have therefore selected the nine years following the revolution as the revolutionary period. An empirical analysis of successive three-year age cohorts confirms that mobility patterns change noticeably eight to ten years after the revolution (see Appendix 6, section 1). Men in the revolutionary period were between seventeen and twenty-five at the time of the revolution.

The remaining group came of age in the postrevolutionary period. We have confined the analysis to those twenty-four or older at the time of the survey, which would make them ten to sixteen at the time of the revolution. The reason for not including younger people is to avoid a well-known bias but the restriction is in practice of little consequence and the substantive conclusions remain the same when younger men are included.[2] In all, there are 628 men in the prerevolutionary period, 271 in the revolutionary period, and 169 in the postrevolutionary period.

These definitions are necessarily somewhat arbitrary in that one might well argue that the revolutionary period should be a year or two longer or shorter than we have specified or that some people come of age somewhat sooner or later than we estimate. But they should be a reasonable approximation. Furthermore, it is likely that errors would weaken our case rather than strengthen it. To see this, suppose that things are different for those in the revolutionary period from the way they were for those coming of age earlier but we mistakenly classify as prerevolutionary some people who truly belong in the revolutionary period, and also misclassify as revolutionary some who actually came of age before. The effect of those misclassifications will be to dilute the apparent differences between the prerevolutionary and the revolutionary cohorts; the supposed prerevolutionary cohort will look a little like the revolutionary cohort (since some of its members really belong to that cohort) and the revolutionary cohort will look something like their prerevolutionary predecessors (since some of those predecessors are mistakenly included in it). The same thing would happen if we make errors in distinguishing between those who came of age during and those who came of age after the revolution. In short, whatever errors we have made here will likely bias our results against our predictions, not in favor of them.

Occupation and Education. To make an appropriate comparison between men in these three cohorts, we must of course compare them at the same points in their life cycle. It would not do, for example, to try to infer revolution's effects on income by comparing the present income or standard of living of (old) men who entered the labor force before the revolution with the incomes of (middle-aged) men who entered in the revolutionary period or with that of (young) men who entered after the revolution. The problem is that a man's position in the life cycle strongly affects his income and living standards—men with more experience in the labor force earn more than men in similar jobs who have less experience, they have had more years to accumulate possessions, they have older and larger families and so may need more money (and so work harder) or perhaps less (if their children can help them out), their values may be different than those of young men at the beginning of their careers, and so on. So if we find a difference between the income of older and younger men, we would not know if that was due to the revolution or was merely a consequence of their different positions in the life cycle. To make appropriate comparisons, we must make use of retrospective data on events that happened at the *same* stage of everyone's life cycle. Fortunately we have appropriate data for both education and respondent's first job.[3] Although both have their weaknesses (discussed in detail in chap. 2), they nonetheless give a good picture of what happened in the early part of men's careers. We measure education in years and occupational status by the procedures described at length in chapter 2 and of course use the same measures for father's education and status as for son's.

METHODS OF ANALYSIS

The analytic procedures we use are ordinary least squares regression. The particular models we estimate are mathematically identical to analysis of covariance (Goldberger 1968) and our exact procedures are described in Appendix 6, section 2. These procedures assume that the relations between variables are, to a reasonable approximation, linear and additive. They are also modestly sensitive to errors in measurement and sometimes to the exact specification of the model estimated.[4] We have dealt in some detail with most of these issues in chapter 2 and provide additional evidence at appropriate points in the text below.

Our statistical tests for differences between time periods use conventional analysis of covariance procedures obtained by the use of interaction terms in ordinary least squares regression (Goldberger 1968) and include age in the analysis to capture secular trends. Since we are comparing two types of society, prerevolutionary and revolutionary, we have adjusted the number of cases to be equal in the two periods; otherwise the results would be affected by the accident that our prerevolutionary cohort is much larger than our revolutionary cohort. This was done by weighting the 628 prerevolutionary cases down to equal the 271 revolutionary cases. In comparing the revolutionary period with the postrevolutionary period we readjusted the weights in an analogous manner, for the same reasons. This weighting makes our statistical tests conservative since the true number of cases is greater than that used in the tests. Since direction was predicted in advance, a one-tailed test is used.

While regression procedures are old and well-tried methods whose strengths and weaknesses are well known, they are not the only ones that might be used here. In particular it has been argued that the log-linear procedures developed by Goodman and others have conceptual advantages for situations such as ours (see Goodman 1979 and the references cited there). We had originally planned to use these procedures at least as supplements to regression but found that they are in practice quite ineffective in dealing with this kind of problem, seemingly for fundamental reasons (see Pescosolido and Kelley 1979), so we have not used them.

With these technical questions out of the way, we can return to substantive issues. We begin by looking at the revolution's effects on

the kind of jobs available to men beginning their careers and then go on
to analyze the subsequent patterns of occupational mobility.

EFFECTS ON THE OCCUPATIONAL STRUCTURE

Before the revolution Bolivia was a poor, predominantly agricultural society with little physical or human capital, and that low level of
economic development largely determined the kind of jobs the economy had to offer. After the revolution Bolivia was still a poor, predominantly agricultural society, with little physical or human capital,
whose occupational structure was still quite limited. As can be seen in
table 7.1, the kind of jobs men took up at the beginning of their careers
was little affected by the revolution. It is a range of jobs typical of
preindustrial societies with the usual small group of high ranking jobs,
a slightly larger group of clerical, business, and modern skilled blue-
collar jobs, followed by a much larger group of traditional crafts jobs.
Agriculture is by far the predominant pursuit, with mostly poor
farmers and farm laborers at the bottom of the hierarchy but a fair
number of middle level and wealthy farmers as well. Prerevolutionary
and postrevolutionary Bolivia was thus typical of countries at its low
level of development (see chap. 3). Revolution cannot overnight create
factories out of potato fields, nor can it make civil engineers out of
illiterate peasants. All that takes time and money; it takes huge
investments in education and physical capital and a time frame of
generations. It is the level of economic development which largely
determines the kind of jobs available, not the edicts of politicians,
revolutionary or otherwise. And at the time of our survey a decade and
a half after the revolution, the economy was still at roughly the same
level of development as before the revolution (see chap. 6) and the
occupations available were therefore characteristic of that level of
development.

There were, nonetheless, some minor changes. The number of men
beginning their careers in elite white-collar jobs, always small, seems to
have dropped even further. The number beginning as wealthy cattle
ranchers may also have declined briefly, only to rise again in the long
run. But there seems to be an expansion, perhaps even a doubling in
the long run, of the number starting in high white-collar jobs, among
them the educated young men who so often seem to gain sinecures in
the bureaucracy and the schools after a revolution. But these jobs are
only a tiny fraction of the labor force so even a doubling, while an
important expansion of opportunities, does not really amount to much
in the broader picture. There seem to have been few systematic
changes in the middle ranking occupations. At the bottom the differences are also small and inconsistent. More men seem to have
started their careers as farm laborers in the revolutionary period but in

150   *Revolution and Inherited Privilege*

TABLE 7.1

REVOLUTION'S EFFECTS ON THE OCCUPATIONAL STRUCTURE. PERCENTAGE
DISTRIBUTION OF FIRST JOB FOR MEN COMING OF AGE BEFORE, DURING,
AND AFTER THE REVOLUTION.

Status	Occupations in the ethnographic classification	Cohort coming of age		
		Before the revolution (percent)	During the revolution (percent)	After the revolution (percent)
Higher classes				
	100 Elite white-collar	3	1	1
	75 Large farmer	2	2	2
	72 Cattle rancher	3	0.5	3
	71 High white-collar	2	3	4
	(Subtotal)[1]	(10)	(6)	(10)
Upper middle				
	66 Skilled modern blue-collar	2	2	2
	62 Clerical and sales	2	4	1
	57 Small business	11	7	10
	(Subtotal)[1]	(16)	(13)	(13)
Lower middle				
	33 Specialized farm	10	6	5
	31 Skilled traditional blue-collar	25	30	27
	31 Unskilled nonfarm	3	3	3
	(Subtotal)[1]	(37)	(40)	(37)
Lower classes				
	12 Tenant farmer	1	3	3
	9 Farm laborer	21	26	16
	4 Small farmer	13	12	19
	0 Small livestock owner	3	1	2
	(Subtotal)[1]	(38)	(42)	(40)
	Total[1]	100	100	100
	Mean occupational status	31	27	30
	Standard deviation of occupational status	25	22	23
	Number of cases[2]	(599)	(255)	(166)

Source: Head of household survey.

[1]Detail may differ from total because of rounding.
[2]Excluding missing data.

the longer run fewer began that way and more began as small farmers.
But on the whole, these are small and not particularly consistent
variations; any detailed analysis of the minor fluctuations would require a much larger sample than the one thousand we have at hand.
But the main point is clear: there was no major change in the range of
jobs available in the decade and a half following the revolution. Nor
does our sample seem to be at all atypical in that respect; on the

contrary, the fragmentary data available for the country as a whole also suggest great continuity in the occupational structure.[5] It would seem that change, if change there is to be, will only become apparent many decades after the revolution as economic development slowly reshapes the preindustrial economy of Bolivia.

A Technical Note on Occupational Hierarchies. There is one technical issue we should raise briefly at this point, and that is the effect that revolution has on the ranking of occupations. Our theory and analysis turn on the question of who gets the good jobs and it would complicate the analysis, to say the least, if revolution made any fundamental changes in the occupational hierarchy, that is, if it reordered the status of occupations. But of course it does no such thing. Not only is the distribution of jobs much the same, but the ranking is unchanged. After the revolution as well as before it, small peasant farmers on the altiplano are still poorer and less skilled than traditional craftsmen, and they in turn poorer than clerical and sales workers, and they in turn poorer than large farmers, and they in turn poorer than men with elite white-collar jobs who are, as always, at the top of the hierarchy. There is not the slightest evidence in any of the anthropological literature, or in the income and educational statistics for postrevolutionary Bolivia, of any real change in the ranking of occupations. And in that Bolivia is in no way atypical since occupational hierarchies are essentially invariant throughout the world, in communist societies as well as capitalist, and in the past as in the present.[6] There may have been small changes in rank (for example in the status of miners whose incomes rose dramatically for a few years before falling back to normal levels) but we have not, after some considerable searching, found any of even the slightest consequence in our data. Aside from changes in the rank of occupations, many other kinds of changes (for example, a leveling down of the status of elite occupations or a leveling up of poor ones) would not affect our conclusions. Leveling down, for example, is a linear transformation that necessarily leaves standardized coefficients unchanged and could not account for our results, since we find that revolution has the same effects on both standardized and unstandardized coefficients. But in fact there is no evidence of changes of any kind in the occupational hierarchy and no persuasive reason to think that there should be any, at least under Bolivian conditions.

OVERALL EFFECTS ON INHERITED PRIVILEGE

IN THE SHORT RUN

As we have seen in chapter 3, before the revolution high status families were able to give their sons a very advantageous start in life, resulting in a high correlation between father's and son's status. We are now in a position to see how the revolution changed that. If it really overturned the old stratification order, discriminating against sons of the old elite and favoring children of the oppressed masses, then there would be a *negative* correlation between father's and son's status in the period just following the revolution.[7] On the other hand, if revolution simply eliminated all vestiges of the inherited privilege of old without putting any new privilege in its place, then there would be neither advantage nor disadvantage in being born into an old elite family and consequently *no* correlation between father's and son's status. A third possibility is that revolution is, at least in this respect, merely a sham which leaves the old elite to pass on its privileges to its children just as in the past. That would leave the correlation between father's and son's status unchanged. We of course argued for a fourth possibility, suggesting that revolution would reduce inherited privilege but not eliminate it.

A First Estimate.   Let us begin with the correlation between father's and son's occupational status, a simple, appropriate, and quite conventional measure of status inheritance. This dropped from .53 before the revolution to .44 during the revolutionary period, a decline of 17 percent (see A in fig. 7.1).[8] This is a substantial decrease in inherited status but by no means the end of it. To put it in a wider perspective, revolution changed Bolivia from one of the world's more rigid societies (noticeably more rigid than the United States, for example) to a more or less average one (about the same as the United States; see chap. 3, fig. 3.5).

An alternative way of measuring status inheritance is the metric regression coefficient, which indicates in concrete terms how much a son can expect to gain from each unit of his father's status. It is more appropriate than standardized coefficients for our purposes and has a clearer intuitive meaning as well.[9] We will therefore focus our discussion mainly on metric comparisons throughout the chapter but will also present results in the perhaps more familiar standardized form graphically and in appendix tables. Exactly the same conclusions follow no matter which figures one considers.

In these metric terms, a son coming of age before the revolution could expect to get just under half a status point for each status point his father had. So, for example, a son born into an elite white-collar family (whose father would have a status of 100) could expect to get about 50 points from his father, enough to get him halfway up the status hierarchy himself, while a son from a poor peasant's family (whose father's status would be 0 or 4) could expect almost nothing.[10] The revolution reduced the advantage enjoyed by the professional's son by about 20 percent, to 40 status points (B in fig. 7.1). That was an

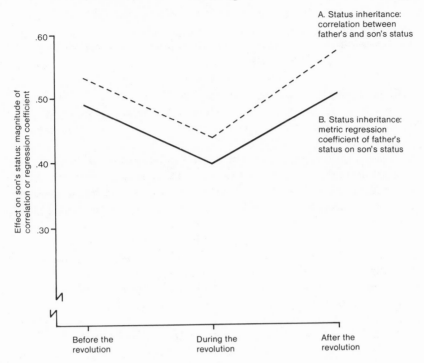

Figure 7.1   Revolution's effect on status inheritance: first estimates. Correlation between father's occupational status and the status of his son's first job (A) and metric regression coefficient (B). Men, 24 years or older, coming of age before, during, or after the revolution. See Appendix 6, section 2, for details and table 6.6A for exact figures. *Source*: Head of household survey; N=628, 271, and 169 before, during, and after the revolution, respectively.

appreciable loss, and a statistically significant one (p < .07), but still left him with 80 percent of his original advantage in hand.

A More Comprehensive Measure of Family Background.   While father's occupational status is a good first approximation to the standing and resources of the family one is born into, we can improve our model by adding a measure of father's human capital.[11] This is better because there are some fathers with high education but modest jobs whose status and resources would be underestimated by a measure focusing just on occupation, while there are others with high occupations but little education whose position would be exaggerated. We call this Model 2. In addition to education, the family's ethnicity (or social race, however one chooses to call it) is another important aspect of family background in Bolivia and we will add it to our other indicators of family background; we call this Model 3. In Bolivia the differences between those of Indian and those of Spanish heritage are, as we have seen, wide. Indians are poorer, less educated, have worse jobs, and had very different experiences in the revolution; indeed, we have seen that they were the main beneficiaries of the revolution while the main costs fell on Spanish speakers. Our measure of social race was described in chapter 2.

Since these more complete measures of family background involve more variables, the results are a little more difficult to present. We will report both the percent of variance explained, a conventional but not very intuitive measure closely related to standardized coefficients,[12] and also another summary related to metric coefficients which is based on a comparison between two sons, one from a privileged family at the top of the Bolivian social hierarchy and the other from a poor peasant family at the bottom. For this last we report the average advantage that one son has over the other, measured by the difference in status between the jobs that sons born into elite families get on the average and the jobs that sons born into peasant families get. For the privileged one, let us take a son whose father works at an elite white-collar job (100 status points), has 11.6 years of education (the average for such workers), and is Spanish. For the other let us take a son whose father is a landless llama herder (0 status points), has 1.2 years of education (the average for such workers), and is Aymara; a small farmer's son or the son of a farm laborer would be in the same position (with fractionally higher status but fractionally lower education). So what we have in effect is a representative of the impoverished majority of the Bolivian population. Regression techniques then provide straightforward estimates of the difference in their sons' prospects.[13] In practice, this way of reporting the results of our analysis and a variety of reasonable alternatives all lead to the same conclusions, as may be seen from the figures and the detailed tables in Appendix 6, but for simplicity we usually will not describe the alternative measures in the text.[14]

In the simplest model, where family background is measured only by occupational status (which we call Model 1), we have seen that the son from an elite family could expect a job 50 status points higher than a poor peasant's son, an advantage the revolution reduced by 20 percent (this is shown as A in fig. 7.2). If we improve the accuracy with which family background is measured by adding father's education to the model, we get virtually identical results (B in fig. 7.2).[15] Finally, if we measure family background even more comprehensively, including father's social race as well as his education and occupation, the results are again virtually identical to those from the other models (C in the figure).[16] In all it is clear that the Bolivian revolution appreciably reduced the advantages of being born into a high status family. And these reductions are all statistically significant ($p < .02$ for all three models).

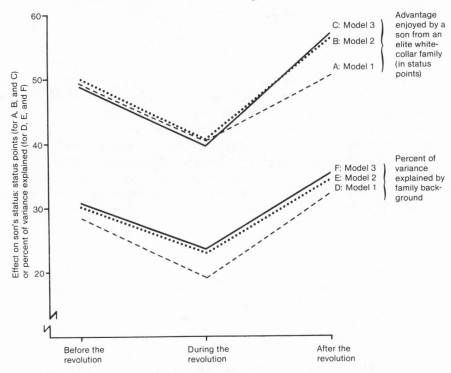

Figure 7.2 Revolution's effect on status inheritance: more comprehensive estimates. Advantage enjoyed by a son from an elite white-collar family compared to a poor peasant's son and also percent of variance explained by family background. Men, 24 years or older, coming of age before, during, or after the revolution. Alternative estimates measuring family background by father's occupational status alone (Model 1); father's occupation and father's education (Model 2); or father's occupation, education, and social race (Model 3). See Appendix 6, section 2, for details and table 6.6A for exact figures. *Source*: Head of household survey.

Farm Origins and Other Variables. In addition to measuring family background in these ways, we have considered a number of other variables, adding farm origin, region, and support for the revolution (among others) to the analysis. Farm origin is the only one that matters and it does not really matter much; including it does not change the substantive conclusions in the slightest (see Appendix table 6.5A, Panel D, for details). Other variables mattered even less.

Summary. Perhaps the best single way of putting this is to say that the revolution reduced the advantage enjoyed by a son born into a family at the top of the Bolivian hierarchy by about a fifth, a decline of 10 status points. That is a noticeable decline, especially in a society where the mean status is 30 points, but it still leaves him with a great advantage, indeed with 80 percent of the advantage he would have had before the revolution.

These results offer no support at all for the notion that revolution entirely overturned the status order, favoring the children of the masses over the offspring of the old elite. Nor do they provide any support for the view that a radical revolution will eliminate all inherited privilege, leaving children from all families competing on an equal basis. Even in the midst of revolution, children from poor peasant families are far from able to compete on equal terms with children from more privileged families. Nor, however, do they support the view that inherited privilege is so deeply rooted in the very fabric of society that it is impervious to revolution. Rather, they are as we predicted (Hypothesis 8): revolution reduces inherited privilege but does not eliminate it.

LONG-RUN EFFECTS ON STATUS INHERITANCE

We have seen that a radical revolution seems to reduce status inheritance in the short run, but what happens then? Does status inheritance decline further as the effects of revolutionary politics come into full fruition, as more and more children grow up in an environment dominated by the revolution, attend schools run by the revolutionary government, and enter an economy long under the sway of revolutionary dictates and the administration of revolutionary leaders? Or do things stay as they were in the revolutionary period, the changes introduced by revolution neither being undermined nor being enhanced? Or does status inheritance increase once again as a new elite emerges and children of the old elite learn how to take advantage of the new rules of the game?

Let us begin simply with the correlation between father's and son's status. During the revolution the correlation was, as we have seen, .44. A decade after the revolution it rose by almost a third to .57, a substantial increase (see fig. 7.1). Put slightly differently, the advantage a son born into an elite white-collar family had over a poor peasant's son increased from 40 status points to 50, an appreciable and significant increase (p < .10). This is, coincidentally, exactly the same advantage elite sons enjoyed before the revolution.

We can measure family background more comprehensively by considering both father's occupation and education (Model 2) or father's occupation, education and social race (Model 3). Measured in either of these ways, the advantage of being born into an elite home rose 16 status points, an increase of 40 percent. These are substantial and statistically significant increases (p < .10 for both models, in spite of the rather modest sample sizes for these periods).

It seems, then, that revolution does lead to the rebirth of inherited privilege, increasing the advantage of being born into a high status home by about 40 percent. These are people coming to adulthood a dozen years after the revolution. They will have received much of their schooling in schools run (and often built) by the revolutionary government and will have entered an economy whose commanding heights were long dominated by nationalized industry. But it seems that status inheritance did not continue to fall, despite what revolutionary leaders would have liked. It did not even stay at the relatively low level it reached in revolutionary times but in fact increased again, reaching or even surpassing its prerevolutionary levels. That is surprising, and surely not what the revolutionary leaders hoped or intended. But this is exactly as we predicted (Hypothesis 9) and supports our theory. To find out how and why this came about and whether it came about for the reasons we posited, it will help to distinguish the revolution's effects on property from its effects on human capital. We do that in the next two sections.

REVOLUTION AND PROPERTY

We have argued that property is especially vulnerable to revolution. Unlike the knowledge and skills that make up human capital, property is readily separated from its owners: land and houses can be taken from their old owners; pensions, rents, and debts can be canceled or devalued; businesses can be regulated or expropriated. We have seen that in fact there was an effective land reform; that inflation did destroy the value of prerevolutionary pensions, rents, and debts; and that the abolition of old monopolies, the rise of unions, and other economic changes undermined most of the privileges of the old business elite. So the revolution appears to have led to a substantial redistribution of income and wealth. We argued that this redistribution should in theory reduce the advantages of being born into an elite home, since part of those advantages come about because the elite use their income and wealth to help their children (Hypothesis 8). With fewer large farms to hand on to their children, fewer and less prosperous businesses to provide their children with jobs or bankroll them in their own ventures, and with less free income to support their schooling, elite families will, we argued, no longer be able to do as much for their children. In this section we will see what happened in actual fact. We must first, however, describe how we measure property's effects, a matter which is not without real difficulty.

Measuring the Advantages of Property

Measuring the effect of father's property is somewhat problematic since we have no direct measure of his income or wealth. No question on that was asked, nor would the answer have been believable had it been asked. But we can get some not unpersuasive indirect estimates. Since property and occupational status are closely correlated, many and perhaps all of the effects of father's property will appear as *direct* effects of father's *occupational* status in models like ours where there is no explicit measure of property but other important aspects of family background are explicitly measured. For this to be a good approximation, three things must be true. First, occupational status must be closely linked with physical capital, which in Bolivia it obviously is (see table 2.4). In part this is built into the definition of occupational status: we have explicit information on father's land ownership and implicit information on the size and value of the land insofar as that is reflected in the presence or absence of hired farm labor and we used that information to distinguish large from small farmers. We also have explicit information on whether the father was an owner or employee, and so can distinguish self-employed businessmen and the like from mere employees; this information was also used as part of the measure of occupational status. And in addition to these definitional overlaps, having a high status occupation is one of the most important reasons for having high income, so there is a strong casual overlap as well. So for these various reasons, the correlations between occupation and our standard of living measure (good surrogate for income) was .58 at the time of our survey and there is every reason to assume that it was at least as high for the previous generation.

Second, we need to have satisfactory measures of the things *other than* property which give sons born into high status families an advantageous start in life. Human capital is the obvious candidate but we have a quite satisfactory measure of that in father's education and language (or social race, as we have called it). Insofar as there is, or was, discrimination against Indians, that is also measured by social race and so presents no further problem. At least under Bolivian conditions, we believe that human capital (including motivational, cultural, and linguistic advantages that are part and parcel of human capital), social race, and property pretty much exhaust the advantages of being born into a high status family. While it is possible that there are other advantages linked to father's occupation and not his human capital (need for achievement, skill in dealing with bureaucracies, personal contacts), under the specific conditions we are dealing with we doubt that they are either large or widespread. So to a reasonable approximation, the effects of father's occupation that are left after we control for his human capital and social race will, we believe, largely reflect his income and wealth,[17] with perhaps some contamination from these other variables. With these assumptions and reservations in mind, we will speak of the direct effect of father's occupational status (measured by the partial regression coefficient in models where human capital is controlled) as reflecting the effect of his property. But that is an attribution that must be treated with some caution, even though we will, for stylistic convenience, not always make the qualification explicit.[18]

SHORT-TERM EFFECTS

The Decline of Wealth. Measured in this way, the advantage that a high status father was able to pass on via wealth and income before the revolution seems to have been very large. At that time, a child born into an elite white-collar family had an advantage that we attribute solely to his father's property of 31 status points over one born into a poor peasant's home, enough in itself to get him almost a third of the way to the top of the status hierarchy (A in fig. 7.3).[19] The revolution reduced that advantage to 17 points, a little over half what it had been, a large and statistically significant drop (p < .01). The pattern is exactly the same in standardized terms (B in fig. 7.3). The revolution reduced the advantage of being born into a wealthy home substantially, in fact almost by half.

We can get an even closer look at what revolution did by distinguishing two basic ways in which being born into a wealthy home is an advantage. One advantage is *indirect* in that children of wealthy homes are able to get more schooling and because they get more schooling they therefore get better jobs. The other advantage is *direct* in that children born into wealthy homes get advantages other than simply education.[20] Although we do not have explicit measures of what these other advantages are, it seems likely that they are in the main the obvious ones: inheriting the family farm, going into the family business, using family funds to start a new venture, and the like.

We have argued that the revolution, by expropriating property, devaluing the currency, destroying old business monopolies, and the like should substantially reduce the direct advantages. And in fact it does, reducing the advantage enjoyed by a son born into an elite white-collar home by more than half, from 23 points to 10 points (A in fig. 7.4). In fact the direct advantage is not significantly different from zero in the revolutionary period (p > .10, two-tailed); given the less than enormous sample size here, it would probably not be wise to conclude that the advantage has disappeared, only that it is substantially reduced. The reduction is clearly significant (p < .01).

The indirect effect through education was small to begin with, sons born into elite white-collar families enjoying an advantage of eight status points before the revolution. The revolution changed this little, reducing it by perhaps a point (not a statistically significant drop; see C in fig. 7.4). In part this is because a good deal of the education we are considering was, presumably, completed before the revolution. So

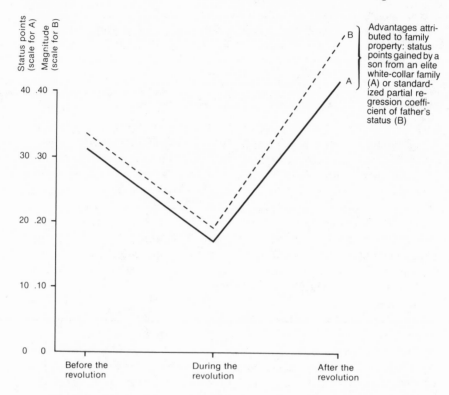

Figure 7.3   Total effects attributed to family property, regardless of how they come about. Advantage enjoyed by a son from an elite white-collar family compared to a poor peasant's son (A) and standardized partial regression coefficient of father's occupation on the status of his son's first job (B). Men, 24 years or older, coming of age before, during, or after the revolution. Estimated from Model 3. The effect of father's occupational status, controlling for his education and social race, is interpreted as reflecting the influence of his property for reasons (and with qualifications) noted in the text. See Appendix 6, section 2, for details and table 6.6A for exact figures. *Source*: Head of household survey.

what we have basically is that revolution undercut the direct advantages of being born into a wealthy home, reducing them by more than half. With property expropriated or devalued there was simply much less to inherit and the society was correspondingly more open to social mobility. This is exactly as we predicted (Hypothesis 8).

LONG-TERM EFFECTS ON PROPERTY

While revolution greatly reduced the advantages of being born into a wealthy home, we have argued that that would not last and that in the

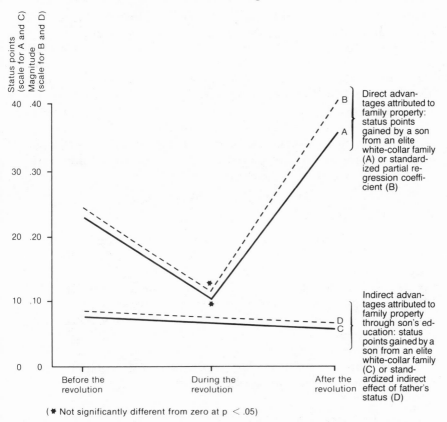

Status points
(scale for A and C)

Magnitude
(scale for B and D)

40 .40

30 .30

20 .20

10 .10

0   0

Before the revolution

During the revolution

After the revolution

B

A

Direct advantages attributed to family property: status points gained by a son from an elite white-collar family (A) or standardized partial regression coefficient (B)

D
C

Indirect advantages attributed to family property through son's education: status points gained by a son from an elite white-collar family (C) or standardized indirect effect of father's status (D)

(✳ Not significantly different from zero at p < .05)

Figure 7.4   Direct and indirect effects attributed to family property. Direct effects of father's occupation are those having nothing to do with his, or his son's, education and indirect effects are those that come about because father's occupation influences his son's education, which in turn affects the status of his son's first job; these effects are attributed to family property for reasons (and with qualifications) noted in the text. Men, 24 years or older, coming of age before, during, or after the revolution. See Appendix 6, section 2, for details and table 6.6A for exact figures. *Source*: Head of household survey.

longer run the advantages conferred by wealth would reappear in new and perhaps more virulent forms. And this is what seems to have happened. The advantage of being born into an elite white-collar home increased from a revolutionary low of 17 status points to 42, an increase of almost 250 percent (significant at p < .05; see A in fig. 7.3). The result was to leave the advantages of wealth at least as great and perhaps greater than they had been before the revolution.

It is once again useful to divide these up into the direct and indirect effects. It turns out that the increase came about entirely because the direct advantages grew enormously, in fact 350 percent, from 10 status points to 36. This is a statistically significant increase (p < .03; see A in fig. 7.4). The small indirect effect through education hardly changed, if anything decreasing by a single point. Thus, inheritance and other of the obvious direct privileges of wealth reemerge less than a decade after the revolution's triumph. And they do not reemerge in a modest and attenuated way but with a vengeance.

In short, by upsetting the transmission of advantages through property, revolution does indeed seem to reduce inherited privilege in the short run. But in the long run—within barely a decade, which is not all that long a run—inequality is reborn. This is exactly as we predicted and strongly supports our theory (Hypotheses 8 and 9).

REVOLUTION AND HUMAN CAPITAL

We have seen that revolution had a dramatic effect on property but not what effect it had, if any, on the role played by human capital in the transmission of advantages from one generation to the next. Neither revolutionaries nor their opponents have generally distinguished between property and human capital in this context and so would presumably have the same hopes and expectations for it as for property. In contrast, we made a sharp distinction between them, arguing that revolution could be expected to disrupt the one but not the other, human capital if anything becoming more valuable after the revolution. In this section we will see what actually happened.

FAMILY BACKGROUND AND EDUCATION

One reason that revolution cannot entirely eliminate inherited advantage was, we argued, that high ranking families would always be able to acquire more education for their children. In part, this probably has to do with money, since prosperous families can better afford to do without their child's labor at home and to pay his school fees. These are the sorts of advantages that revolution could well undermine. But there are other, more important, advantages to do with values and motivation, and with the skills and knowledge parents are able to impart to their children and use themselves in guiding a child's progress through school. These, we argued, are the sort of thing that a revolution probably cannot change, and because it cannot change them, revolution cannot eliminate inherited advantages in education. We are in a position now to get some evidence of this.

It turns out that the Bolivian revolution was unable to eliminate the educational advantages that come from being born into a high ranking family. Before the revolution, high status families were able to provide great advantages to their children. In our usual comparison a child born into the elite white-collar family could expect to get nine years more education than the llama herder's son. In the midst of revolution this great advantage dropped only fractionally, barely 4 percent, leaving the elite son with a very large and highly significant advantage (p < .001; see A in fig. 7.5). And in the long run the advantages of birth increased again, rising by a quarter and leaving children of elite families with a large and significant advantage indeed (p < .001). Thus even in the midst of a radical revolution, coming from a high ranking family conferred a massive educational advantage.

This advantage was passed on mainly through human capital, which seems to be the reason it was so little affected by the revolution (table 6.5A gives the details). In standardized terms, the effect of

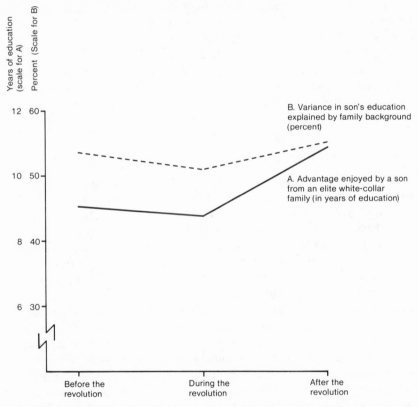

Figure 7.5   Human capital: The influence of family background on education before, during, and after the revolution. Advantage enjoyed by a son from an elite white-collar family compared to a poor peasant's son in years of schooling (A) and percent of variance in son's education explained by father's education, occupation, and social race (B). Men, 24 years or older, coming of age before, during, or after the revolution. Estimates from Model 3C; see Appendix 6, section 2, for details and table 6.6A for exact figures. *Source*: Head of household survey.

father's education was about twice that of father's occupation before the revolution and in the course of revolution father's education retained, or if anything increased, its importance.[21] But the effect of father's occupation, an effect that we are inclined to attribute largely to money and property, seems to have declined by about a quarter in the midst of revolution, leaving father's human capital over three times as important an influence on son's human capital (the decline, however, was not statistically significant). In the long run, father's occupation appears to have once again recovered its former importance (the increase was significant at $p < .05$), leaving the influence of family background on education much as it was before the revolution.

In sum, the Bolivian revolution appears to have had little effect on the educational advantages that high status families were able to provide for their children. These advantages were mainly a consequence of the parents' human capital and revolution left them unchanged, if not actually higher than before. The remaining advantages, ones that we attribute to income and property, may have declined somewhat in the midst of revolution, but not much, and not for long. In the end, the educational advantages of birth were as large, if not larger, than before the revolution.

HUMAN CAPITAL AND STATUS INHERITANCE

We have seen that even in the midst of revolution, educated parents were able to get much more schooling for their children than poorly educated parents were able to get for theirs. But were they able to get them better jobs as well, or was the advantage confined only to education? It certainly was not so limited before the revolution; on the contrary, families with human capital were able to get substantially better positions for their children. In terms of our usual comparison of a son born into an elite family (whose father, an elite white-collar worker, had 11.6 years of education) and one born into a family at the very bottom of the hierarchy (whose father was a llama herder with 1.2 years of education), the elite son would on the average have obtained a first job 14 status points higher than the poor family's son solely because of his father's greater education.[22] But in the period immediately following the revolution, father's education seems to have become somewhat more important, the advantage increasing 35 percent (A in fig. 7.6). This is in striking contrast to revolution's effects on property, where it led to a decrease of about the same amount. Although this 35 percent increase is appreciable in substantive terms, it is not statistically significant with our sample size ($p = .11$). We can fairly safely say that the revolution did not lead to any decrease in the advantages that families with human capital were able to confer on their children but that, if it made any difference at all, it increased the advantage.[23]

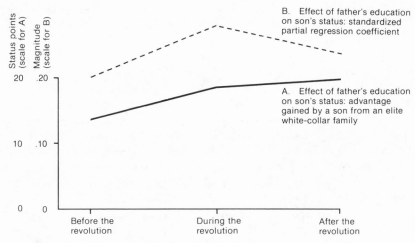

Figure 7.6: Effect of father's human capital on the status of his son's first job before, during, and after the revolution. Advantage enjoyed by a son from an elite white-collar family owing to his father's education (A) and standardized partial regression coefficient of father's education (B). Men, 24 years or older, coming of age before, during, or after the revolution. Estimates from Model 3; see Appendix 6, section 2, for details and table 6.6A for exact figures. *Source*: Head of household survey.

We argued that human capital would, in the longer run, remain valuable in the postrevolutionary economy, as indeed it would in any economy. And in fact it seems to have remained as important as it was in the revolutionary period. A son born into an elite family could on the average have expected a first job 19 status points higher than a son born into an impoverished peasant family. That was essentially the same as the advantage such a son would have had during the revolution and if anything higher than he would have had before the revolution.

In short, even a decade and a half after the revolution, it was still a substantial advantage to be born into a well-educated home. The revolution was not able to eliminate or even reduce the inequality that springs from cultural and linguistic advantages of elite homes. On the contrary, that advantage remained both in the short run and in the long run and was, if anything, slightly larger than in prerevolutionary times. Human capital seems to be immune to revolution.

THE RELATIVE IMPORTANCE OF PROPERTY AND HUMAN CAPITAL

At this point it is useful to bring together our results for property and human capital and look at the importance of one relative to the other. A major theme of our argument has been that property is, in the short run, vulnerable to disruption and redistribution by revolution, but that human capital is not. Thus the short-run effect is to temporarily shift the basis of stratification away from the domination by property toward a system more heavily influenced by human capital (Hypothesis 3).

We have seen the changes separately for property and human capital but have not yet explicitly compared the two. In doing so at this point, a comparison of metric coefficients would be useless since they are in different units, but we can usefully compare the standardized partial regression coefficients of education (our measure of human capital) and of father's occupational status (which we interpret as reflecting property). We can also compare the advantages conferred by father's education and occupation on sons born to, respectively, elite white-collar and poor peasant homes. Both comparisons, given in figure 7.7, show the same pattern. Before the revolution, property was substantially more important than human capital, in fact roughly twice as important (compare A and B or C and D). The revolution greatly reduced the advantages conferred by property, leaving it no more important than human capital during the revolutionary period, as we predicted. But that lasted less than a decade. In the longer run property grew once more in importance, equaling or exceeding its influence in prerevolutionary times, while human capital did not change appreciably. The result was to shift the basis of the stratification system once again in the direction of property.

THE RETURNS TO EDUCATION

In this section we digress briefly from our focus on the way advantages are passed from one generation to the next to look at the occupational advantages a son gets from his *own* human capital, that is, what he gains in occupational status because of his education. One of the major themes of our argument is that this advantage remains, or even grows, in the midst of revolution and in its aftermath as well. We now bring some evidence to bear on these arguments.

Short-Run Effects.   In prerevolutionary Bolivia, as elsewhere in the world, well-educated men tended to get much better jobs (see fig. 7.8). For example, a man who completed six years of primary school could expect a job 14 status points higher than a man without schooling, other things being equal. During the revolution education became even more valuable, with each year of education worth, on the average, about 15 percent more than before. It is thus quite clear that the revolution did not overturn the stratification order in the sense of letting the illiterate compete on anything like equal terms with the educated. Rather, those with human capital continued to have a large and statistically very significant advantage ($p < .001$). This is exactly as we predicted (Hypothesis 1).

While it is evident that having human capital remained advanta-

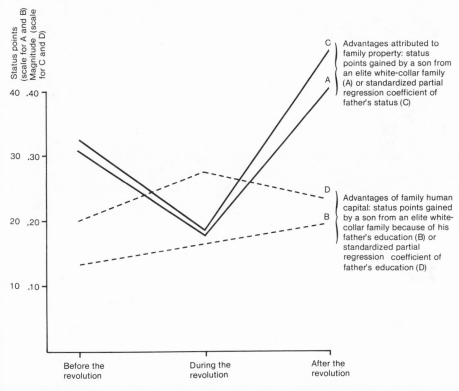

Figure 7.7   Relative importance of family property and human capital in determining the status of son's first job before, during, and after the revolution. Advantage enjoyed by a son from an elite white-collar family because of his father's occupation (an advantage attributed to family property for reasons, and with qualifications, noted in text) and standardized partial regression coefficient of father's occupation. Advantage enjoyed by a son from an elite white-collar family because of his father's education and standardized partial regression of father's education. Men, 24 years or older, who came of age before, during, or after the revolution. See Appendix 6, section 2, for details and table 6.6A for exact figures. *Source*: Head of household survey.

geous after the revolution, it is less evident that the advantage increased as we argued it might. There was an increase, to be sure, but it was modest in magnitude and not statistically significant with a sample of this size ($p > .10$).

Long-Run Effects. In the long run, education clearly remained a valuable source of occupational status (fig. 7.8). A man who completed primary school, for example, could expect a large and statistically significant advantage of some 10 status points after the revolution ($p < .01$). This advantage was, however, somewhat smaller than it was during the revolution and may even be fractionally smaller than before

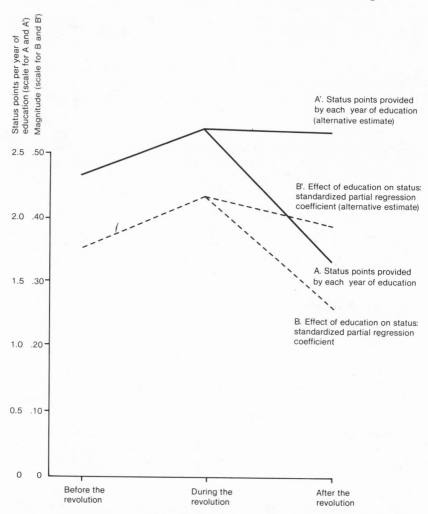

Figure 7.8   Effect of son's education on the status of his first job before, during, and after the revolution. Metric (A) and standardized (B) partial regression coefficients of son's education for men, 24 years or older, coming of age before, during, or after the revolution, with alternative (and probably better) estimates for the postrevolutionary period as described in the text (A' and B'). Estimates based on Model 3B; see Appendix 6, section 2, for details and table 6.6A for exact figures. *Source*: Head of household survey.

the revolution. But given the sample sizes, the decline is not statistically significant, so it may be best to assume that there was no change.

There is a further consideration in that a plausible alternative estimate suggests that education's effects were just as large after the revolution as during or before it. We suspect that in the postrevolutionary period some men reported minor and transient jobs they took when school was out of session, or between periods of schooling, or in the army and the like, and that these jobs do not reflect the full advantages they eventually obtained from their education.[24] Older cohorts are presumably less likely to report such minor experiences in the remote past. But since the postrevolutionary period in our data is only six years long, we can obtain an alternative estimate of the effects of education by replacing first job by current occupation. Since the oldest of these men are only 30, their current job is still one very early in their occupational careers. Making this change gives results shown as A' and B' in fig. 7.8. These results suggest that there was little or no decline in the advantages conferred by education in the postrevolutionary period.[25] A primary education was worth about 16 status points both during and after the revolution, in both cases slightly more than the 14 status points it was worth before the revolution.

Thus education remained valuable long after the revolution, its influence remaining both large in absolute terms and statistically significant. This is quite consistent with our theoretical predictions, which stressed the continuing value of human capital. But it is by no means clear that it became more important in the midst of revolution, as we argued it might. Education seems to have retained, but not increased, its value.

Alternative Measures of Education

For these analyses we have scored education in years, a simple, conventional, and effective procedure. There are various more complex scoring procedures that could be used instead but in fact they seem only to complicate the exposition while leading to exactly the same substantive conclusions. We experimented with a number of them, including dummy variables to capture nonlinearities (for example, separate dummy variables for no schooling, elementary schooling, secondary schooling, and advanced education); the inclusion of quadratic as well as linear terms, to capture curvilinear effects; various interaction terms involving social race, including interactions between social race and the dummy variables; and, finally, extensive tabular analyses making no assumptions at all about functional form. In general the simple, linear form turned out to be an excellent approximation, the alternative forms explaining little additional variance and adding little of substantive interest. There were some noticeable interactions with social race but they are not particularly relevant to the issues at hand and, in any case, are largely taken into account when we analyze Spanish and Indians separately later in the chapter. In short, we are confident that the results presented in the text, based on the simple years of schooling measure, quite satisfactorily capture the role of education in Bolivia.

ADVANTAGES OF BIRTH AMONG THE SPANISH AND THE INDIANS

As has been stressed in previous chapters, there was a major cleavage in prerevolutionary society between Spanish and Indians, or what is the same thing, between those who grew up in homes speaking the national language and those from Amerindian-speaking homes. The revolution of 1952, at least in rural Bolivia, was primarily of benefit to the Indians; it was in large part a revolution of landless Indians against Spanish landowners. The bulk of the Spanish-speaking population, neither masters nor serfs, nonetheless suffered substantial economic loss from the revolution and from its aftermath (chaps. 5 and 6). Since they are socially and economically distinctive and bore the brunt of the revolution, it is useful to see how the revolution affected them. According to our theory, they should show the same pattern as we predicted for the society as a whole, if anything more clearly, since the redistribution and economic disruption fell most heavily upon them (as they had the most property to lose), while the new opportunities opened up in postrevolutionary society were especially accessible to them because of their greater human capital. After seeing how revolution affected the Spanish, we will see how it affected the Indians, the remainder of the population.

Revolution Among the Spanish

Short-Term Effects. Among the Spanish-speaking population the revolution first led to a decline in status inheritance, just as it had for the Bolivian population as a whole. There are several ways to measure the change but all give the same picture (see fig. 7.9). Perhaps the simplest summary is to note that the advantage of being born to a well-educated, elite white-collar father declined by about a quarter during the revolution, from 41 status points to 31.[26] But that still left a large and statistically significant advantage (p < .001).

Let us try to distinguish revolution's effects on property from its effects on human capital. For reasons set out earlier, we can plausibly attribute the effects of father's occupation (in models where human capital is explicitly taken into account) mainly to his property. These are the effects which are, we argued, vulnerable to revolution. And in fact they declined precipitously during the revolution, by some 60 percent, leaving an elite white-collar son with an advantage of only 10 status points.[27] Indeed that advantage is not even significantly different from zero, at least with a sample of our size (p > .10).[28] These effects can, as we have seen earlier, be further divided into two parts, the direct effect that a father's property has on his son's status and the indirect effect that it has through the son's education, and these two are

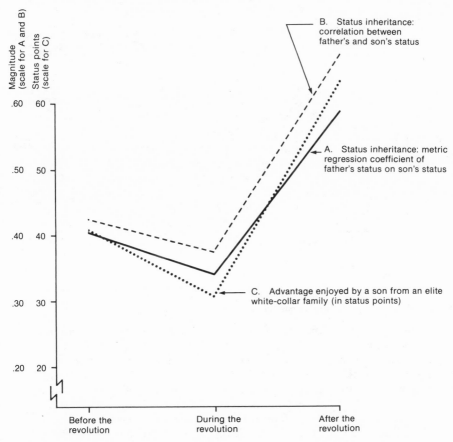

Figure 7.9 Revolution's effect on status inheritance among Spanish-speaking Bolivians. Correlation between father's occupational status and the status of his son's first job and the metric regression coefficient of father's occupation (estimated from Model 1); advantage enjoyed by a son from an elite white-collar family compared to a poor peasant's son (estimated from Model 2). Men, 24 years or older, coming of age before (N=245), during (N=94), or after (N=63) the revolution. See Appendix 6, section 2, for details and table 6.6A for exact figures. *Source*: Head of household survey.

shown in figure 7.10.[29] They tell a very interesting story. The direct advantage of being born into an elite white-collar home—advantages which presumably reflect the inheritance or purchase of businesses and farms and other such direct advantages of having a wealthy family—were large before the revolution, amounting to some 18 status points (A in fig. 7.10). But the revolution destroyed them entirely, leaving a *disadvantage* of 6 points, a significant decline even with the small sample size (p < .06). It seems highly unlikely that wealth per se would ever be a disadvantage, but it is quite possible that political

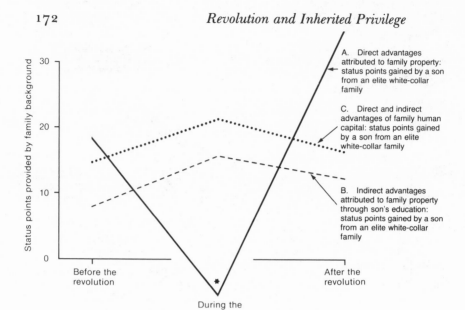

Status points provided by family background

A. Direct advantages attributed to family property: status points gained by a son from an elite white-collar family

C. Direct and indirect advantages of family human capital: status points gained by a son from an elite white-collar family

B. Indirect advantages attributed to family property through son's education: status points gained by a son from an elite white-collar family

Before the revolution

During the revolution

After the revolution

(✽ Direct effect not significantly different from zero at $p < .05$)

Figure 7.10   Effects attributed to family property and human capital among Spanish-speaking Bolivians. Direct effects of father's occupation are those having nothing to do with his, or his son's, education and indirect effects are those that come about because father's occupation influences his son's education which in turn affects the status of his son's first job; these effects are attributed to family property for the reasons (and with the qualifications) noted in the text. The effects of father's education are attributed to family human capital. Men, 24 years or older, coming of age before, during, or after the revolution. See Appendix 6, section 2, for details and table 6.6A for exact figures. *Source*: Head of household survey.

considerations would make it one. If new revolutionary rulers distrusted the offspring of the old wealthy elite, they might well discriminate against them. This seems to have happened in Russia in the years immediately following the revolution and in China for some decades afterward. With a sample of this modest size, however, the disadvantage is not significantly different from zero and so it is probably safer to conclude that in Bolivia the revolution entirely destroyed the direct advantage of having a wealthy family, but not that there was any clear penalty attached to it. The indirect advantages, reflecting the influence of a family's property on education and through that indirectly on occupational status, show no such dramatic decline but if anything increase during the revolution, growing from 8 to 16 status points (B in fig. 7.10). This change came about not because property influenced education more during the revolution but because the little education it did provide became a greater advantage.

Human capital was also quite important before the revolution and remained equally important afterward. Our elite son (whose father we assume had just over eleven years of education) could reasonably have expected, on the basis of his father's education alone, to get a first job 15 status points higher than our poor peasant's son (whose father had only one year of education) (C in fig. 7.10). The revolution raised that advantage over 40 percent, a very substantial increase. Thus among Spanish-speaking Bolivians, it seems that the revolution *reduced* the advantages to the son of property in the family by about 60 percent but at the same time *increased* the advantages of human capital by about 40 percent.

Long-Term Effects. We have seen that in the short run the revolution virtually eliminated the advantages of wealth and now ask whether this situation lasted or whether wealth once again became important (as we predicted it would). As it turned out, the advantage, no matter how measured, grew dramatically, far exceeding its prerevolutionary levels (fig. 7.9). The advantage enjoyed by the son of an elite white-collar family, for example, more than doubled, from 31 status points to 64 (C in the figure).

The advantages conferred by property grew strikingly, an elite white-collar son's advantage growing almost five times as large after the revolution as during it. In fact the direct effects of property, representing the most direct forms of inheritance, changed even more strikingly. An elite white-collar son stood to *lose* six status points from the direct effects of his father's wealth in the revolutionary period but to gain 36 status points afterward, a change of no less than 40 status points (A in fig. 7.10; the change is significant at p < .08). In contrast, human capital shows a very different pattern. The effects of father's human capital may have declined to roughly their prerevolutionary level once again (C in fig. 7.10), or on an alternative estimate, remained at roughly the level they reached in the revolutionary period.[30] The indirect effects of father's property that come about through his son's education, which were always small, stay about the same or decline slightly (B in fig. 7.8).

In all, we have seen that revolution's effects on Spanish Bolivians are essentially the same as for the society as a whole but if anything more dramatic. The pattern of changes is exactly as we predicted and thus clearly supports our theory.

STATUS INHERITANCE AMONG INDIANS

The same pattern observed for the Spanish speakers seems to hold, although with somewhat different emphasis, for those born into Aymara-speaking families, the group which gained most as a result of the revolution.[31]

Short-Term Effects. The now familiar decline in status inheritance from prerevolutionary days shows up quite clearly once again (fig. 7.11). The decline was about a third, from 45 status points for an elite white-collar worker's son (not that there were many among Indians) to 28 (a decline significant at p < .01). But that still left the elite with a substantial and statistically significant advantage (p < .001).

We can once again try to separate revolution's effects on property from its effects on human capital but must do so a little differently than before. The difficulty is that very few Indian fathers had any schooling at all, with an average of only a third of a year. This paucity of data, together with the modest sample size in later time periods,[32] makes estimates of the effects of father's education very unreliable. We have

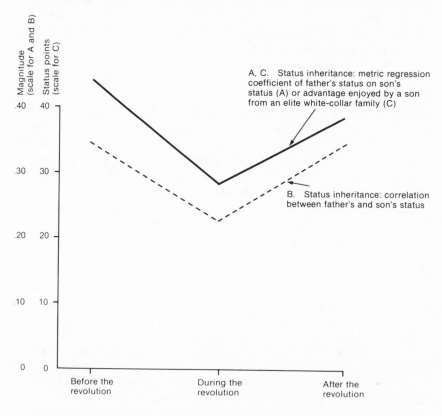

Figure 7.11   Revolution's effects on status inheritance among Indians. Correlation between father's occupational status and the status of his son's first job, metric regression coefficient of father's occupation, and the advantage enjoyed by a son from an elite white-collar family (estimated from Model 1). Men, 24 years or older, coming of age before (N=368), during (N=169), or after (N=103) the revolution. See Appendix 6, section 2, for details and table 6.6A for exact figures. *Source*: Head of household survey.

therefore eliminated it from the analysis. Subject to this qualification and the usual reservations about attributing the direct effects of father's status to his property, the estimates are shown in figure 7.12. The direct effects of family property—those that presumably come from the inheritance of the family farm or business and the like— declined by about a quarter during the revolution, from 30 status points to 22 (a decline significant at p < .06). This is the same pattern we have seen before, and the predicted one, although smaller than for the Spanish population. That it is smaller may reflect different experiences in the revolution since among Indians more than Spanish, those who lost property in the inflation and the economic disorders of the revolution were offset by others who gained in the land reform. The indirect advantages of wealth, those that come about because more prosperous families are more successful in educating their children and so indirectly improving their chances in the job market, were always negligible among Indians and remained so after the revolution (B in fig. 7.12). For Indians property was always the crucial

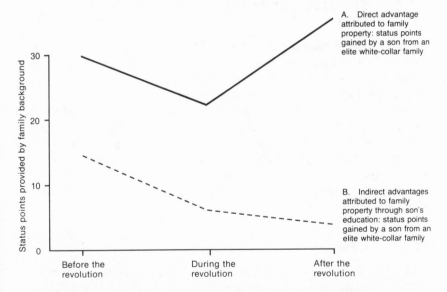

Figure 7.12 Effects attributed to family property among Indians. Direct effects of father's occupation are those having nothing to do with his son's education and indirect effects are those that come about because father's occupation influences his son's education, which in turn affects the status of his son's first job; these effects are attributed to family property for the reasons (and with the qualifications) noted in the text. No estimate of the effects of family human capital are possible for reasons noted in the text. Men, 24 years or older, coming of age before, during, or after the revolution. See Appendix 6, section 2, for details and table 6.6A for exact figures. *Source*: Head of household survey.

question, especially landed property (which they did not, of course, lose in the revolution). Indian families did not have enough education to make much difference to their children (indeed, not enough for us to analyze).

Long-Term Effects.   In the long run, the advantage that high status fathers were able to pass on to their children increased among Indians, as among other groups (fig. 7–11). The increase was over a third, a substantial figure although the advantage remained smaller than in prerevolutionary times. The family's property was, once again, the reason: the advantage of having an elite father grew from 22 to 35 status points, an increase of about 60 percent which left the advantage larger than in prerevolutionary times (A in fig. 7.12).

In short, the revolution seems to have affected the Indian population in much the same way as it did the Spanish population and the rural population as a whole. And its effects were precisely those we predicted.

INHERITED PRIVILEGE AFTER POLAND'S COMMUNIST REVOLUTION

Up to now we have applied our model only to the Bolivian experience, and by and large the model fits. But Bolivia was in many ways an incomplete revolution in which, after redistributing land and nationalizing large industry, small-scale capitalism and private wealth were allowed to reemerge.[33] We do not know how our model would work under a regime that nationalized even small merchants, artisans, and traders and prevented even small capitalists from reemerging after the revolution. Testing our theory on such a revolution would be most informative and, fortunately, there are data for one such regime, Poland, a communist regime following World War II. We will therefore consider them briefly.

DATA AND SETTING

The Polish revolutionary experience was quite obviously different from the Bolivian process in numerous ways. To begin with, Poland is a much richer, more advanced, and more industrialized society. Its revolution, moreover, was imposed from the outside and most crucially of all, it was a communist revolution. This was a revolution directed by a powerful bureaucracy, which was totally and successfully committed to the social control of wealth and the forcible redistribution of property with a long-term policy of opposition to the accumulation of physical capital and its use as a source of social mobility.

The Polish data are from a survey by the government's Central Statistical Office conducted in 1968. It was a representative sample of

3,482 heads of families and single people running households who maintained themselves by work in the socialized, nonagricultural sector of the economy. The socialized sector at that time accounted for 95.4 percent of all persons employed outside agriculture. These data were analyzed in a valuable paper by Zagorski (1971) and we have based our analysis on his tables.[34]

The only data relevant to our purposes show the relation between father's occupation and respondent's first job separately for those who began working in four periods: before World War II, during the war, the beginning of the revolutionary communist period (1945–1955), and a postrevolutionary period (1956–1968). This allows us a reasonable estimate of status inheritance in traditional times, in a subsequent period when Poland was defeated in World War II, in the midst of a revolutionary communist transformation of society, and finally a period under a stable communist regime.

The occupational data distinguish only between manual, non-manual, and (for the fathers) farm.[35] Although crude, this well-known white-collar/blue-collar distinction should, on the experience of other countries, prove to be a reasonable if imperfect alternative to more rigorous coding. Both male and female respondents are included, but experience in other countries consistently suggests that patterns of status inheritance are essentially the same among men and women, so this is unlikely to make any substantial difference (see Treiman and Terrell 1975*b* and the references cited there).

REVOLUTION AND STATUS INHERITANCE

Prewar Poland was a very rigid society, with a correlation between father's and son's status of .63, a very substantial figure putting it among the most rigid societies in the world (see fig. 3.5). During World War II, Poland was dismembered, Russia conquering one half and Nazi Germany the other. World War II also brought tremendous destruction and loss of life. But these disasters did not greatly affect status inheritance (see fig. 7.13). For Poles coming of age during the war, the correlation between father's and son's occupational status was .58, less than 10 percent below the prewar figure. But then came the more thorough communist revolution, imposed by force and with rigor. That did indeed reduce status inheritance, but only to .43, a reduction of about a third in comparison with the prewar period. That is a substantial reduction, but by no means the elimination of inherited privilege. On the contrary, status inheritance remained large and statistically significant ($p < .001$). Indeed, in the decade following the communist revolution the amount of inherited privilege in Poland was no less than in the United States or in many other capitalist societies (see fig. 3.5).[36]

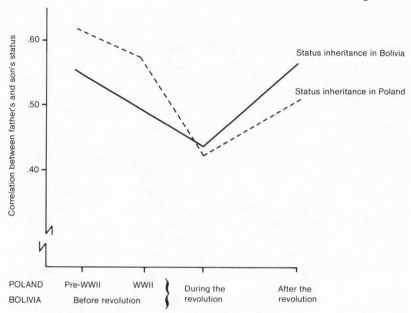

Figure 7.13   Revolution's effect on status inheritance in Poland. Correlation between father's occupational status and the status of his son's first job for male and female heads of household coming of age prior to 1939 (N=443), between 1940 and 1944 (N=229), 1945 to 1955 (N=1560), and 1956 to 1968 (N=1041). See the text for details. Corresponding figures for Bolivia from figure 7.1. *Source*: Calculated from Zagorski 1971:7.

So Poland's communist revolution did indeed reduce the privilege of birth. And the communist government stayed in power, with little effective opposition. Compared to Bolivia, they were much less vulnerable to the capitalist preferences of their peasants and small businessmen. Their ideology was strongly opposed to inherited privilege and it was something they worried about. They had confiscated virtually all capital save small peasants' farms and, unlike Bolivia, kept control of even small productive enterprises in a way that prevented the accumulation of new capital. They also adopted educational policies giving explicit preference to peasants' and workers' children. So with all that, were they able to gradually destroy inherited privilege? Or at least to prevent it from growing any larger? On this evidence, they were not able to do so (fig. 7.13). In the postrevolutionary period the correlation between father's and son's status in fact *increased* from .43 to .51, an increase of 19 percent. It seems that revolution leads to the rebirth of inequality even after a thorough communist revolution.

So the Polish data agree perfectly with our theoretical predictions. That two countries as diverse as communist Poland and rural Bolivia show the predicted pattern is strong evidence for our theory.

OTHER EVIDENCE ON COMMUNIST SOCIETIES

Other data on Poland also suggest that the communist revolution there had effects of the sort we have predicted. Inequality in income and in nonmonetary privileges (which come to much the same thing and are tax-free in the bargain) appears to be growing faster than the general standard of living and has, indeed, become a political issue of some consequence.[37] There is also some indirect evidence of increasing status inheritance (Tellenback 1978:438–439).

Nor does Poland appear to be exceptional. Evidence that inequality has endured in socialist and communist societies is widespread (for Eastern Europe see Dobson 1977; Lane 1971; Lipset and Dobson 1973; Matthews 1978; and Szelenyi 1978; for China, Chinn 1978 and Frolic 1978). And, while the relevant data are rarely published, there is some evidence that inequalities are growing with time (Anderson 1975; Volgyes 1978:512–514). Nor are the parallels confined to inequality. Recently published survey data on Hungary clearly suggest that status inheritance followed exactly the same pattern as in Poland—a decline when the communists came to power followed by an increase beginning a decade or two later (Andorka 1978:313–316; Simkus 1980:fig. 1). And human capital is deeply implicated in all this. That it is both valuable and inherently resistant to revolution is apparent in the "red versus expert" debates that surface with great regularity in communist societies, in China as well as Eastern Europe (Frolic 1978:410–413; Khrushchev 1970:18–21; Lipset and Dobson 1973). And it is clear that the main way in which high ranking families are able to pass their advantages on to their children is through education; their children simply do much better in school (Dobson 1977; Tellenback 1978). Thus, the pattern of changes evident in Bolivia and Poland is, we believe, a very general one.

CONCLUSION

SUMMARY

In this chapter we investigated revolution's effects on inherited privilege. Analyzing data from the head-of-household survey, we found that revolution appreciably reduced the advantage of being born into a high status family. This was true for rural Bolivia as a whole, for the Spanish and Indian populations separately, and for a very different revolution under very different circumstances, the communist revolution in Poland. The reason for this seems to have been that the revolution redistributed land, wealth, and other forms of property and virtually eliminated the advantages of being born into a wealthy home insofar as those advantages came through inheritance, from gift or loan of land or capital, or from entering the family business. Before the revolution these advantages were large but during the revolution they were very small for rural Bolivia as a whole. Indeed, for Spanish-speaking Bolivians, who bore the brunt of redistribution, they disappeared entirely.

But inherited privilege did not disappear in rural Bolivia, nor among the Spanish or Aymara, nor in Poland. On the contrary, even in the midst of revolution children born into elite families continued to have a substantial advantage in the competition for good jobs, an advantage perhaps four-fifths as large as they had enjoyed before the revolution. This seems to have come about because revolution could not reduce the crucial role played by human capital. It could not redistribute it. Nor could it eliminate the advantages of being born into a well-educated family but instead left these advantages at least as large as in prerevolutionary times and, if anything, larger. Education, language, and other skills were passed from parent to child as effectively in the midst of revolution as they were before, and conferred at least as great an occupational advantage on the child. Human capital seems to be immune to revolution.

In the longer run, revolution seems to have set loose forces which caused inherited privilege to grow once again. Within two decades it had grown substantially in rural Bolivia as a whole, and among the Spanish and Indians separately, and also in Poland. In some cases it even exceeded its prerevolutionary value and in others it remained a little lower, at least within the span of time covered by our data. The reason that inherited privilege grew so quickly after the revolution seems to have been that inequality in the distribution of income, land, and property grew apace, so that the advantages of being born into a prosperous home increased. In short, revolution leads to the rebirth of inequality and inherited privilege.

THEORETICAL IMPLICATIONS

We had predicted these results in advance (Kelley and Klein 1974, 1977) and so they strongly support our theory. We predicted that a radical revolution would in the short run reduce status inheritance, because it redistributes property, but not eliminate it, because it cannot redistribute human capital (Hypothesis 8). That is what happened. We predicted that in the short run a radical revolution causes a shift in the basis of stratification, making human capital more valuable relative to physical capital (Hypothesis 3), and that too it did. Finally, we predicted that in the long run radical revolutions create forces which cause status inheritance to begin to grow once again (Hypothesis 9). That too happened both in Bolivia and Poland. We argued that education would remain as valuable a source of occupational status during and after the revolution as it had been earlier, and that it clearly did. However, we went on to argue that it might in fact become *more* valuable during the confusion and disorganization of the revolutionary period, and possibly later, and the evidence on that is equivocal. During the revolution a father's education did become more valuable to his son and a son's education became more valuable for himself. But these gains, although in striking contrast to the dramatic drop in the value of property, were not large and not statistically significant. In the long run, changes in the effect of human capital were modest and none were statistically significant. So it seems reasonable to conclude that human capital is impervious to revolution, remaining as valuable in the midst of revolution as it was before, but not that it actually becomes more valuable than previously. But except for this, the weight of the data strongly supports our analysis. The fact that this complex pattern of changes appeared as predicted suggests that our theory is not entirely without merit as an explanation for revolution's effects on inequality and social mobility.

8
Conclusion

REVOLUTION: THE BOLIVIAN EXPERIENCE

Before the revolution Bolivia was one of the more rigidly stratified societies, with enormous differences between elite and mass in education, language, and skills; in income, wealth, and property; and in power, privilege, and prestige. This inequality was especially clear in the countryside where a small group of Spanish-speaking landlords held almost feudal sway over a large discontented mass of Indian peasants, extracting three or four days a week of free labor, requiring deference and respect, and monopolizing commerce in return for granting access to the land. The landlords controlled the government, the police, the courts, and the army and used them to ruthlessly suppress any unrest by force of arms. Given this great inequality, there was very little social mobility. Instead, a man's position in life was strongly shaped by the accident of birth, those born into prosperous and well-educated Spanish-speaking homes generally getting higher status jobs than the majority so unfortunate as to be born into poor, illiterate, Amerindian-speaking peasant homes. But in its great inequality and pervasive status inheritance, Bolivia was by no means unusual in comparison with other societies at its modest level of economic development. What was unusual was the dramatic way in which it changed.

In a few days in the April of 1952, armed groups of civilians, municipal police, and tin miners under the leadership of the MNR seized the capital, defeated and disbanded the national army, and established worker and civilian militias as the dominant military force in the nation. The crucial tin industry was nationalized and the government took control of most modern manufacturing, leaving it with two-thirds of the nation's capital and a dominant role in the national economy. But the most fundamental changes were in the countryside. Peasants were armed, their militias becoming the dominant military force in the countryside, and revolution swept away the old hacienda system. Work records were burned, landlords' homes sacked, and the landlords themselves driven into exile in the capital or abroad; the land reform was thorough and permanent. Not only was land redistributed but the disruption and inflation accompanying the revolution destroyed savings, devalued rents and pensions, and effectively redistributed urban property.

These changes reduced inequality in income and property, leaving the poor better off and the society as a whole less stratified in the aftermath of revolution. And by doing that the revolution almost eliminated the advantages that wealthy families had in the past been able to pass on to their children. No longer could a lucky few count on their fathers buying them an advantageous start in life. But in destroying the physical basis of wealth and status, the revolutionary regime of necessity left untouched an even more pervasive and important source of inequality: human capital. Education, skills, language, administrative abilities, and other attributes of human capital cannot be redistributed. And they remained valuable even in the midst of revolution. Because human capital remained, so did inherited privilege. The ability of well-educated families to pass their skills on to their children remained, and the advantage their children obtained from that was as large as before the revolution. Indeed, so crucial and enduring is human capital that the revolution was able to reduce inherited privilege by only a fifth.

After the initial destruction of property and the disorder and confusion of the few years immediately following the revolution, a new set of forces became evident in the countryside. With the landlords no longer around to extract the peasants' surplus and keep them all more or less equally poor, differences between one peasant and another began to emerge. Those with the most land, capital, or education, or the greatest skills or motivation, were able to get the full advantage and soon were noticeably better off than their peers. Furthermore, the revolution produced a variety of other changes which made both human capital and property more productive and hence more valuable. By freeing peasants from their weekly labor obligations, it enabled them to travel away from the land, to buy in cheaper urban markets, to trade, and to take secondary jobs during the slack season. With this newly found freedom, the abolition of the old elite's commercial monopolies, and the assistance of their powerful syndicate organizations, peasants took over the bulk of the marketing and transport. All of this meant higher prices for peasants when they sold farm produce and lower prices when they bought manufactured goods. The greatest benefit from these new opportunities again came to those with the land, education, linguistic skills, finances, contacts, and motivation to take advantage of them, and therefore increased inequality among both Indian peasants and among the other rural and small-town residents who, though better off than the Indians, were also effectively exploited by the elite before the revolution. In all it seems that inequality declined in the first few years following the revolution but then began to grow slowly and steadily in subsequent decades.

The rebirth of inequality led in turn to a clear increase in inherited privilege as families with income and property were once again able to buy their children an advantageous start in life. Indeed, the advantages of being born into a wealthy family more than tripled in the decades following the revolution, leaving status inheritance at least as great as it had been before the revolution and possibly greater. And this pattern of a short-run decline followed by a long-term reemergence of inherited privilege is not unique to Bolivia but also appeared under very different circumstances following Poland's communist revolution.

THEORETICAL IMPLICATIONS

These results strongly support our theory and not because it was conceived post hoc.[1] We argued that radical revolutions can be expected to redistribute income and physical capital, making for a more equal distribution of wealth and income in the short run. Hence a revolution will, we predicted, lead to a decline in status inheritance and, in fact, it did. But advantages are also, and perhaps predominantly, passed on through education and other forms of human capital and we argued that these were virtually immune to revolutionary disruption; hence we predicted that status inheritance would not by any means disappear after the revolution. Nor does it in actual fact. In the long run we predicted that inequality would reemerge because revolutionary liberation allows previously exploited groups to make fuller use of their human capital, physical capital, and other resources; that, we showed, can be expected to lead to greater inequality and more status inheritance. That prediction was clearly confirmed. In all, these results give substantial support for our theory and some warrant for believing that our predictions would be borne out in other revolutionary times and places.

We claim that any revolution that frees peasants from their traditional exploitation will in the short run improve their standard of living, reduce inequality in the society as a whole, and reduce inherited privilege. At this stage the peasants and the radical revolutionary intelligentsia will have the same goal, the overthrow of the traditional elite and the end of exploitation, but that will not last. Revolution inadvertently sets loose forces which, if unchecked, will in the long run allow inequality and inherited privilege to grow steadily and the result will be a rural stratification system of a familiar capitalist type with rich peasants playing the role of capitalist entrepreneur. Thwarting these forces is never easy and often impossible. Liberal policies, or even moderate socialist policies which allow a mixed economy, will hardly repress these deeply rooted forces. They involve the property of modest family farmers and the opportunities for small traders, small businessmen, government bureaucrats, and the holders of human capital to accumulate wealth and pass it on to their children. By giving in to these forces, accepting the new status quo, and abandoning any further redistribution in the countryside, a revolution can maintain the allegiance of the new elites, leaving a peaceful, prosperous, and highly stratified countryside. The Bolivian and Mexican revolutions, for example, seem to have taken this conservative course. The only viable alternative is a radical attempt to root out even the smallest vestiges of private property, as in China or Cuba. Among other things, this requires extensive economic planning, a large and effective bureaucracy with unusual commitment and incorruptibility, the power to overcome strong opposition in the countryside, and the willingness to bear the substantial human costs involved. In this, the experience of Poland and other eastern European communist societies is instructive. In spite of the virtual abolition of urban private property and the institution of a fully socialist economy, not to mention the political upheaval of the war years and the communist revolution, status inheritance never disappeared and, within a couple of decades of the revolution, began to increase once again in the midst of a still communist society. It seems to have taken longer to grow again in Poland than in Bolivia, perhaps twice as long, but inequality did reemerge and did so well within a generation.

The basic reason for this is that human capital is virtually immune to revolution. Confiscating land and machines is easy compared to controlling human capital and only China during a brief period in the 1960s has been willing to bear the costs of a determined assault on it and even that assault seems to have failed. It is not by choice that governments pay a premium to those with human capital but because skills are necessary for economic and administrative efficiency and it is far cheaper to pay for them than to do without; human capital is well rewarded not just in capitalist societies but in socialist systems and in virtually every moderately complex economy, ancient as well as modern.[2] Revolutionary governments are as little able to undermine human capital as any other governments. And whenever differences in education, skills, language, or other kinds of human capital remain, they will eventually lead to inequality and to inherited advantage, revolution to the contrary notwithstanding.

REFORMULATION OF THE THEORY

On the whole, the Bolivian and Polish data strongly support our theory, increasing our confidence in the basic argument. But there are nonetheless two reasons to offer a modest reformulation. The first is largely stylistic: in its present form we have not clearly specified which of the many changes introduced by a radical revolution lead to which consequences. We went into this in some detail in the theory chapter, using our computer simulation to provide some leverage on the question, and are inclined now to incorporate those conclusions in the formal statement of our hypotheses. The second reason for change is that the Bolivian experience did not strongly support our claims about human capital becoming *more* important in the aftermath of revolution, although neither did it refute them; the changes were largely in the predicted directions, but they were small and few were statistically significant. Although we are still inclined to believe our original arguments on this, the fact remains that the evidence for the rest of the theory is very much stronger and prudence suggests a tactical withdrawal (if not a hasty retreat) on the one question. Both the underlying logic of our analysis and the evidence are clearly consistent with a simpler and less extreme claim than our original: that revolution leaves the value of human capital *unchanged*. It does not decrease it, and for that we have clear evidence from Bolivia and elsewhere in the world, but may not increase it either. This is not, in fact, very much of a modification of the original argument. Indeed, in the computer simulation of chapter 1 we made no use of our original assumption that human capital became more valuable; all our conclusions follow on the assumption that we now adopt, the assumption that its value remains unchanged by revolution.

We will recast our theory by separating the effects of revolution into four parts: those that follow from redistribution and the end of the traditional exploitation of the old elite; those that follow from revolution's inability to redistribute or devalue human capital; those that follow from the destruction and disorganization of the revolutionary period; and, finally, those that follow from the new opportunities and economic growth that come in revolution's train. In this reformulation we follow our original logic closely and reorganize the presentation in a way that closely parallels our detailed discussion of the computer simulation of the theory in chapter 1; we will therefore cover the ground with the brevity that befits a recapitulation and leave the fuller discussion to chapter 1.

A: REDISTRIBUTION AND THE END OF EXPLOITATION

The most fundamental characteristic of a radical revolution is that it redistributes income, land, and physical capital, taking from the old elite and giving to the poor. That is what revolution is all about. It leaves those who were exploited by the old regime better off than they were before, reduces inequality between rich and poor, and reduces inherited privilege in the society as a whole.

But redistribution in and of itself, quite apart from any of the other consequences of revolution, creates inequality among the previously exploited according to our theory. There are always differences among them in education, knowledge, and skills; in land and physical capital; in strength, motivation, diligence, and luck; and in the myriad other things that lead to differences in income between one person and another. But before the revolution these differences in endowments led to only modest differences in income because the old elite was able to arrogate most of the returns for its own use. A peasant with land and skills, for example, was enriching his landlord as much, or more, than he was enriching himself. And the exactions of the old elite fell most heavily not on the poorest peasants at the margins of subsistence—for they had nothing to give—but their more fortunate brethren. By ending that exploitation, revolution allows the more fortunate among the peasants and other subordinate groups to reap the full advantage of their fortune, to accumulate for themselves and for their children. The result is growing inequality among them, and growing inherited privilege among their children. So redistribution has two faces, two equally fundamental sides of the same coin: equality and social mobility on the one side and, on the other, inequality and inherited privilege. In short, we argue that:

Hypothesis A. A radical revolution redistributes income and property.

Hypothesis A1. Redistribution benefits those who were previously exploited, increasingly so as they come to utilize more fully their human capital, land, physical capital, and other resources.

Hypothesis A2. By allowing them full benefit from their human capital, land, physical capital, and other resources, redistribution causes economic inequality among previously exploited groups to grow.

Hypothesis A3. Redistribution causes inherited privilege to grow among the previously exploited because it increases economic inequality among them and so increases the advantages transmitted from one generation to the next through property.

Hypothesis A4. In the society as a *whole*, redistribution causes economic inequality to decline.

Hypothesis A5. Redistribution causes inherited privilege in the society as a *whole* to decline, because it causes economic inequality, and hence the advantages transmitted through property, to decline.

See chapter 1, especially figures 1.1, 1.2, and 1.6, for details.

B: Human Capital

Revolutions change society by redistribution, taking from the rich and giving to the poor. They can fairly easily take land from landlords and factories from capitalists; revolutions also can, albeit with much more difficulty, take the modest property of small peasants, independent craftsmen, and small merchants. But they cannot take human capital from its owners; it can be destroyed, to be sure, but not expropriated. Nor can revolutionary societies do without human capital. To run even a simple society requires an educated elite. Business and government require various record-keeping and administrative skills; hospitals require doctors and nurses; armies require quartermasters and artillerymen; factories, whether they make iron breastplates or automobiles, require skilled workers; even small traders and commercial farmers benefit greatly from elementary record-keeping and simple accounting. And to run a complex society requires a truly vast range of skills, from computer programmers to electrical engineers, theoretical physicists, and aircraft mechanics. And because human capital is so useful in so many ways, those who have it can use their strong bargaining position to extract higher incomes and other rewards. Only a handful of societies have even attempted to eliminate these privileges and none with success; even after monumental efforts in China during the Cultural Revolution, the attempt failed. Nor can a society prevent these privileges from being passed on from one generation to the next. Throughout the world and throughout history, well-educated, highly skilled parents are more successful than the less educated and skilled in acquiring human capital for their children. In short:

Hypothesis B. A radical revolution cannot redistribute or devalue human capital.

Hypothesis B1. Because it cannot eliminate human capital, a radical revolution cannot eliminate economic inequality.

Hypothesis B2. Because it cannot redistribute or devalue human capital, a radical revolution cannot eliminate inherited privilege but instead leaves untouched the advantages transmitted from one generation to the next through human capital.

See chapter 1 for details (especially figs. 1.3, 1.5, and 1.6).

C: DESTRUCTION AND DISRUPTION

Radical revolutions are not quiet and peaceful affairs but rather are accompanied by much destruction and disruption. Some property is destroyed outright and in the midst of the changes, confusion, and uncertainty of the revolutionary period, marketing, finance, and production are disrupted. Savings, pensions, bonds, and other investments are devalued by inflation or repudiated outright. Much of the wealth and property accumulated over the past generation is lost and much current production sacrificed, and the losses fall most heavily on those who had saved the most in the past or could produce the most in the present. So both income and economic inequality decline, and less status is passed on through property since there is less property to pass on. These disruptions only last for a while, perhaps a decade. In short:

Hypothesis C. A radical revolution destroys accumulated wealth from the past and, in the short run, disrupts the economy.

Hypothesis C1. The destruction and disruption following a radical revolution lead to a short-run decline in income for the society as a whole.

Hypothesis C2. The destruction and disruption following a radical revolution in the short run reduce economic inequality in the society as a whole.

Hypothesis C3. The destruction and disruption following a radical revolution lead to a short-run decline in inherited privilege in the society as a whole because they reduce the advantages transmitted from one generation to the next through property.

Details are given in chapter 1 (especially figs. 1.2 and 1.3).

D: NEW OPPORTUNITIES

A radical revolution typically opens up new opportunities for the previously exploited.[3] The end of old elite's monopolies and the elimination of regulations and restrictions imposed by old vested interests create new opportunities in commercial agriculture, marketing, transport, and commerce. The destruction of serfdom, corvée labor and other obligations tying peasants to the land opens up new opportunities for them in other geographical areas and outside of agriculture altogether. Economic development, a goal of almost all radical revolutions (although not necessarily an achievement at all), has the same effect, opening up new opportunities in industry, government, and commercial agriculture. But these opportunities do not go to all equally but rather go mainly to those with the human capital, land, physical capital, motivation, or other resources to exploit them most effectively. The profitable new opportunities increase the incentive for the previously exploited to acquire human capital and property, and increase the opportunities for them to do so, and so lead to greater investments among them. So economic inequality grows—often very rapidly indeed—and inherited privilege grows with it. In all:

Hypothesis D. A radical revolution opens up new opportunities for the utilization of human capital, land, physical capital, and other resources.

Hypothesis D1. New opportunities increase the income of previously exploited groups.

Hypothesis D2. New opportunities increase investments in human capital and property among the previously exploited, since they increase incentives to have them and opportunities to acquire them.

Hypothesis D3. New opportunities increase economic inequality among the previously exploited, more so when the opportunities are larger.

Hypothesis D4. New opportunities increase inherited privilege among the previously exploited by increasing the advantages transmitted from one generation to the next through property, more so when the new opportunities are large.

E: THE LEVEL OF INEQUALITY AND INHERITED PRIVILEGE IN POSTREVOLUTIONARY SOCIETY

In the generation or two following a radical revolution, the level of inequality in the society as a whole will grow and eventually stabilize. Our argument clearly implies that it grows from its revolutionary low, and grows steadily for about a generation. But it is far from clear whether the amount of inequality, and hence of inherited privilege, will in the end remain above or below its prerevolutionary level. The difficulty is that inequality in the society as a whole depends crucially on the rate of economic growth following the revolution and on the nature of the postrevolutionary elite. If economic growth is rapid and if the new elite is itself exploitative, then inequality is likely to be higher than before (see chap. 1, especially figs. 1.6 and 1.7). Otherwise it is likely to be lower. But the nature of the new elite and the level of economic growth depend largely on factors outside the scope of our theory. Thus we have clear predictions about the short-term consequences but the long-term are more problematic:

Hypothesis E1. In the society as a *whole*, economic inequality following a radical revolution will first decrease, then begin to increase again, and eventually stabilize. The level at which it stabilizes will be higher if there is rapid economic growth or if the new postrevolutionary elite is relatively exploitative, lower if there is little economic growth or the new elite is not exploitative, and in all may, or may not, be higher than in prerevolutionary times.

Hypothesis E2. Inherited privilege in the society as a whole following a radical revolution will first decline, then begin to increase again, and finally stabilize at a level which may or may not be higher than in prerevolutionary times, depending on whether inequality is greater or less than before.

GENERALIZATION OF THE THEORY

Our predictions about the effects of redistribution and ending exploitation (Hypotheses A1 to A5) and those about the effects of new opportunities (Hypotheses D1 to D4) apply not only to radical revolutions but, we believe, to *any* social changes which reduce exploitation or increase economic opportunities. Such changes include the political changes which have reduced the exploitation of, or increased opportunities for, blacks or women in the United States, untouchables in India, aborigines in Australia, nationalists in former colonies throughout the world, and other previously exploited groups. They also include the economic "revolutions" which increase opportunities by liberating people from stifling restrictions or increase their productivity by technical means. Examples of these are the gradual changes which destroyed feudalism, the Green Revolution in agriculture, and the introduction of cash crops or a market economy in nonmarket societies. Insofar as these various changes increase opportunities for previously subordinate groups they should, according to our theory, have exactly the same effects as the increase in opportunities that follows a radical revolution; our predictions turn entirely on the new opportunities, not on features unique to radical revolutions. And insofar as these changes redistribute income or end exploitation, this should have the same effects as the redistribution following a radical revolution; those effects are consequences of the redistribution itself, not things peculiar to radical revolutions.

Specifically, with the decay of feudalism serfs were liberated from heavy taxes and stifling restrictions on their productivity very much like those Bolivian peasants labored under before the revolution. The effects should therefore be much the same, an increase in income but also an increase in inequality among them, and there is some evidence that they were (Kieniewicz 1969:181). In agriculture's Green Revolution, improvements in seed and farming techniques led to much higher yields and so increased peasants' incomes. But peasants who already had the skills and enterprise needed to adopt these new techniques, and the money to afford the fertilizer and pesticides required by them, stood to gain more than poor and unskilled peasants; as a consequence inequality among the peasantry seems to have increased (Havens and Flinn 1975). With the introduction of cash crops or a market economy in nonmarket societies—as has happened in many African societies well within this century as well as in more remote times and places—all seem to have benefited. But chiefs, lineage leaders, and anyone else who could use their position in traditional society to acquire education or fertile land benefited more and so inequality and inherited privilege increased (Kelley and Perlman 1971). Blacks and other minorities have gained economically in recent decades in the United States but we would predict that inequality and inherited privilege among them would therefore rise, and there is some evidence that they did (Featherman and Hauser 1976). In the many societies which have emerged from colonialism in recent decades, new opportunities appeared for those who supported the nationalist cause. But those among them with more education, property, or political power would, we predict, have reaped the largest benefits and in time inequality will therefore grow and an inherited status increase.

In short any changes that end exploitation, that redistribute from the rich to the poor, that liberate people from stifling restrictions, or that provide new opportunities through political reform or technical innovation, have a dual nature. They improve the lot of the poor and previously exploited, providing them with higher incomes and the chance to benefit fully from their education and skills, from their land and capital, and from all their abilities and resources. But that all means growing inequality among them. And as inequality grows, the more successful have ever larger advantages to pass on to their children, and so inherited privilege grows as well. Thus the revolution that brings redistribution and new opportunities in one hand inevitably brings inequality and inherited privilege in the other. Revolution leads to the rebirth of inequality.

Appendix 1

1.1 A FORMAL MODEL

In this appendix we develop the formal model underlying our theoretical argument. The first section develops a simple model for the effect of revolution on income and income inequality. The second section presents our model of inherited privilege. The third and final section presents some further results from the computer simulation of the model of income and income inequality described in chapter 1.

INCOME AND INCOME INEQUALITY

The Model. We first develop a model of radical revolution's effects on income and the accumulation of wealth, and hence on inequality. Hourly rates of pay for unskilled workers before the revolution, pay_u, are determined by various production and supply conditions, employers' monopoly powers, geographic restrictions (which, for example, prevent peasants from taking up trading and urban jobs or moving to high wage areas), and the like. We assume that wage rates also depend on human capital (H), property used in work (P), and on motivation, ability, luck, and the like (call them O) which can to a reasonable approximation be combined into a single aggregate resource $(H+P+O)$ with wages proportional to it.[1] The return to this combined resource reflects both the economic return and the costs imposed by restrictions on the type and location of work peasants are allowed to undertake, the property they are allowed to own, employers' monopoly powers, and the like. Wage rates for all workers are then (pay_u + pay_s $(H+P+O)$), all workers receiving pay_u and advantaged workers receiving a bonus proportional to their resources. For simplicity we assume that this is the same throughout the life cycle but other reasonable assumptions (e.g., Mincer 1974: chap. 1) would lead to the same qualitative conclusions. By reducing the costs imposed on pay_u and pay_s a revolution increases both components of workers' pay.

Earnings depend on the number of hours worked for pay. Yearly earnings, EARNED, will be hours worked for pay times the wage rate, less any per capita taxes (e.g., head taxes) or in all:

$$\text{EARNED} = \text{hours} \; (\text{pay}_u + \text{pay}_s \cdot (H+P+O)) - \text{head tax} \quad [\text{Eq. 1}]$$
$$= \text{hours} \cdot \text{pay}_u - \text{head tax}$$
$$+ \text{hours} \cdot \text{pay}_s \cdot (H+P+O)$$

The second line separates earnings into a part that is the same for everyone (unskilled wages minus head taxes) and a part that depends on the worker's human capital and other resources. Labor taxes (common in quasifeudal societies) simply subtract some hours from those worked for pay; taxes that are, taken all together, approximately a fixed proportion of income (e.g., some combination of progressive, flat rate, and regressive taxes) also in effect subtract working hours. Revolution in an exploited peasant countryside will reduce taxes, effectively increasing the number of hours worked for pay and hence increase earnings and the variance in earnings, i.e., increase inequality.

Wealth is accumulated savings from the past plus inherited wealth, both invested at interest. Assume that people save approximately a fixed percent (call it save) of both their wage income and the interest (call it int) they earn on accumulated capital. Then wealth in the nth year of someone's working life, WEALTH_n, depends simply on their accumulated wealth from the past, WEALTH_{n-1}, on savings from interest, $\text{save} \cdot \text{int} \cdot \text{WEALTH}_{n-1}$, and on savings from the year's wage earnings, $\text{save} \cdot \text{EARNED}$, giving:

$$\text{WEALTH}_n = \text{WEALTH}_{n-1} + \text{save} \cdot \text{int} \cdot \text{WEALTH}_{n-1} \quad [\text{Eq. 2}]$$
$$+ \text{save} \cdot \text{EARNED}$$
$$= (1 + \text{save} \cdot \text{int}) \; \text{WEALTH}_{n-1}$$
$$+ \text{save} \cdot \text{EARNED}$$

By induction, wealth at time n can be expressed as a function of inherited wealth, WEALTH_o, and the accumulated savings from each year in the past:

$$\text{WEALTH}_n = (1+\text{save} \cdot \text{int})^n \; \text{WEALTH}_o \quad [\text{Eq. 3}]$$
$$+ (1+\text{save} \cdot \text{int})^{n-1} \text{save} \cdot \text{EARNED}$$
$$+ (1+\text{save} \cdot \text{int})^{n-2} \text{save} \cdot \text{EARNED}$$
$$+ \ldots + \text{save} \cdot \text{EARNED}$$
$$= (1+\text{save} \cdot \text{int})^n \; \text{WEALTH}_o \; + \frac{(1+\text{save} \cdot \text{int})^{n-1}}{\text{int}}$$
$$(\text{hours} \cdot \text{pay}_u - \text{headtax})$$
$$+ \frac{(1+\text{save} \cdot \text{int})^{n-1}}{\text{int}} \; \text{hours} \cdot \text{pay}_s \cdot (H+P+O)$$

The second line is obtained by summing the geometric series and then substituting the earnings expression from Eq. 1 and simplifying.[2] It gives current wealth explicitly in terms of the accumulated advantages from inherited wealth (first term), plus the accumulated savings everyone will have from their labor (second term), plus the accumulated savings from the bonus paid to workers with human capital, property, and related resources (third term).

Total yearly income from all sources in the $(n+1)^{th}$ year, $INCOME_{n+1}$, depends on the same factors. It is simply the interest earned on the wealth accumulated in previous years plus the amount earned by working during the current year:

$$INCOME_{n+1} = int \cdot WEALTH_n + \ hours \cdot pay_u \qquad [Eq.\ 4]$$

$$- \ head\ tax \ + hours \cdot pay_s \cdot (H+P+O)$$

The first term is the return from accumulated wealth, the second is the income everyone earns by working, and the third term is the bonus earned by workers with human capital, property, or other resources.

Implications.   With these results in hand, we are in a position to lay out the argument underlying each of our hypotheses. Let us begin with Hypothesis 1 (which states that a radical revolution cannot redistribute human capital and hence cannot entirely overturn the old stratification order, but instead leaves those with human capital better off than those without it both in the short and in the long run) and Hypothesis 2 (in the short run a radical revolution produces a more equal distribution of income and property but cannot entirely eliminate income inequality). The claim, argued on substantive grounds, is that a radical revolution cannot eliminate human capital (H), and at least some of the other resources lumped together as O (e.g., differences in motivation or strength), and that workers with human capital or other resources will inevitably be paid for those resources. The implication is that inequality in income and eventually in wealth will persist after the revolution since part of that inequality is due to differences in human capital and other resources (as indicated in the third term of both Eqs. 3 and 4). Indeed, inequality among the previously exploited population that arises from these sources will actually increase after the revolution, since revolution reduces taxes and eliminates other restrictions on productivity, so increasing *pay_s* and hours, and hence increasing the returns on human capital and other resources (third term of Eqs. 3 and 4). Revolution, however, will reduce or even eliminate accumulated wealth (first term of Eqs. 3 and 4) and redistribute some property (which therefore reduces the variance of $H+P+O$ in the third term of both equations). Since peasants are poor and their exploiters rich (or at least richer than peasants), that clearly reduces the standard deviation of wealth in the society, i.e., they reduce inequality. The transfer of property from rich landlord to poor peasant, the abolition of free labor that peasants previously provided for landlords, and the loss to inflation of accumulated savings, pensions, and other assets held by the middle and upper classes reduce the income and wealth of advantaged groups or increase income and wealth of the previously disadvantaged, and so reduce inequality.

As a consequence of revolution's ability to redistribute wealth and property but not human capital, that is, as a consequence of Hypotheses 1 and 2, we have Hypothesis 3 (in the short run, a radical revolution causes a shift in the basis of stratification, making human capital more valuable relative to physical capital as a source of income and occupational status). Reducing the variance of P but not of H in Eq. 4 reduces the effect of one but not the other on income, leaving H relatively more important than in prerevolutionary times.

Hypothesis 4 (in both the short and the long run, those who were exploited under the old regime are better off after a radical revolution) comes about because revolution reduces taxes (head tax is smaller afterward or, for proportional taxes, peasants in effect have more hours to work on their own account); that increases the second and third components of both wealth and income. By destroying the old elite's monopolies, removing restrictions on geographic mobility, allowing peasants to take up a wider range of jobs, or the like it increases both pay_u and pay_s and that also increases the second and third components of both wealth and income. New opportunities and incentives for peasants to invest in human capital increase the third component. Revolution may allow peasants to use their physical capital more effectively, which increases the interest rate and therefore increases all three components of wealth and the first component of income. Anything that increases wealth of course increases the first component of income in subsequent years.

The claim that, by allowing them to more fully utilize their human capital, land, physical capital, and other resources, radical revolutions set loose forces which in the long run cause economic inequality among previously exploited groups to increase steadily (Hypothesis 5) comes about because a radical revolution has several effects which increase the first and third components of wealth (Eq. 3) and income (Eq. 4) and hence increase their standard deviations.[3] As we have seen, revolution is likely to increase the number of hours that peasants can work for their own benefit (by abolishing the landlord's rights to free labor) which increases inequality both because it increases peasants' total earnings (and hence the standard deviation of earnings) and because even larger benefits go to peasants with human capital or other advantages. With higher returns available on human capital, peasants have more reasons to invest, which increases income and inequality. And the variance in human capital is likely to increase as well (if only because education depends in part on ability and family background), and that further increases inequality of income and wealth. Greater inequality in one generation will also increase the inequality in inherited wealth and hence inequality in the future. Revolution may well increase the rate of savings, since peasants have more income from which to save and are free to enjoy the benefits of their savings, and that can markedly increase inequality in wealth since people with human capital or inherited wealth preserve more of their advantages; that subsequently leads to more inequality in income. Finally, if revolution in the long run leads to higher interest rates, perhaps by stimulating economic growth or opening up new investment opportunities, that will increase inequality in the same way that increased savings would.

Hypothesis 6 (in the long run, radical revolutions lead peasants and other previously exploited groups with little human capital to acquire more but also create a more unequal distribution of human capital among them) turns on two arguments. First, by increasing the returns on education (pay_s), reducing the taxes paid on these turns (i.e., increasing hours), and perhaps increasing profits from investing them, a radical revolution makes investment in human capital more attractive on purely economic grounds (Becker 1964; Mincer 1974). The second argument turns on the effect of this on inequality among the peasants or other exploited groups which previously had little human capital. If their levels are very low, say the 80 or 90 percent illiterate which is common enough among peasant groups, then increasing education will move some out of the ranks of illiteracy and increase the standard deviation, that is, increase inequality, with the result that some now have the pay and other advantages of education where none had such advantages before.[4]

Finally, Hypothesis 7 (in the society as a *whole*, inequality following a radical revolution will first decrease, then begin to increase again and eventually (a) stabilize at a level below its prerevolutionary value if the general population remains well off and there is little economic development among previously exploited groups but (b) continue to increase and perhaps in time exceed its prerevolutionary levels in poor societies in which there is substantial economic development among previously exploited groups) depends on a simple model. As a rough approximation, we can imagine there are four classes in the society as a whole—peasants and other members of the rural masses who have no appreciable human capital, peasants and others with human capital, the working- and middle-class population of the towns, and the urban elites—and that within each class everyone has the same wealth and income.[5] The average income (or wealth) in the society as a whole is simply the weighted average for all four classes, and income inequality is the standard deviation of income, which is a simple function of the squared deviation from the mean. Before the revolution, all peasants are poor, the elite is rich, and town population is somewhere in between. Revolution makes the elite poorer and peasants richer, bringing everyone closer to the mean and reducing inequality. Peasants with human capital then begin to improve their positions steadily, which further reduces inequality when they are still below the mean, has little effect when they are near the mean, and eventually increases inequality if they rise above the mean. Whether they get that far depends on how high the mean was to start with, how much richer they become, and what happens to the mean while all this is going on. If the mean is low at the beginning, if the revolution leads to steady economic development in the countryside (so that peasants with capital continue to grow richer), and if wealth among the town dwellers and urban elites does not grow, then many rich peasants will exceed the mean. Inequality in the society will increase and may eventually exceed its prerevolutionary value, particularly when town dwellers and the elite are a small part of the total population. Without steady economic development and with a large gap between peasants and the rest of the society inequality will remain low. In other situations there are conflicting tendencies, the outcome depending on which are stronger. More complex models with more classes and wealth distinctions within classes lead to the same qualitative conclusions.

That completes our analysis of revolution's effects on inequality. But inequality has profound implications for status inheritance and it is to those that we now turn.

1.2 REVOLUTION AND STATUS INHERITANCE

The Model.   We offer a model of status inheritance which is based on the assumption that status is passed from one generation to the next by the transfer of scarce and valuable resources.[6] We assume that those resources are, to a reasonable approximation, of two kinds only: human capital on the one hand and on the other money and property. In competing for jobs, workers with more of these resources have the advantage over those with less, so that a worker's occupational status is some monotonically increasing function of his or her human capital (H), property (P), and luck and other advantages (O_1), each appropriately weighted (by b_1, b_2, and b_3). We assume that the function is to a reasonable approximation additive:

$$[S = f\ b_1H + b_2P + b_3O_1] \qquad\qquad [Eq.5]$$

Since human capital, property, and other advantages always help, b_1, b_2, and b_3 are always greater than zero.

To determine how much status is passed on from one generation to the next, we need to know how much of a child's human capital, property, and other advantages come from his parents. Let us say that he gets a certain amount, b_4, of his father's property, a certain amount, b_5, of his father's human capital, and a certain amount of wealth from other sources, O_2, unrelated to his father's status. Designating father's property and human capital by lower case p and w, respectively, that gives:

$$p = b_4p + b_5h + O_2 \qquad \text{[Eq.6]}$$

Since having a wealthy or well-educated father is always an advantage, or at least no disadvantage, b_4 and b_5 are always greater than or equal to zero. A child's human capital depends similarly on his father's property and human capital and on other, unrelated things (O_3) :

$$H = b_6p + b_7h + O_3 \qquad \text{[Eq. 7]}$$

We assume there is always some educational advantage to having well-educated or prosperous parents, so b_6 and b_7 are greater than zero.

We can now derive an approximate expression for the correlation between the status of father and child. First we substitute the right-hand sides of Eqs. 6 and 7 into Eq. 5, getting an expression for the son's status in terms of his father's property and human capital. Collecting terms and (without loss of generality) combining those involving O_1, O_2, and O_3 into a single term, O, this gives:

$$S = f\ [(b_1b_6+b_2b_4)\,p + (b_1b_7+b_2b_5)\,h + O] \qquad \text{[Eq.8]}$$

In dealing with Eq. 8 we make use of the well-known fact that correlations are little affected by monotonic transformations, so that correlations with status will be approximately equal to the correlation with the weighted sum of w, h, and O. The only important difference is that the variance in status is fixed by the nature of the jobs available. Now to get the correlation between father's and son's status, r_{sS}, we multiply both sides of Eq. 8 by father's status, s, sum over the population and divide by N (where we have assumed, without loss of generality, that w, h, and O are measured as deviations from their means). That gives:

$$r_{sS} = (a/c)\,r_{sp}\,\sigma_p + (b/c)\,r_{sh}\,\sigma_h \qquad \text{[Eq. 9]}$$

where a is the coefficient of w from Eq. 8, b is the coefficient of h in the same equation, and c is a nasty expression involving the variances of w, h, and O.[7] Except for its appearance in c, O has dropped out since we assumed that these other factors were not correlated with father's status.[8] What is left is the correlation between father's and child's status expressed as the weighted sum of two terms. The weights are all positive by previous assumptions. The two correlations on the right-hand side of Eq. 9, that between father's status and his property (r_{sp}) and between his status and his human capital (r_{sh}), we also assume to be positive for the same reasons that we assumed property and human capital were valuable for the child in his quest for a high status occupation.

What is left is the part that is crucial for our purposes: the standard deviation of father's property (σ_p) and father's human capital (σ_h), that is, measures of inequality in the distribution of father's property and human capital. From Eq. 9 it is clear that status inheritance will be greater whenever either of these is greater, that is, that there will be more status inheritance whenever property or human capital are more unequally distributed among fathers.[9] This is the crucial link between inequality and social mobility: whatever increases inequality will also increase status inheritance and, conversely, whatever decreases inequality will decrease status inheritance.

All our predictions about status inheritance apply not only to the correlation between parents' and child's status, but also to the corresponding metric regression coefficients expressing the advantages of birth in metric terms. We have assumed that the jobs available are, in the short run and to a reasonable approximation, fixed by the nature of the economy and not by the characteristic of workers seeking jobs. The variance in occupational status is thus fixed so that the metric regression coefficient will be the same as the correlation (if the variance in parents' and child's occupational status is the same) or at least some fixed multiple of it (if the variance has changed).

Implications. A direct implication of this result is Hypothesis 9 (which states that by creating greater inequality in property and human capital, in the long run radical revolutions cause status inheritance among previously exploited groups to increase steadily and eventually exceed its prerevolutionary level). Revolution increases inequality for reasons we set out earlier (Hypotheses 5 and 6) and we have just shown in Eq. 9 why status inheritance follows along, paralleling the changes in inequality. The same argument applies to inequality and status inheritance in the society as a whole. We argued that inequality in the society as a whole is affected by revolution in a particular way (Hypothesis 7) and from Eq. 9 it follows that status inheritance is affected in the same way (Hypothesis 10).

Finally, it is worth looking in detail at Hypothesis 8 (because a radical revolution redistributes property but cannot redistribute human capital, in the short run it reduces the advantage of being born into a family with property but not the advantage of being born into a family with human capital, so reducing status inheritance but not eliminating it).

Revolution leads to a decrease but not disappearance of inequality of income and property (Hypothesis 2), leading also to a decrease but not a disappearance of status inheritance (Eq. 9). But we can say even more than that. By reducing σ_p in Eq. 9, revolution reduces the importance of property and, indeed, could even eliminate it since revolution can entirely redistribute property. This will not happen to human capital, however. Indeed, we have seen that there is good reason to believe that human capital will remain after a revolution and some reason to think that it will become more important an influence on occupational status (Hypothesis 3). That would increase b_1 in Eq. 5 and hence b in Eq. 9 and so give father's human capital a stronger effect on his child's status during the revolution. So we can actually specify Hypothesis 8 more precisely than we have before, in a way, moreover, that we will be able to explicitly test in chapter 7.

Hypothesis 8*a*. In the short run, revolution reduces or even eliminates the effect of father's income and property on his son's occupational status.

Hypothesis 8*b*. In the short run, revolution leaves unchanged or perhaps increases the effect of father's human capital on his son's occupational status.

Inequality and Status Inheritance in Socialist Society

Before leaving our formal model, there is one special case that is of sufficient importance to warrant special attention. We have been discussing the model as though postrevolutionary society would have both human capital and private ownership of physical capital. But the model in fact applies even to societies where physical capital is expropriated during the revolution and never allowed to reappear. In such societies the patterns we have just described will reappear but the effects of revolution will be longer lasting and the reemergence of inequality slower.

This is, however, a matter of sufficient importance to warrant consideration in some detail. Let us begin with inequality in wealth. If a socialist government is able to entirely eliminate inherited wealth, inequality in wealth will depend entirely on the wealth accumulated over a single lifetime and will be a simple function of the third term in Eq. 3:

$$\frac{(1 + \text{save} \cdot \text{int})^n - 1}{\text{int}} \text{hours} \cdot \text{pay}_s \cdot (H + P + O),$$

since the first term drops out and the second is the same for everyone. As long as workers with human capital are paid more than others there will be variance in wealth, that is, inequality, more so when savings are larger, interest rates higher, people work longer hours, or skills are more highly rewarded. These things being equal, inequality will be less than in capitalist societies only because the contribution of inherited wealth, the first term of Eq. 3, is less. How much difference this makes is an empirical question but the fragmentary evidence available from capitalist societies suggests that inherited wealth is of little consequence, so the difference may not be especially large.

Inequality of income is in part a function of the interest obtained from inherited wealth and so will be less in a socialist society (Eq. 4). But it also depends in the same way on wealth accumulated in the course of a single lifetime, which we just discussed, and on the returns to human capital, *hours·pay$_s$* (H+P+O). These will not be zero even in a socialist society and, other things being equal, will be smaller only if skill differentials are smaller. In fact, the rather fragmentary data available from capitalist societies suggests that income inequality arising from differences in wealth, especially differences in inherited wealth, is only a small part of the total. So inequality may not be that much smaller.

As for status inheritance, even if wealth cannot be handed on directly from one generation to the next, fathers with higher income or greater wealth are likely to be able to help their sons acquire human capital if only because they can more easily afford to forego the income the child would contribute to the household by quitting school and going to work. And in a society where children generally live at home until they marry or even longer, as in the USSR, this may be an important consideration. But even if a socialist society is able to undermine these and other indirect advantages of wealth, governments cannot effectively prevent human capital from being passed from one generation to the next except at ruinous cost, as is clear from the now extensive evidence from eastern Europe (Anderson 1975; Lipset and Dobson 1973). Even in the total absence of direct and indirect effects of wealth and income, status inheritance will be, from our Eq. 9:

$$r_{sS} = (b/c) \, r_{sh} \, \sigma_h,$$

and all of these terms are positive. Other things being equal, there will be less status inheritance following a socialist revolution than following a capitalist one, how much less depending on the size of the other term in Eq. 9. But the difference may not be enormous since cross-cultural studies of status inheritance strongly suggest that human capital is a crucial factor (see, for example, table 3.6).

A socialist revolution will thus be somewhat different than a capitalist one. Wealth will play a smaller role but human capital remains with the same consequences as in capitalist societies. In our model, some terms drop out of the crucial equations but others remain and are alone quite sufficient to establish our conclusions. Inequality will be somewhat less than after a capitalist revolution, but inequality there will be, and status inheritance; even socialist revolutions lead to the rebirth of inequality.

1.3 SOME FURTHER RESULTS FROM THE COMPUTER SIMULATION

A basic difficulty with the simulation model is that it is difficult to rigorously show that the conclusions follow from all reasonable settings of the initial parameters, not just those we present in the text. A great many more variants than those we used represent reasonable and plausible initial conditions, far too many to cover exhaustively. Here we present results from a large number of choices of initial conditions in an attempt to show that, at least for some futher alternatives, the basic conclusions follow.

In choosing which alternatives to present, we have taken two approaches. One is to present a variety of plausible types of societies. For example, we present a model where the elite is much smaller than in our baseline model and the peasantry poorer, thus creating an archetypical exploitative agrarian society. We also offer one more in keeping with the European experience, with a large elite and a prosperous but highly taxed peasantry. These and other ideal types are set out in table 1.1A.

A second approach is to set the basic parameters we previously used at two extreme values, one on the high side and the other one low. For example, we set the return to human capital and property at half what it was in the baseline model (that is, to 5 percent instead of 10 percent) as a low estimate and twice the baseline figure as a high estimate. These results are also presented in table 1.1A. In both of these approaches, the new models are in accord with our arguments in chapter 1 and with our formal hypotheses.

TABLE 1.1A

PREDICTED EFFECTS OF REVOLUTION ON INCOME INEQUALITY FOR VARIOUS
ALTERNATIVE VERSIONS OF THE MODEL. INEQUALITY IS MEASURED BY THE
STANDARD DEVIATION AND EXPRESSED AS A PROPORTION OF THE
PREREVOLUTIONARY LEVEL OF INEQUALITY FOR THE CORRESPONDING
GROUP. SIMULATION RESULTS FOR (A) THE BASELINE MODEL,
(B) OTHER IDEAL-TYPICAL SOCIETIES, AND
(C) VARIANTS OF THE BASELINE MODEL.

Model (all are identical to the baseline model except for the differences specified)	*Years after the revolution:*	*Inequality among previously exploited peasants*			*Inequality in the society as a whole*		
		5	15	45	5	15	45
A. *BASELINE*[1] A typical peasant society. The economy grows at the equivalent of 2½ percent per year for the generation following the revolution and the new elite is half as exploitative as the old		72	182	348	10	85	147
B: *OTHER IDEAL-TYPICAL SOCIETIES* 'Asian' agrarian society with a tiny elite and an enormous and very poor peasantry. Elite is 1 percent of the population and peasants 79 percent. Poor peasants are exactly at subsistence and big peasants have incomes only 25 percent above it		74	204	485	11	148	260
Large elite with a prosperous but highly taxed peasantry in the 'European' style. Elite is 8 percent of the population; big peasants 25 percent with incomes 4 times subsistence; small peasants 50 percent with incomes half again subsistence		62	177	320	14	78	136
A large, rich but relatively benign elite. Elite is 10 percent of the population with human capital giving an income 4 times the subsistence level; taxes are only 10 percent (one-fifth of the baseline model's level)		36	119	232	53	128	216
Exploitation of a small minority. Elite is 10 percent of the population; the							

TABLE 1.1A (continued)

Model (all are identical to the baseline model except for the differences specified)	Years after the revolution:	Inequality among previously exploited peasants			Inequality in the society as a whole		
		5	15	45	5	15	45
urban middle and working class is very large (70 percent) and the exploited peasantry small (20 percent)		72	181	344	10	80	143
C: VARIANTS ON THE BASELINE MODEL							
C1: Different income hierarchies[2]							
Elite has twice as much human and physical capital as in the baseline model		72	182	348	13	90	154
Elite has half as much human and physical capital		72	182	348	10	82	144
Proportional taxes are half again as large		145	308	584	8	84	144
Proportional taxes are half as large		48	141	270	17	90	159
Peasants have twice as much human and physical capital		72	181	325	9	80	139
Peasants have half as much human and physical capital		73	184	403	13	89	154
C2: Overall level and sources of income[2]							
Rich: cost of subsistence is half as much as in the baseline model		65	170	365	7	70	120
Poor: cost of subsistence is twice as much		79	196	363	14	100	176
Human capital is twice as much for all classes		80	184	387	13	84	144
Human capital is half as much for all classes		67	181	356	9	86	150
Physical capital is twice as much for all classes		66	180	329	9	77	133
Physical capital is half as much for all classes		81	186	379	13	95	165
C3: Class size and structure[2]							
Elite is half as large (hence has twice the tax income per capita)		72	182	348	8	82	141
Elite is twice the size (hence half the tax income)		72	182	348	15	90	157

TABLE 1.1A (continued)

Model (all are identical to the baseline model except for the differences specified)	Years after the revolution:	Inequality among previously exploited peasants			Inequality in the society as a whole		
		5	15	45	5	15	45
Agricultural classes only; no urban middle class		72	182	348	19	107	185
C4: Savings[2]							
Twice as much income is saved		39	133	584	6	62	218
Half as much income is saved		95	206	267	14	97	123

[1]Details are given in chapter 1. In this model, all classes earn a subsistence income from the unskilled component of their labor. In addition, the elite, urban middle and working classes, and big peasants get the equivalent of another subsistence income from their land and property while small peasants get a fifth of a subsistence income from theirs. The elite gets a further subsistence income from their human capital, the urban classes get two-fifths of one, big peasants one-fifth, and small peasants nothing from theirs. All these incomes are increased by half in the postrevolutionary period; this roughly corresponds to a 2½ percent annual rate of economic growth for the generation following the revolution. In prerevolutionary times the elite takes half the other classes' income above the subsistence level, in revolutionary times nothing, and in postrevolutionary times the new elite takes half as much as the old elite.

[2]All of these models are identical to the baseline model except for the changes shown. Differences between these and the corresponding baseline figures in Panel A are in effect estimates of the partial derivative and show the effect of the indicated change on income inequality, evaluated at the parameter settings of the baseline model.

Appendix 2

2.1 AN EXPOSITORY NOTE ON CORRELATION AND REGRESSION ANALYSIS

Let us begin with correlations and then go on to regression analysis. Readers unfamiliar with correlations may wish to know, to begin with, what is a large correlation and what is a small one. That is always a somewhat subjective question, on the lines of asking whether a glass is half full or half empty, but some useful guidance can be obtained from familiar benchmarks. One benchmark is the correlation between father and son for traits like height that are transmitted genetically. The theoretically expected value, as well as that empirically observed, is about .50. The correlation between father's and son's IQ, which presumably reflects substantial components of both environmental and genetic influence, is also, coincidentally, about .50.

Another way of getting some perspective on the matter is to consider the correlation corresponding to some simple tables. By way of illustration, let us think of the relation between father's and son's occupational status. To make matters simple, we will divide occupational status in the middle of the distribution, so that half the people are counted as high status and half low. (We lose a good deal of information by dividing into only two categories and would not do so in a proper analysis, but here it makes the illustrations much clearer.) Some hypothetical tables that might result are shown in table 2.1A. We can get, by simple inspection, some intuitive idea of the strength of the relation represented there. Tables A, B, and C are hypothetical examples of tables where the correlation between father's and son's status is high, .50, while tables D, E, and F are examples where the correlation is modest, only .20. In these simple examples, the correlation is exactly equal to the percentage difference (divided by 100). For example, in table A 60 percent minus 10 percent equals 50 percent, for a correlation of .50. Where the variables are not exactly split into equal halves the correlation will be a little lower than the percentage difference but the correspondence is still close.

These hypothetical tables can also illustrate partial regression coefficients, figures of which we make much use in subsequent analysis. Let

TABLE 2.1A

HYPOTHETICAL EXAMPLES ILLUSTRATING THE CORRESPONDENCE BETWEEN
TABLES AND VARIOUS REGRESSION STATISTICS. BOTH
VARIABLES ARE DICHOTOMIZED AT THE
MIDPOINT AND SCORED SO THAT
HIGH = 1 AND LOW = 0

Examples where the correlation (and the regression coefficient) is about .50

	Table A		Table B		Table C	
	Father high	Father low	Father high	Father low	Father high	Father low
Son high	60	10	80	30	90	40
Son low	40	90	20	70	10	60
	100%	100%	100%	100%	100%	100%

Examples where the correlation (and the regression coefficient) is about .20

	Table D		Table E		Table F	
	Father high	Father low	Father high	Father low	Father high	Father low
Son high	50	30	70	50	90	70
Son low	50	70	30	50	10	30
	100%	100%	100%	100%	100%	100%

us introduce a third variable into the analysis by supposing that table A
shows the relation between father's and son's occupation only for those
fathers who had never been to school, while table B shows the same
relation for those fathers who had been to primary school, and table C
shows it for fathers with secondary or higher education. Then each
table represents the effect of father's occupational status when father's
education is explicitly taken into account (what would be called in
technical terms the effect of father's occupation controlling for father's
education). The corresponding *metric partial regression* coefficient is
equal to the difference in proportions we have been discussing, i.e., .50.
Analogously, if we think of tables D, E, and F as representing fathers
with different levels of education, then we have an example where the
metric partial regression coefficient would be smaller, .20. These coefficients would be the same whether or not fathers were evenly divided
between high and low status. *Standardized partial regression* coefficients
(or *paths* in the sociological terminology) are closely akin to (partial)
correlations and would also be equal to the difference in proportions in
these simple examples but would be a little lower if fathers and sons are
not divided equally into high and low status. In more realistic examples
where the relation between father's and son's occupation is not quite
the same in each of the three tables, the regression coefficients will be a
weighted average of the difference in proportions in each of the tables.

There is an important difference between standardized and un-standardized regression coefficients which is not illustrated in these simple examples: the metric coefficients depend on the units used. If, for example, we gave high status fathers a score of 100 rather than 1, the metric regression coefficients would all be 100 times larger while the standardized coefficients would be unchanged. That makes it difficult to compare metric partial regression coefficients for two variables that are scored very differently—say, for example, education scored in years and occupation scored from a low of zero to a high of 100. Even if they are equally important, the metric coefficient expressing the influence of education will look larger than the metric coefficient expressing the influence of occupation, since education has in practice a range of only zero to roughly 20 in contrast to occupation's range of zero to 100. For this reason, standardized partial regression coefficients are used to assess *which* variable is more important. For example, we might want to know whether father's education or father's occupation is a more important influence on son's occupation. The illustrative analysis in table 2.2A suggests that father's occupational status would be more important since it has a standardized partial regression coefficient of .37 while father's education has one of only .22; one can think of these as correlations expressing the separate influence of father's occupation and education, respectively. If we had done the analysis in tabular form with all variables evenly divided between high and low, the tables showing the influence of father's occupation would look something like tables A, B, or C in figure 2.1A (although not quite so dramatic, since they correspond to a standardized coefficient of .50 instead of .37), while the tables showing the influence of father's education would look something like tables D, E, or F.

Except for such comparisons, however, metric regression coefficients are usually more meaningful than standardized ones, mainly because they express the relationship in meaningful units. To continue with the example in table 2.2A, father's education has a metric coefficient of 1.5 which means essentially this: if two fathers are otherwise the same except that the first has one more year of education than the second, then on the average the first's son can expect to get an occupation one and a half status points higher than the second's son. Analogously, the coefficient of .35 for father's occupational status means that, if two fathers are otherwise the same except that the first has a job one status point higher than the other, then on the average the first's son can expect to get a job about one third of a status point higher than the second's son. Another way of putting it is that if the first father is one hundred status points higher than the second (the first being, say, a lawyer while the second is a landless llama herder), the first's son can expect to get a job 35 status points higher than the second's son (say a primary school teacher as opposed to a carpenter).

210

TABLE 2.2A

ILLUSTRATIVE REGRESSION ANALYSIS PREDICTING SON'S OCCUPATIONAL STATUS
ON THE BASIS OF FATHER'S OCCUPATIONAL STATUS AND EDUCATION FOR
PREREVOLUTIONARY BOLIVIAN MEN. OCCUPATIONAL STATUS IS SCORED FROM A
LOW OF ZERO TO A HIGH OF 100 AND EDUCATION IS IN YEARS.

Independent variables	Standardized partial regression coefficient or path coefficient (β)	Metric partial regression coefficient (b)
Father's occupational status (0 to 100)	.37	.35
Father's education (years)	.22	1.5
(Percent of variance explained, R^2)		(30)
(Constant)		(20)

Source: Table 3.6, panel 2, first two columns.

We have so far focused on differences between one son and another, but there is a simpler sort of question that regression analysis can answer. Suppose, for example, that we want to know what status of job a lawyer's son might expect to obtain. The prediction is that he would get 35 points because of his father's high occupation (the metric coefficient of .35 times 100, which is his father's status), plus something from his father's education (if his father had 14 years of education, then it would be the metric coefficient for father's education, 1.5, times the 14 for a total of 21), plus an amount that all sons get regardless of their father's position (this is a constant, 20, shown on the last line of the table) for a total of 76 (which is about the status of a large farmer or cattle rancher).

In addition to the metric and standardized regression coefficients, it is usual to show the percentage of variance explained, R^2. In our example this shows how well we can predict son's occupational status on the basis of father's occupation and education (the two predictor or "independent" variables in the jargon). There are several ways to interpret this but the simplest is, oddly enough, to convert the percent to a proportion and take the square root (the square root of .30 in our example, which is .55). The result is a correlation much like the ones we have already discussed. The difference is that it reflects the joint influence of all the predictor variables taken together. In our example it means that if one combines father's education and occupation into a single variable in an appropriate way (one might think of this as a summary measure of "family background"), that new measure would have a correlation of .55 with son's occupation. That would correspond to a table like A, B, or C (only slightly more dramatic). So by looking at the square root of the proportion of variance explained, one gets back to more familiar ground.

In giving this brief and informal introduction to correlation and regression, we have of course left many important things unsaid. They are covered in a variety of standard textbooks.

Appendix 3

3.1 REPRESENTATIVENESS OF THE RISM SAMPLE

This appendix shows that the RISM survey data are representative of the population of the six towns from which they were drawn. The evidence comes from a comparison of all heads of household in the anthropological census of the towns with those who were also interviewed in the survey. We were able to identify 606 heads of household who were interviewed in both the census and the survey; the remaining 524 heads in the survey could not be identified due to omissions in the census, modest differences in geographic coverage, problems with identification numbers in Villa Abecia, and various errors and omissions in the surviving census records. We compare results for the interviewed heads with results for the target population, the 1,217 male heads of households, 20 or older, in the full census (excluding Villa Abecia). We weighted the interviewed heads by a procedure like that used to weight the survey, matching the target population's distribution by town and literacy. This adjusts for differential sample weights and makes the analysis comparable to the results reported in the text.

The census data are much less reliable than the survey data and are not directly comparable with them: (1) Language is coded monolingual Aymara, bilingual, and Spanish, with considerable bias for reasons indicated in the text. These were scored 1, 2, and 3 since bilinguals are in practice Aymara speakers who have Spanish as a second language. (2) Education is in years. (3) Occupation was recorded only briefly and coded into an ad hoc system which, among other problems, did not preserve the crucial distinction between large, medium, and small farmers. Also, census takers not infrequently confused secondary with primary occupations, particularly for peasants. For the present analysis we recoded occupations into an appropriately modified version of the procedure described earlier; this gives scores from 0 to 100.

There is no real difference between those interviewed in the survey and the target population. Table 3.1A gives the data. The means and standard deviations for language, education, and occupational status are virtually identical. The regressions on occupation are also essential-

TABLE 3.1A

COMPARISON OF THE HEAD OF HOUSEHOLD SAMPLE WITH THE TARGET
POPULATION. POPULATION RESULTS ARE FOR ALL HEADS OF HOUSEHOLD IN THE
SIX COMMUNITIES, WHILE SAMPLE RESULTS ARE BASED ON THAT SUBSET OF THE
TARGET POPULATION WHO WERE ALSO INCLUDED IN THE HEAD OF HOUSEHOLD
SURVEY. ALL DATA ARE FROM THE ANTHROPOLOGICAL CENSUS. CORRELATIONS,
MEANS, STANDARD DEVIATIONS, AND REGRESSIONS ON OCCUPATIONAL STATUS
FOR BOLIVIAN MALE HEADS OF HOUSEHOLD, 20 OR OLDER.

Statistics	Entire target population			Those also in the survey sample		
	Language	Education	Occupation	Language	Education	Occupation
Correlations						
Language		.44	.15		.41	.10
Education	.44		.32	.41		.30
Occupation	.15	.32		.10	.30	
Means	2.0	3.1	51	2.0	3.2	54
Standard deviations	0.7	3.4	30	0.7	3.4	28
Regression statistics						
b's on occupation	.63*	2.75	—	−.99*	2.52	—
's on occupation	.01*	.31	—	−.02*	.31	—
Percent of variance explained			10			9

Source: RISM census. N = 1,217 for the entire target population and 606 for those also in
the survey sample.

   *Not significant at p < .05.

ly the same. Each year of education is worth two and one half status
points in the survey sample compared to two and three quarters in the
full census and the standardized coefficients are identical. Language
has no net effect in either. The percent of variance explained is much
the same in both. This is substantial evidence that the sample is
representative of the population from which it was drawn.

3.2 AN OCCUPATIONAL CLASSIFICATION FOR RURAL BOLIVIA

   This appendix lists the occupational classification used by the Research
Institute for the Study of Man Bolivia Project to classify occupations in
the head of household survey. It is an extension of the International
Labor Office's (1958) International Standard Occupational Classification, with additions and extensions appropriate to rural Bolivia. These
specific occupations are in turn grouped into fourteen categories
devised by the authors and these categories are the basis of the analyses
reported in the text. The original classification was in Spanish and any

ambiguities should therefore be resolved in light of the Spanish terms rather than the authors' English translation.

1. Elite White-Collar

architect	(arquitecto)
chemist	(químico)
map maker	(cartografo)
philosopher, theologian	(filósofo, teólogo)
veterinarian	(veterinario)
physician	(médico)
pharmacist	(farmacéutico)
bishop	(obispo)
judge	(juez)
attorney	(procurador)
rural district governor	(corregidor)
subprefect	(subprefecto)
industrialist, owner of a small factory	(industrial, dueño de pequeña fábrica)
one who lives on his rents	(rentista)
school principal	(director de escuela)
secretary general of a worker's union	(secretario general del sindicato)
engineer	(ingeniero)
topographer	(topógrafo)
accountant	(contador)
agronomist	(agronomista)
dentist	(dentista)
clergyman, priest	(cura, pastor, sacerdote)
lawyer	(abogado)
notary	(notario),
court clerk, etc.	(escribano)
court clerk, actuary	(actuario)
mayor of city or town	(alcalde)
chief of the Criminal Bureau of Investigation	(jefe del Departmento de Investigaciones Criminales)
congressman	(diputado nacional)

2. Large Farmer

farmer, farm owner, unspecialized farmer with in addition at least one *paid* employee outside the family (agricultor general). Information on employees and land ownership was obtained from separate questions.

3. Cattle Rancher

cattle rancher, dealer in cattle	(ganadero)

4. *High White-Collar*

nurse	(enfermera)
assistant social researcher	(asistente social, investigador social)
vaccinator	(sanitario vacunador)
secondary school teacher	(profesor de escuela secundaria)
judge's secretary	(secretario de juez)
artist, painter	(artista, pintor)
publicity advertising agent	(publicista comercial)
radio or TV announcer	(locutor)
first undersecretary to the mayor	(oficial mayor de la alcaldía)
director of public works	(jefe de obras públicas)
tribal chief	(jilicata, San Miguel)
contractor	(contratista)
construction foreman	(constructor)
union official	(funcionario del sindicato)
administrator of a cooperative	(administrador de cooperativas)
insurance agent	(agente de seguros)
midwife	(partera)
primary school teacher	(profesor de escuela primaria)
private tutor	(profesor particular)
legal advisor without degree	(titerillo, abogado no profesional)
interior decorator	(decorador de interiores)
journalist	(periodista)
writer	(escritor)
police official	(intendente)
prison warden	(alcalde de cárcel)
political leader of peasants in a town or village	(cacique)
officer of the armed forces	(oficial de fuerzas armadas)
hotel manager	(hotelero)
political party official	(funcionario de partido político)
administrator of a cattle raising project	(administrador del proyecto ganadero)
photographer	(fotógrafo)

5. *Skilled Modern Blue-Collar*

aviation technician	(técnico de aviación)
telegraph operator	(telegrafista)
radio operator	(operador del radio)
lathe mechanic	(mecánico tornero)

mechanic	(mecánico de coches, camiones, motocicletas, etc.)
plumber	(plomero)
electrician	(electricista)
builder and repairer of telegraph lines	(constructor y reparador de líneas telegráficos)
petroleum refiner	(refinador de petrol)
detective	(detectivo)
truck driver	(camionero)
telephone operator	(telefonista)
radio technician	(radiotécnico)
dental technician	(mecánico dental)
mechanic's assistant	(ayudante de mecánico)
mechanic, unspecified type	(mecánico sin especificar)
radio mechanic	(mecánico de radio)
movie projectionist	(operador de cine)
printer	(litógrafo)
works with a long stick or drill in construction or mines	(barretero, trabaja con un barratero)
topographer's assistant	(ayudante de topógrafo)

6. *Clerical and Sales*

member of an administrative group	(miembro del grupo administrativo)
typist	(mecanógrafo)
office worker	(oficinista)
public employee	(empleado público)
sales person	(vendedor entiendas)
bank employee	(empleado de banco)
office secretaries and kindred	(secretarios de oficina y similares)
collector of money	(cobrador)
shop assistant	(ayudante de tiendas)

7. *Small Business*

merchant middleman who buys goods (coffee, coca, etc.) and resells them at a profit	(vendedor propietario, ventas al por mayor)
timber merchant, lumber dealer	(maderero)
private businessman, wholesale merchant	(rescatador—cafe, coca, etc.)
working proprietor not elsewhere classified	(vendedor proprietario, ventas al por menor)

8-A. Specialized Farmers

horticulturist	(horticultor)
chicken farmer	(avicultor)
bee keeper	(apicultor)
coffee, coca, or fruit planter, etc.	(agricultor de cafe, coca, fruta, . . .)
wine maker, vinyard owner	(viñatero)

8-B. Specialized Farm Workers

cowboy	(peón ganadero)
tractor driver	(tractorista)
or agricultural machine operator	(operador de maquinaria)
miller, agricultural	(molinero, obrero agrícola)
worker in a flower shop or greenhouse	(peón florista o horticultor)
agricultural worker, wine bottler, slaughter house worker, etc.	(obrero agrícola, embotellador de vino, derribador de ganado, molinero)

9. Skilled Traditional Blue-Collar

actor	(actor)
musician	(musico)
dancer	(bailarín)
peddler	(vendedor ambulante)
dressmaker, seamstress	(modista, costurero)
hatmaker	(sombrerero)
shoemaker, sandlemaker	(zapatero, abarquero)
lasso maker for cattle	(hace lazos para asuntos de ganadería)
leather worker	(talabartero)
jeweler	(joyero)
tinker	(mecánico que arregla arte-factos domésticos, calenta-dores, etc.)
builder of canoes or boats	(constructor de canoas o botes)
sawer	(aserradero)
carpenter's assistant	(ayudante de carpintero)
builder of carts or wheels	(constructor de carretones o ruedas)
mason	(albañil)

construction worker who puts stucco on an unfinished structure	(estuquero)
flagstone maker, makes jars, jugs of clay, etc.	(losero, hace tinjas, potes de barro, tiestos, etc.)
baker	(panadero)
butcher	(carnicero)
mat or rug maker	(estero, hace esteros)
policeman	(policía)
restaurant or boarding house cook	(cocinero en restaurante, pensíon)
bartender	(cantinero)
barber's assistant	(ayudante de peluquero)
male witch	(hechicero)
fortune teller	(adivino or brujo)
faith healer	(curandero)
tailor	(sastre)
tailor's assistant	(ayudante de sastre)
mattress maker, feather bed maker	(colchonero)
shoemaker's assistant	(ayudante de zapatero)
sandalmaker, a piece of coarse leather tied on the soles of the feet, worn by peasants	(abarquero)
blacksmith	(herrero)
metal worker	(hojalatero)
solderer, house to house	(soldador, técnico soldador)
carpenter	(carpintero)
sawer's assistant	(ayudante do aserradero)
cabinet maker	(ebanista)
house painter	(pintor de casas)
mason's assistant	(ayudante de albañil)
dealer in glass, glassmaker, etc.	(vidriero, trabaja en fábrica de vidrios, botellas, etc.)
adobe brick maker	(adobero)
tile maker	(tejero, hace tejas)
miller	(molinero)
seller or maker of chocolate	(chocolatero)
works in a noodle factory	(fidero, trabaja en una fábrica de fideos)
candle maker	(velero, hace velas de cero)
jailer	(carcelero)
cook, private household	(cocinero de casa)
women's hairdresser	(peinador de mujeres)

barber   (peluquero de hombres)
dyer   (tintorero)

10. *Unskilled Nonfarm*

newspaper salesman   (vendedor de diarios)
cart transporter   (transportista con carretones)
messenger   (mensajero)
spinner, weaver   (hilandero, trejedor)
road worker   (obrero en construcción de
                                             caminos)
manual laborer, transporter of   (cargador y alzador)
   wares
night-watchman   (sereno)
servant, housemaid   (criada de casa)
doorman   (portero)
superintendent   (cuidador de casa)
ironing woman   (planchadora)
muleteer   (mulero, transportista con
                                             mulas)
bargeman, boatman   (lanchero, botero)
driver's assistant   (ayudante de camionero;
                                             ayudante de chofer)
packer   (empaquetador)
day laborer   (jornalero)
soldier   (soldado)
waiter in a restaurant or board-   (mozo en restaurante, pensión)
   ing house
domestic gardener   (jardinero doméstico)
washing woman   (lavandera)

11. *Tenant Farmer*

general farmer who does not   (agricultor general)
   own his land

12. *Farm Laborer (Peon)*

farm worker   (peón)
vineyard worker   (peón viñatero)
fisherman   (pescador)
rubber worker   (siringuero)
general farm worker   (peón general)
hunter   (cazador)
wood cutter, dealer in wood   (leñador)

13. Small Farmer

general farmer who does not (agricultor general)
  employ paid workers; may or
  may not have members of his
  family working for him

14. Small Livestock Owner

small livestock owner, llamas, (pequeño criador de animales,
  goats, pigs, etc. llamas, cabras, corderos, etc.)

3.3   MEASURES OF OCCUPATIONAL STATUS

Our analysis is based primarily on the "ethnographic" occupational classification described in detail in chapter 2. We prefer this measure to others since it does full justice to local circumstances and conditions. But classifying occupations is a notoriously tricky business and there is always a risk that our measure either missed something that was important or that it somehow capitalized on some unique local aspect of occupational status very different from that typical of other countries, and so reduced the general applicability of our results. To investigate these possibilities, we developed two additional, very different measures of status based on concepts and procedures developed in crosscultural research and then compared them to results using our preferred ethnographic measure. In this appendix we first describe the alternative measures and then show that in practice they produce results remarkably similar to those produced by our ethnographic measure. This provides substantial evidence that our measure is appropriate and effective, both in the sense of capturing the important variations in the Bolivian context and in the sense of measuring much the same thing as other status scores.

Alternative Occupational Status Scores

We constructed our alternative measures by using an occupational classification quite different from the fourteen-category ethnographic scheme we developed for our measure. The alternative classification was devised by Treiman (see Treiman 1977: 203–208 for details). It is based on the International Labor Office's (1958) Standard International Occupational Classification: namely professional and technical, administrative and managerial, clerical, sales, production, service, and agricultural. These groups are quite heterogenous so Treiman subdivided them on the basis of prestige.[1] For example, he divided the professional and technical group into higher professionals (those with prestige scores of 58 or higher) and lower professionals (those with prestige scores below 58) and so on for other categories. We have experimented with a considerable number of different divisions but this has not led to any useful modifications except for farm occupations in some societies where, as in Bolivia, it is useful to make more distinctions than Treiman does. This classification seems to be satisfactory in the sense that it captures what is important about occupations. For Bolivia and the United States we ran a series of analyses of income, first entering a set of dummy variables representing the Treiman classification and then adding other characteristics of occupations (e.g., prestige, mean education of incumbents). We consistently found that the additional variables were unimportant, adding nothing to our ability to explain income differences. We also ran similar analyses of the effect of father's occupation on son's education and on son's occupational status with similar results.

Cross-Cultural Status Scores. We experimented with a wide variety of procedures for assigning status scores to the fourteen categories of Treiman's classification but in the end settled on a variant of the "predictive" canonical procedure suggested by Duncan-Jones (1972: 205–208). The underlying assumption is that socioeconomic status (SES) is intimately involved with education, income, and father's occupation and that in fact these variables are related only because of their links to socioeconomic status. If this is true and if Treiman's classification adequately captures the socioeconomic variation among occupations, then it follows that a single scoring scheme will maximize the ordinary product-moment correlation between respondent's socioeconomic status on the one hand and his education, income, and his father's socioeconomic status on the other. This maximal scoring scheme can be found by a canonical analysis of respondent's occupation and any one of the three other variables. Of course in the real world, these assumptions are met only approximately and there are errors in the data, so it is preferable not to rely on any one of these but on a procedure that takes all into account simultaneously. This can be done by a canonical analysis where respondent's occupation (scored as a set of dummy variables without assumptions about rank) is one set of variables and the second set consists of education, income and father's occupation. Further discussion and cautions are given elsewhere (Kelley and Treiman 1978: 51–63; Duncan-Jones 1972; Kendall and Stuart 1967: chap. 16). Scores produced by canonical procedures are identified only up to a linear transformation, so there is no natural metric. We have adopted the conventional metric, scoring the highest ranking occupation 100 and the lowest zero. We call this the *local* canonical score.

Having developed what seems a plausible way of measuring occupational status, we then applied it to survey data from fourteen other societies around the world.[2] It turns out that socioeconomic status hierarchies are much the same everywhere in the world. The correlations between status hierarchies in sixteen societies throughout the world average .84. And the similarity holds not just for Western industrial societies but is equally apparent for the developing societies of Latin America, Africa, and Asia; correlations between industrial societies and developing societies average .82. Even Poland, though communist for several decades, is little different from the rest of the world. Since socioeconomic status seems to be essentially the same throughout the world, it is reasonable to construct a single scale for use throughout the world. We did this by simply averaging the scores for each country.[3] For the world as a whole, high professionals—the traditional free professionals—are clearly at the top of the socioeconomic hierarchy. Administrators are well behind, closely followed by low professionals, high clerical workers, and high sales workers. Then there is a distinct gap. Below the gap, the bottom end of the white-collar hierarchy (low clerical and low sales) overlaps with the top of the blue-collar hierarchy. Middle and small farmers follow[4] and farm laborers are at the very bottom. This scale, which we call the *cross-cultural* canonical scale, is used at various points in the book when we want to compare Bolivia with other societies (see Kelley, Treiman, Robinson, Roos, and Thompson 1980 for details).

EQUIVALENCE OF DIFFERENT STATUS SCORES

In practice, it turns out that these very different measures of occupational status produce results that are for all practical purposes interchangeable. Current occupational status as measured by our ethnographic procedure is correlated .93 with status as measured by the local SES scale, this in spite of the fact that the scores are based on different ways of grouping occupations and different ways of assigning scores to the groups.[5] More crucially, use of any one of these measures would lead to essentially the same substantive conclusions. As table 3.2A shows, the correlations among several variables related to stratification (father's education and occupation; son's education, occupation, and income) are essentially the same when occupational status is measured by ethnographic scores as when occupational status is measured by local canonical scores or with cross-cultural canonical scores. These three quite different measurement procedures lead to virtually identical results, strong evidence that our measurement procedures are satisfactory.

Appendix 3

TABLE 3.2A

CORRELATIONS BETWEEN THREE ALTERNATIVE MEASURES OF OCCUPATIONAL
STATUS AND SELECTED OTHER VARIABLES IN BOLIVIA.

Variable	Measure of occupational status		
	Ethnographic scores[1]	Local canonical scores[2]	Cross-cultural canonical scores[3]
Son's occupation and:			
Father's occupation	.61	.60	.49
Father's education	.55	.53	.47
Son's education	.61	.64	.60
Son's standard of living	.60	.58	.49
Father's occupation and:			
Father's education	.69	.71	.65
Son's education	.61	.62	.57
Son's standard of living	.52	.52	.44

Source: Head of household survey. N = 1,116, excluding missing data.

[1] These scores, described in chapter 2, are used in most of our analyses in the text.

[2] These scores, described in Appendix 3, are derived from a canonical analysis of the Bolivian head of household data.

[3] These scores, described in Appendix 3, are the average of canonical scores for 16 societies throughout the world. They are used at several points in the text where we compare Bolivia with other societies.

Appendix 4

THE OPEN-ENDED QUESTIONS

This appendix gives the text of the open-ended questions analyzed in chapter 5. The Spanish originals are given first, followed by our English translation. The answers were of course recorded and coded in Spanish, and English translations are only for the benefit of readers unfamiliar with Spanish. The questions were items 68 to 77 in the original interview schedule.

<small>SPANISH TEXT</small>

Temas de Conversación: Yo ahora quisiera comentar con usted algunas cosas que se hablan en este pueblo y me gustaría tener su opinión.

68. Dicen que la tierra tiene que ser de quien la trabaja y no del dueño que no la trabaja.
69. Se dice que con la reforma los campesinos han conseguido la tierra pero ahora que la tienen no la trabajan. ¿Como le parece?
70. También se dice que con la revolución del 52 los ricos y la gente decente han perdido todo y ahora ya no pueden esperar nada. ¿Como le parece?
71. Se habla de que todas las cosas estaban mejor antes de la revolución de 52. ¿Usted, que opina?
72. A mí me han dicho que los campesinos son distintos de los cholos y de la gente decente. ¿Usted está de acuerdo con esto?
73. Si un campesino va a vivir al pueblo o a la ciudad puede considerarse cholo o decente.
74. ¿Como le parece que un campesino se case con una decente?
75. La gente decente, o la gente bien, nunca puede bajar de categoría. ¿Usted, que opina?
76. Me han dicho que en este pueblo la gente no se ayuda mutuamente, que cada uno trata de aprovecharse de los demás y que ni vale la pena ser un . . . . (decir aqui Coroiqueño, o Reyesaño, etc.)
77. Se dice que si uno no tiene muñeca está fregada para cualquier cosa que quiere conseguir. ¿Como le parece?

ENGLISH TRANSLATION

Themes of Conversation: I would now like to discuss with you a few things which they are talking about in this town, and I would like to have your opinion.

68. They say that only those who work the land should own it.

69. They say that with the agrarian reform the campesinos have gotten control over the land but now that they have it they do not work it. What do you think?

70. Also, they say that with the revolution of 1952 the wealthy and upper-class people have lost everything and now they can expect nothing. What do you think?

71. They say that everything was better before the revolution of '52. What is your opinion?

72. To me they have said that campesinos are different from cholos and the upper class. Do you agree with this?

73. If a campesino goes to live in the town or the city, he can be considered a cholo or "decente."

74. What do you think about a male campesino marrying an upper class woman?

75. The upper class can never lose status. What do you think?

76. They have told me that in this town the people don't help each other and that each one tries to take advantage of the others and that it's not worth it being a . . . [member of this particular town].

77. They say that if one doesn't have connections, one cannot get anything. What do you think?

Appendix 5

FURTHER DETAILS ON EDUCATION AND INCOME

In this appendix we present further details on some of the calculations described more briefly in chapter 6. The first section deals with our estimates of revolution's effects on education and educational inequality and the second with our estimates of its effect on income inequality.

5.1 EDUCATION AND EDUCATIONAL INEQUALITY

We would like to assess the revolution's effect on education and educational inequality but the difficulty is that some changes were taking place even before the revolution. As described in chapter 6, the basic strategy is to circumvent this by using data from the prerevolutionary cohort to estimate what the changes would have been in the absence of revolution.

Education is determined mainly by family background (see chap. 3) and, especially among Indians, by a secular trend for education to increase over time (or what is the same thing, for education to decrease with age). We therefore estimate the prerevolutionary pattern on the basis of age, father's education (*FED*), and father's occupational status (*FS*), confining our attention to the prerevolutionary cohort. Education and age are in years, while occupational status is measured by the ethnographic scale which has a low of 0 and a high of 100; these variables are defined in chapter 2 and the cohorts are defined in chapter 7. Differences between Spanish and Indians are large enough, and interesting enough on substantive grounds, that we estimated two separate equations, one for Spanish and one for Indians (where Indians are those of Aymara or cholo social race, as defined in chap. 2). The estimates, obtained by ordinary least squares regression, are as follows:

$$(\text{for Spanish})\ ED = -.0008\ AGE + .452\ FED$$
$$+ .0325\ FS + .960 \qquad (R^2 = .38)$$

(for Indians) $ED = -.0139\,AGE + .505\,FED + .0452\,FS$
$+ .784 \qquad (R^2 = .46)$

These estimates are based on the figures given in table 6.4A and refer to the prerevolutionary cohorts in the head of household survey (N = 245 for Spanish and 368 for Indians).

Estimates of what, in the absence of revolution, educational levels would have been in later times were obtained by inserting the appropriate means in these regression equations. For example, the estimate for the Spanish in the revolutionary period was obtained by multiplying the average age of the Spanish in the revolutionary period (35.3 years) by the age coefficient in the Spanish equation (−.0008), multiplying the average level of father's education for the Spanish in the revolutionary period (3.80 years) by the appropriate coefficient (.452), multiplying their fathers' average status (38.4) by its coefficient (.0325), and finally adding all of these together with the constant (.960) to obtain an estimated educational level of 3.9 years. In fact, the Spanish in this period obtained 4.4 years of education, the difference between that and the expected level presumably reflecting the increased opportunities brought about by the revolution. Estimates for Indians, and for other time periods, were obtained similarly. The estimates, shown in figure 6.5 in the text, are given in more detail here in table 5.1A, line 2).

Estimates of expected trends in educational inequality were obtained by a straightforward extension of these estimates. We measure inequality by the standard deviation of education (for reasons set out in chap. 1). We assume that if there had been no revolution, the standard deviation of education for the Spanish would be the same as in the prerevolutionary period. Similarly, we assume that the standard deviation for Indians would have remained unchanged but for the revolution. The changes we actually observe (a modest decrease in the standard deviation for the Spanish and an appreciable increase for Indians), we attribute to the revolution. For the population as a whole, the standard deviation of education will depend on the standard deviations for Spanish and Indian subpopulations and on the difference in the mean level of education of Spanish and Indians. So we estimate what would have happened in the absence of a revolution by assuming that the standard deviations for Spanish and Indians respectively would have remained unchanged from prerevolutionary times, and that the means would have been those we estimated above. Extrapolation of prerevolutionary trends in this way implies that the mean level education of Indians would have come closer to the mean for the Spanish, and hence that educational inequality in the society as a whole would have declined (line 5). We infer revolution's effects by comparing this predicted decline with the actual changes (line 6).

TABLE 5.1A

Revolution's Effects on Education. Predicted and Actual Levels of Education and Educational Inequality for Cohorts Coming of Age Before, During, and After the Revolution for the Indian and Spanish Populations Separately. Male Heads of Household, 24 or Older.

Variable[1]	Spanish			Indian (Aymara and Cholo)			All[2]		
	Before revolution	During revolution	After revolution	Before revolution	During revolution	After revolution	Before revolution	During revolution	After revolution
1. Actual education (mean years)	4.41	4.32	4.99[b]	0.71	1.45[a,b]	1.97[a,c]	2.22	2.51[b]	3.15[a,c]
2. Expected educational attainment if prerevolutionary trends continue unchanged[2] (mean years)	—	3.89	3.90	—	1.03	1.32	—	2.05	2.30
3. Increase in education attributed to the revolution (line 1 − line 2) expressed as a percentage of line 2	—	+11	+28	—	+41	+49	—	+22	+37
4. Actual educational inequality (standard deviation of education)	4.71	4.41	4.59	1.73	2.19[a]	2.45[a]	3.75	3.47	3.70[d]
5. Expected inequality if prerevolutionary trends continue unchanged (standard deviation)	—	4.71	4.71	—	1.73	1.73	—	3.42	3.43
6. Increase (+) or decrease (−) in inequality attributed to the revolution (line 4 − line 5) expressed as a percentage of line 5	—	−6	−3	—	+27	+42	—	+1	+8
7. (Number of cases)	(245)	(94)	(63)	(368)	(169)	(103)	(628)	(271)	(169)

Source: Head of household survey. See table 6.4A for the underlying data.

[1] Variables are defined in chapter 2 and cohorts in chapter 7.

[2] Includes 26 cases unclassified on social race.

[a] Difference between this and the prerevolutionary mean (or standard deviation) statistically significant at p < .05, one tailed.

[b] Difference between lines 1 and 2 statistically significant at p < .05, one tailed.

[c] Difference between lines 1 and 2 statistically significant at p < .05, one tailed.

[d] Difference between lines 4 and 5 (last two columns only) statistically significant at p < .05, one tailed.

5.2   DETAILS ON THE ESTIMATE OF INCOME INEQUALITY

This appendix describes the calculations underlying the estimates of inequality used in chapter 6. The basic logic and assumptions were described there and here we supply some of the technical details.

The basic data are from the Ministry of Planning. These are currently the most respected data available from Bolivian government sources and are used by almost all analysts but are nonetheless decidedly imperfect (Whitehead 1969). The main biases are likely to be consistent over- or underestimates but these are not especially serious for present purposes since we are concerned not with absolute levels of inequality but with changes over time, and they will not be affected by any consistent bias. The labor force data are from the Ministry of Planning's *Diagnóstico del Sector Agropecuario* (1974:table I.6). This gives the distribution of the labor force by sector for each year between 1966 and 1972 and the average for 1950−1952. Only an agricultural versus nonagricultural breakdown is given for 1950−1952, so we borrowed the nonagricultural breakdown from the 1950 census. Except for the mineral sector, we estimated the missing labor force figures for the years 1953 to 1965 by interpolation between the known figures for 1950−1952 and 1967 using a compound interest formula. The changes in the size and distribution of the labor force are small enough that this seems to introduce little error. For example, 69 percent of the labor force was in agriculture in 1950−1952 and 67 percent in 1966. We took the figures for 1950−1952 to reflect the middle year, 1951, and adjusted the 1950 and 1952 figures by the same compound growth formula. We assumed that changes in employment in the mineral sector followed those in its dominant tin mining component, for which the annual data are available (Thorn 1971:172). Our estimates are shown in table 5.2A.

The figures for gross domestic product from each sector of the economy are also from the Ministry of Planning (reported in Wennergren and Whitaker 1975:table 2.5), and are shown in table 5.2A. These are by year from 1950, so no interpolation is necessary.

The remaining computations are straightforward. We estimated per-worker productivity in any one sector and year simply by dividing the gross domestic product of the sector by the number of workers. This effectively assumes that each worker in the sector was equally productive, an assumption that was discussed in chapter 6. For reasons also discussed there, we use this as an estimate of the worker's income. At this point we have estimates of the number of workers in each sector and the income of each worker and can compute income inequality in the society as a whole for any one year by the usual elementary formula.

We also make alternative estimates adjusting for changes in the prices of tin and the growth of the petroleum industry. We did this by valuing tin production at average prices for 1950–1952. For petroleum, we simply assumed a constant output for the entire period, set at a value equal to the average for the whole period. These adjusted figures are shown in table 5.2A.

TABLE 5.2A

GROSS DOMESTIC PRODUCT AND NUMBER OF WORKERS BY SECTOR AND
ESTIMATED INCOME INEQUALITY IN THE SOCIETY AS A WHOLE. INEQUALITY
IS MEASURED BY THE STANDARD DEVIATION OF INCOME AND EXPRESSED
AS A RATIO OF THE AVERAGE FOR 1950–1952. BOLIVIA, 1950–1972.
ESTIMATES AS DESCRIBED IN THE TEXT.

| Year | Number of workers (100's) | | | | | Gross domestic product (millions of 1958 pesos) | | | | | | Inequality | |
	Agri-culture	Minerals	Petro-leum	Industry	Services	Agri-culture	Minerals (actual)	(adjusted)	Petro-leum[1]	Industry	Services	Not adjusted	Adjusted[2]
1950	8323	389	50	1106	2259	1097	531	562	13	495	1227	.924	.967
1951	8505	393	50	1108	2340	1114	596	603	11	522	1357	1.024	1.027
1952	8693	407	50	1111	2423	1094	620	582	11	525	1459	1.053	1.007
1953	8884	451	50	1114	2510	967	594	635	12	498	1287	.933	.979
1954	9080	466	50	1117	2599	946	494	525	35	587	1366	.861	.894
1955	9280	501	50	1119	2692	1008	525	509	57	622	1397	.877	.858
1956	9484	531	50	1122	2788	953	463	489	66	573	1340	.790	.799
1957	9693	511	50	1125	2887	945	449	507	69	405	1406	.761	.793
1958	9906	466	50	1127	2990	1066	280	323	67	443	1505	.673	.695
1959	10124	461	50	1130	3097	1084	325	434	70	435	1436	.662	.730

1960	10347	467	50	1133	3208	1084	287	369	70	477	1576	.678	.715
1961	10574	462	50	1135	3322	1137	306	377	59	478	1587	.656	.704
1962	10807	458	50	1138	3440	1126	321	379	57	529	1733	.706	.740
1963	11045	454	50	1141	3564	1189	361	405	63	564	1831	.747	.764
1964	11288	460	50	1144	3691	1213	391	441	52	614	1931	.773	.799
1965	11536	466	50	1146	3823	1281	392	420	45	674	2099	.802	.814
1966	11790	479	59	1149	3959	1328	434	465	82	757	2205	.871	.847
1967	12050	490	60	1450	4050	1289	439	497	234	781	2367	1.116	.856
1968	12270	485	50	1499	3232	1352	464	530	233	830	2598	1.339	1.063
1969	12490	500	49	1550	4383	1239	513	539	223	839	2795	1.215	.943
1970	12710	525	49	1633	4531	1294	597	540	160	884	2910	1.112	.934
1971	12940	510	50	1696	4692	1345	570	543	234	909	3020	1.239	.935
1972	13170	525	50	1758	4861	1381	561	581	204	967	3321	1.199	.987

Source: See the text for sources and details on the estimations.

[1] The adjusted figure for petroleum is 92 for all years.
[2] Adjusted for changes in the price of tin and growth in the petroleum industry.

Appendix 6

FURTHER DETAILS ON INHERITED PRIVILEGE

This appendix gives further details on our estimates of inherited privilege. It is in three sections. The first gives some regression results by time periods much narrower than those used in the text. The second describes the regression analyses underlying the results of chapter 7. The final section gives the basic data for the analysis of chapter 7, a variety of additional analyses only briefly mentioned in the text, and the exact figures for the results reported graphically.

6.1 REGRESSION RESULTS BY NARROWER TIME PERIODS

Here we show regression results for fifteen separate age cohorts. This gives more detail than the simple division into prerevolutionary, revolutionary, and postrevolutionary cohorts used in the text but results in analyses based on some very small samples, which are therefore subject to substantial random variation. The most characteristic effect of the revolution was to reduce the advantage that families could pass on by their property and so we show estimates of that. We measure it by the unstandardized regression coefficient of father's occupational status in a regression equation predicting the status of son's first job on the basis of his father's education and occupational status (the assumptions underlying this approximation are described in the text in detail). This is the Model 2 described in the text and the next section. We have not included father's social race (which would be Model 3) because it is so highly colinear with father's education and occupation that it puts undue strain on the decidedly modest sample sizes we are dealing with here.

The results are shown in table 6.1A. They quite clearly show the pattern we have seen in the text using the simpler division into three time periods. Property was important before the revolution but became very much less so for sons coming of age at the time of the revolution and for about a decade thereafter. But then in the longer run it became important once again. The main exception to this is the seemingly anomalous results for the men who were 35 to 36 at the time

TABLE 6.1A

THE EFFECT OF FATHER'S OCCUPATION STATUS ON STATUS OF SON'S JOB FOR 15
AGE COHORTS OF BOLIVIAN MALE HEADS OF HOUSEHOLD: METRIC PARTIAL
REGRESSION COEFFICIENTS OF FATHER'S OCCUPATION
FROM A MODEL ESTIMATING SON'S STATUS FROM FATHER'S
STATUS AND FATHER'S EDUCATION (MODEL 2).

Age at time of survey	Metric partial regression coefficient	Number of cases
20–25	.42	37
26–30	.51	129
31–32	.12	53
33–34	.11	56
35–36	.64	60
37–38	.07	71
39–40	.26	77
41–43	.25	70
44–46	.57	77
47–49	.33	58
50–54	.29	84
55–59	.54	68
60–64	.41	70
65–74	.31	81
75 and over	.67	64

Source: Head of household survey.

of the survey; we see no logical explanation for this and are inclined to attribute the results to chance.

6.2   DETAILS ON THE REGRESSION MODELS

This section gives details on the regression calculations reported in chapter 7. The main outlines of the analysis were given there and we focus here on technical details and the statistical tests.

VARIABLES

The variables used in the analysis were described in detail in chapter 3, so we mention them only briefly here.

Son's occupational status (*S*) is the occupational status of the son's first job. Status is measured by the ethnographic scoring procedure described in chapter 3. *Father's occupational status* (*FS*) is also measured by the ethnographic procedure.

Father's education (*FED*) and *son's education* (*ED*) are measured in years of schooling completed.

Father's social race (FRACE) is the father's ethnic-linguistic background, scored so that Spanish is 1 and Aymara 0.

Time Period, prerevolutionary period, the revolutionary period, and the postrevolutionary period, is distinguished in the manner described in chapter 7.

Missing data are not much of a problem with these variables, averaging less than one percent for son's occupation and education, four percent for father's occupation, eight percent for father's education, three percent for father's social race, and less than one percent on time period. Computations were based on pair-wise present data, a procedure known to give better estimates than the main alternative, which is to confine the analysis to those for whom there is no missing data on any variables.

ESTIMATING THE MODEL

We estimate the model for each time period separately using ordinary least squares regression (OLS) estimates. Some estimates are further restricted to Spanish or Aymara respondents, respectively. Three models are reported in the text.

Model 1. This is the simplest model, where family background is measured only by father's occupational status. The regression equation is:

$$\hat{S} = a_1 + b_1 \, FS \qquad\qquad\qquad\qquad \text{[Model 1]}$$

where a_1 is the intercept and b_1 the metric (or unstandardized) regression coefficient. The standardized regression coefficient of course comes from the same equation, expressed in a different metric and in this simple model is the same as the correlation between father's and son's status. Some results reported in figures 7.1, 7.2, 7.9, and 7.13 are from this regression equation.

Model 2. In this model family background is measured by two variables:

$$\hat{S} = a_1 + b_2 \, FS + b_3 \, FED \qquad\qquad\qquad \text{[Model 2]}$$

This model produces results that are virtually identical to those from the next, more comprehensive Model 3, so let us defer any discussion for a moment. Results from this model are reported in figure 7.2. Note, however, that Model 3 sometimes reduces to Model 2 (for example, when applied to the Indian population).

Model 3. This uses the most comprehensive measure of family background and is our preferred model:

$$\hat{S} = a_3 + b_4\,FS + b_5\,FED + b_6\,FRACE \qquad\qquad \text{[Model 3]}$$

FED provides a comprehensive measure of the family's human capital and *FRACE* adjusts for ethnic-cultural differences between Spanish and Aymara. (For the results in chapter 7, where we deal separately with the Spanish and Aymara populations, this of course reduces to Model 2, since *FRACE* drops out.) We interpret the coefficient of *FED* in this equation (i.e., b_5) as a measure of the influence of family *human capital*; that is reported in figures 7.6, 7.7, and 7.10. We interpret the coefficient of father's occupational status, b_4, as a rough approximation to the total influence of father's *property*. The assumptions involved in this interpretation are discussed at length in the text and the results are reported in figures 7.3, and 7.7. The estimates are given in table 6.2A.

Model 3B. Models 1, 2, and 3 all measure the total influence of family background without asking how that influence comes about. But for some purposes it is useful to know more about the process and we learn more by explicitly including the son's education in the analysis.

$$\hat{S} = a_4 + b_7\,FS + b_8\,FED + b_9\,FRACE + b_{10}\,ED \qquad \text{[Model 3B]}$$

In this model, the coefficient of father's status, b_7, is interpreted as the *direct effect of family property*, i.e., that part that comes about through outright gift, purchase, inheritance, or the like. The coefficient of father's education, b_8, analogously reflects the direct effect of father's education but this is in practice equal to zero, for reasons explained theoretically in chapter 1. Estimates from Model 3B are shown in figures 7.4, 7.8, 7.10, and 7.12. (The estimates for the Aymara population given in figure 7.12 do not include *FED* for reasons explained in the text and of course do not include *FRACE*, and so reduce to a very simple model depending on *FS* and *ED* only.)

The effect of son's *human capital* is of course shown by the coefficient of education, b_{10}, in Model 3B. This appears in figure 7.8.

Model 3C. All the models we have discussed so far predict the status of a son's first job. But none can ask exactly parallel questions about the effects of family background on son's education. We make such estimates simply by replacing son's status, *S*, in Model 3, by son's education, *ED*, and proceeding exactly as before. The results are shown in table 6.2A and reported in the text in figure 7.5.

Computing Direct and Indirect Effects

We sometimes want to find, for example, that part of the effect of father's occupation that is indirect via education and that part that is direct in the sense of not having anything to do with education. These

TABLE 6.2A

EFFECTS OF FAMILY BACKGROUND ON THE STATUS OF SON'S FIRST OCCUPATION (COLUMNS 1–6) OR EDUCATION (COLUMNS 7–9) FOR PREREVOLUTIONARY (PreR), REVOLUTIONARY (Revol), AND POSTREVOLUTIONARY (PostR) COHORTS. STANDARDIZED AND UNSTANDARDIZED PARTIAL REGRESSION COEFFICIENTS ESTIMATED FROM MODELS 3 AND 3C BASED ON DATA IN TABLE 6.3A.[1] UNITS ARE SHOWN IN PARENTHESES.

Independent Variables	Son's Occupation²			Son's Occupation²			Son's Education³		
	PreR (1)	Revol (2)	PostR (3)	PreR (4)	Revol (5)	PostR (6)	PreR (7)	Revol (8)	PostR (9)
Standardized Partial Regression Coefficients (betas)									
1. Father's occupational status	.33	.19	.47	.25	.11*	.41	.24	.17	.26
2. Father's Education	.20	.28	.24	.03*	.03*	.09*	.49	.57	.56
3. Social race	.09	.09*	-.11*	.06*	.08*	-.11*	.08	.02*	-.01*
4. Son's education	—	—	—	.35	.43	.26	—	—	—
5. (% of variance explained, R²)	(31)	(24)	(36)	(37)	(27)	(39)	(54)	(51)	(55)
Unstandardized Partial Regression Coefficients (b's)									
6. Father's occupational status (Top=100, bottom=0)	.31	.17	.42	.23	.10*	.36	.035	.025	.035
7. Father's Education (years)	1.3	1.8	1.9	0.2*	0.2*	0.7*	.48	.58	.71
8. Social race (Spanish = 1, Indian = 0)	5	4*	-5*	3*	4*	-5*	0.6	0.2*	-0.1*
9. Son's Education (years)	—	—	—	2.3	2.7	1.7	—	—	—

Source: Head of household survey.

[1] The number of cases for the pre-revolutionary, revolutionary and post-revolutionary periods respectively is 628, 271, and 169.

[2] Scored in the same way as father's occupation with a top of 100 and a bottom of 0.

[3] In years.

*Not significantly different from zero at p < .05, two tailed.

calculations are straightforward (Alwin and Hauser 1972). We first compute the total effect of father's occupation from Model 3 above. We then add son's education to the model, obtaining Model 3B above. The regression coefficient for father's occupation in this equation reflects its direct influence apart from father's education and social race and, crucially, son's education. It will in general be smaller than the total effect (since some of the advantage of having a high status father comes about because it confers an educational advantage). In fact it can be shown that the difference between the total effect and the direct effect $(b_4 - b_7)$ is exactly equal to the *indirect* effect through education. Let us illustrate this by an example. Before the revolution, in the regression equation predicting son's first job on the basis of his father's occupation, education, and social race, father's occupation has a standardized partial regression coefficient of .47; that is the total effect. But when son's education is added to the equation, the regression coefficient of father's occupation drops to .41; that is its direct effect net of son's education. The difference between these two, $.47 - .41 = .06$ is the indirect effect, reflecting the part of the total effect that comes about indirectly through education rather than by inheritance and the like. Exactly the same procedures apply to computing effects in metric rather than standardized terms. Results from these calculations are reported in figures 7.4, 7.10, and 7.12.

6.3 BASIC DATA AND SUPPLEMENTARY TABLES

This section gives the basic correlations, means, and standard deviations underlying the analysis in chapter 7. These are given in tables 6.3A for the population as a whole and table 6.4A for the Spanish and Indian populations separately.

The analysis of chapter 7 is largely based on Model 3, the model which provides the most comprehensive measurement of family background and the one we prefer. Estimates for that model were reported in detail in table 6.2A in the preceding section. Estimates for a variety of other models are shown in less detail in table 6.5A. The models include the less comprehensive Models 1 and 2. Finally, table 6.6A gives the figures for all the results reported graphically in chapter 7.

238

Appendix 6

TABLE 6.3A

CORRELATIONS, MEANS, AND STANDARD DEVIATIONS FOR BOLIVIAN
MALE HEADS OF HOUSEHOLD, 24 OR OLDER, COMING OF AGE
IN THE PREREVOLUTIONARY, REVOLUTIONARY, OR POSTREVOLUTIONARY
PERIODS. UNITS ARE SHOWN IN PARENTHESES.

Variable and cohort[1]	Father's status	Father's education	Social race	Son's education	Son's status
Father's occupational status (0 to 100)					
Prerevolutionary		.687	.594	.628	.526
Revolutionary		.723	.519	.593	.437
Postrevolutionary		.646	.495	.611	.571
Father's education (years)					
Prerevolutionary	.687		.539	.702	.480
Revolutionary	.723		.510	.703	.462
Postrevolutionary	.646		.499	.717	.487
Social race (0 or 1)					
Prerevolutionary	.594	.539		.487	.398
Revolutionary	.519	.510		.400	.332
Postrevolutionary	.495	.499		.395	.242
Son's education (years)					
Prerevolutionary	.628	.702	.487		.559
Revolutionary	.593	.703	.400		.556
Postrevolutionary	.611	.717	.395		.533
Status of son's first job (0 to 100)					
Prerevolutionary	.526	.480	.398	.559	
Revolutionary	.437	.462	.332	.556	
Postrevolutionary	.571	.487	.242	.533	
Means					
Prerevolutionary	25.5	1.91	.400	2.22	31.3
Revolutionary	22.0	1.56	.357	2.51	27.4
Postrevolutionary	25.6	1.49	.378	3.15	29.7
Standard deviations					
Prerevolutionary	26.4	3.81	.490	3.75	24.7
Revolutionary	23.7	3.40	.480	3.47	21.6
Postrevolutionary	26.8	2.90	.486	3.70	23.5

Source: Head of household survey. N=628, 271, and 169 in prerevolutionary, revolutionary, and postrevolutionary cohorts respectively.

[1]Variables defined in chapter 2 and cohorts in chapter 7. Occupational status is in the ethnographic metric.

TABLE 6.4A

CORRELATIONS, MEANS, AND STANDARD DEVIATIONS FOR SPANISH
AND INDIAN MALE HEADS OF HOUSEHOLD, 24 OR OLDER, COMING OF AGE
IN THE PREREVOLUTIONARY, REVOLUTIONARY, OR POSTREVOLUTIONARY
PERIODS. FIGURES FOR SPANISH ABOVE THE MAIN DIAGONAL
AND FOR INDIANS BELOW IT; UNITS ARE SHOWN IN PARENTHESES.

Variable and cohort[1]	Father's status	Father's education	Age	Son's education	Son's status	Means	Standard deviations
Father's occupational status (0 to 100)							
Prerevolutionary		.588	−.063	.478	.423	43.9	28.9
Revolutionary		.727	−.156	.673	.377	38.4	28.3
Postrevolutionary		.548	−.194	.621	.676	42.4	30.1
Father's education (years)							
Prerevolutionary	.426		−.094	.592	.413	4.58	4.96
Revolutionary	.220		−.169	.754	.448	3.80	4.65
Postrevolutionary	.546		−.070	.757	.534	3.51	3.96
Son's age (years)							
Prerevolutionary	−.063	−.101		−.059	.067	54.8	11.5
Revolutionary	−.004	−.053		−.159	−.226	35.3	2.53
Postrevolutionary	−.064	−.127		−.292	−.060	27.4	1.91
Son's education (years)							
Prerevolutionary	.553	.576	−.176		.539	4.41	4.71
Revolutionary	.165	.434	.009		.610	4.32	4.41
Postrevolutionary	.329	.404	−.142		.690	4.99	4.59
Status of son's first job (0 to 100)							
Prerevolutionary	.343	.218	−.200	.332		43.2	27.7
Revolutionary	.229	.227	.019	.323		37.1	25.6
Postrevolutionary	.344	.358	−.154	.199		36.5	26.3
Means							
Prerevolutionary	11.9	0.33	56.3	0.70	23.2		
Revolutionary	12.9	0.29	34.9	1.45	22.0		
Postrevolutionary	15.2	0.46	27.5	1.97	24.9		
Standard deviations							
Prerevolutionary	14.3	1.39	13.8	1.73	18.6		
Revolutionary	13.9	0.98	2.5	2.19	17.2		
Postrevolutionary	18.0	1.27	2.2	2.45	20.3		

Source: Head of household survey. N=245, 94, and 63 for the Spanish in the pre-revolutionary, revolutionary, and postrevolutionary cohorts respectively and for Indians 368, 169, and 103 respectively.

[1]Variables defined in chapter 2 and cohorts in chapter 7. Occupational status is in the ethnographic metric.

TABLE 6.5A
Various Models of the Influence of Family Background on the Status of Respondent's First Job, for Bolivian Male Heads of Household, 24 or Older, in Prerevolutionary (PreR), Revolutionary (Revol), and Postrevolutionary (PostR) Cohorts Separately. Metric Partial Regression Coefficients.

Model and independent variables[1]	Cohort					
	PreR	Revol	PostR	PreR	Revol	PostR
1. Number of cases for panels A to D	(628)	(271)	(169)	—	—	—
Panel A: Model 1						
2. Father's occupation	.49	.40	.50	.27	.15	.34
3. Son's education	—	—	—	2.5	2.8	1.9
4. (Percent of variance, R^2)	(28)	(19)	(33)	(36)	(33)	(38)
5. (Constant)	(19)	(19)	(17)	(19)	(17)	(15)
Panel B: Model 2						
6. Father's occupation	.35	.20	.39	.25	.13*	.33
7. Father's education	1.5	1.9	1.6	0.3*	0.4*	0.4*
8. Son's education	—	—	—	2.4	2.7	1.7
9. (Percent of variance, R^2)	(30)	(24)	(35)	(36)	(33)	(38)
10. (Constant)	(20)	(19)	(17)	(19)	(17)	(15)
Panel C: Model 3						
11. Father's occupation	.31	.17	.41	.23	.10*	.36
12. Father's education	1.3	1.8	1.9	0.2*	0.2*	0.7*
13. Social race	5	4*	−5*	3*	4*	−5*
14. Son's education	—	—		2.3	2.7	1.7
15. (Percent of variance, R^2)	(31)	(24)	(36)	(37)	(33)	(39)
16. (Constant)	(19)	(19)	(18)	(19)	(17)	(16)
Panel D: Farm origins						
17. Father's occupation	.26	.08*	.42	.19	.03*	.35
18. Father's education	1.3	2.0	1.7	0.2*	0.4*	0.5*
19. Farm origin	− 9	− 9	2*	− 8	− 7	3*
20. Son's education	—	—	—	2.3	2.6	1.7
21. (Percent of variance, R^2)	(32)	(26)	(35)	(38)	(34)	(38)
22. (Constant)	(29)	(29)	(15)	(27)	(25)	(12)
Panel E: Respondents of Spanish origin only						
23. Father's occupation	.26	.10*	.48	.18	−.06*	.36
24. Father's education	1.4	2.0	1.6*	0.3*	0.3*	−0.3*
25. Son's education	—	—	—	2.4	3.8	2.7
26. (Percent of variance, R^2)	(22)	(21)	(50)	(33)	(37)	(58)
27. (Constant)	(25)	(26)	(11)	(23)	(23)	(9)
28. (Number of cases)	(245)	(94)	(63)	—	—	—
Panel F: Respondents of Indian origin only						
29. Father's occupation	.45	.28	.39	.30	.22	.35

TABLE 6.5A (continued)

Model and independent variables[1]	Cohort					
	PreR	*Revol*	*PostR*	*PreR*	*Revol*	*PostR*
30. Son's education	—	—	—	2.2	2.3	0.8*
31. (Percent of variance, R^2)	(12)	(05)	(12)	(15)	(14)	(13)
32. (Constant)	(18)	(18)	(19)	(18)	(16)	(18)
33. (Number of cases)	(368)	(169)	(103)	—	—	—

Source: Head of household survey. Calculated from data in tables 6.3A and 6.4A.

[1]Variables defined in chapter 2 and cohorts in chapter 7.
*Not statistically significant at $p < .05$, two tailed.

TABLE 6.6A
MORE EXACT DATA FOR THE ANALYSIS REPORTED
GRAPHICALLY IN CHAPTER 7.[1]

Figure (see text for full description)	Before the revolution	During the revolution	After the revolution
For Figure 7.1			
A. Correlation	.526	.437	.571
B. Metric regression coefficient	.491	.398	.500
For Figure 7.2			
A. Advantage estimated by Model 1	49.1	39.8	50.0
B. Advantage estimated by Model 2	49.8	39.8	55.6
C. Advantage estimated by Model 3	49.2	39.6	56.0
D. Percent of variance, Model 1	27.5	19.1	32.7
E. Percent of variance, Model 2	30.3	23.5	35.0
F. Percent of variance, Model 3	30.8	24.1	35.9
For Figure 7.3			
A. Metric regression coefficient	31.0	17.0	41.5
B. Standardized coefficient	.332	.187	.474
For Figure 7.4			
A. Direct, in status points	22.9	10.3	35.6
B. Direct, standardized	.246	.113	.406
C. Indirect, in status points	8.1	6.7	5.9
D. Indirect, standardized	.086	.074	.068
For Figure 7.5			
A. Advantage, in years	9.08	8.72	10.83
B. Variance explained	53.3	51.0	55.2
For Figure 7.6			
A. Advantage, in status points	13.6	18.4	19.0
B. Advantage, standardized	.202	.279	.235
For Figure 7.7			
A. Property, in status points	31.0	17.0	41.5
B. Human capital, in status points	13.6	18.4	19.8
C. Property, standardized	.332	.187	.474
D. Human capital, standardized	.202	.279	.235

TABLE 6.6A (continued)

Figure (see text for full description	Before the revolution	During the revolution	After the revolution
For Figure 7.8			
A. Metric coefficient	2.33	2.69	1.67
A'. Metric, alternative estimate	2.33	2.69	2.67
B. Standardized coefficient	.354	.432	.263
B'. Standardized, alternative estimate	.354	.432	.387
For Figure 7.9			
A. Metric regression coefficient	.405	.341	.590
B. Correlation	.423	.377	.676
C. Advantage of elite son	40.9	30.9	63.9
For Figure 7.10			
A. Direct advantage of property	18.4	−5.8	35.7
B. Indirect advantage of property	7.9	15.6	12.1
C. Advantage of human capital	14.6	21.1	16.1
For Figure 7.11			
A and C. Metric and advantage	.445	.284	.389
B. Correlation	.343	.229	.344
For Figure 7.12			
A. Direct advantage of property	29.9	22.4	35.3
B. Indirect advantage of property	14.7	6.0	3.6
For Figure 7.13			
Bolivia	.526	.437	.571
Poland	.631 .577	.427	.510

Source: Head of household survey. Table 6.5A gives number of cases (see line 1 for figures 7.1 to 7.8 and lines 28 and 33 for figures 7.9 to 7.12).

[1]Variables defined in chapter 2 and cohorts in chapter 7. Further details on calculations given in Appendix 6, section 2.

Notes

1. Theory of Revolution's Effects

1. We use the term *peasants* broadly to include not only the ideal type "rural cultivators whose surpluses are transferred to a dominant group of rulers that uses the surplus both to underwrite its own standard of living and distribute the remainder to groups in society that do not farm but must be fed for their specific goods and services in turn" (Wolf 1966:3–4) but also farm laborers and other landless agricultural workers.

2. Specifically, Hypotheses 1, 4, 5, 6, 7, 9, and 10 apply.

3. Conceptually we would like to just add these up and take the average but arithmetic turns out to obstruct conceptual clarity: the positive differences always balance the negative ones, so the sum is always zero. We can avoid this annoyance by squaring the differences and then adding up all the squared differences and taking the average. This gives the variance. We could use that as a measure but it is more customary, and conceptually equivalent in any case, to use its square root, which is the familiar standard deviation. The other familiar inequality measure, the Gini coefficient, is much the same. It begins with the same differences between all possible pairs but gets around the arithmetical annoyance by taking the absolute value of the differences and then averaging those. See the excellent discussions by Paglin (1975:601) and Allison (1978).

4. The correlation between the Gini and the corresponding measure based on the standard deviation, computed over the income distributions of 56 countries, is .84 (computed from Paukert 1973:table 6), and other popular measures are highly correlated with the Gini and so presumably with the standard deviation (Alker and Russett 1964 report correlations averaging .87 computed over various data of practical interest).

5. We do this as part of our computer simulation of the theory, showing that the changes in the standard deviation of income implied by our theory are closely paralleled by changes in the Gini coefficient.

6. Inflation does not actually destroy savings and the like in the way that fire destroys buildings; no real resources are destroyed. Rather, it effectively transfers the value from the saver to the government which is running the money-printing presses. But the consequences for the individual saver, and for inequality and social mobility, are much the same as destruction since his money is lost with little or no benefit to himself.

7. There will, of course, be some political positions opened up for the revolution's supporters but these are few and, since we are dealing with effects on the population at large rather than for the governmental elite, they can reasonably be ignored. Nonetheless, it is worth noting that success in the revolutionary party, and in the revolutionary government afterward, is not unlike success in other large organizations. It depends heavily on education and training, that is to say, on human capital, and so indirectly on family background; it is no accident that virtually all revolutionary leaders are well educated and that most come from privileged homes (for it is such homes that are best able to educate their children). So in this way inequality remains within the revolutionary party, in ways not unlike in the general population.

8. Especially for the peasantry (tied to the land, they were usually subject to effective

control and stringent restrictions) and residents of small rural towns (also subject to effective control) but less to residents of large urban areas and perhaps not at all for workers in large plantations and rural industries, since revolution does not basically change their opportunity structure and their wages are often subject to political control afterward.

9. In principle peasants might devote their new opportunities solely to leisure rather than accumulation, working only long enough to earn their customary wage. But in practice they are poor enough, and materialistic enough, not to do that (Miracle and Fetter 1970).

10. The social and economic restraints which prerevolutionary peasants created to restrict inequality will in practice be eroded, if not destroyed, by revolution and the expansion of economic opportunities. In much of traditional Latin America, for example, the fiesta system effectively exchanged wealth for prestige, inhibiting the growth of economic inequality (Cancian 1965). As a man's career progressed he took on an orderly system of lesser fiesta offices which paralleled his growing power and influence, culminating in his fifties with a major political role in the traditional community government and sponsorship of a major and expensive fiesta. After the revolution peasants are usually unwilling to exhaust their savings in this way, in part because the economy provides alternative attractions but in part because the prestige obtained by sponsoring a fiesta declined. Much of the prestige came from the intimate association with power in the traditional political system and revolution breaks that down, creating new sources of power separate from the traditional offices and usually dominated by younger, more cosmopolitan leaders with little involvement in the fiesta system.

11. Although the rest of our theory is strongly supported by our data from Bolivia, the claim that education becomes *more* valuable after the revolution is not, although neither is it refuted. The evidence is perhaps most consistent with a claim that education remained equally valuable afterward (see chaps. 6 and 7 for details).

12. The standard deviation, our measure of inequality, is of course a simple function of the (squared) deviation from the mean. As peasants get closer to the mean the deviation decreases, and as they get further away from it, it increases.

13. Inequality actually begins to increase somewhat before they reach the mean. As they improve their position, that will usually raise the mean for the society as a whole and poor peasants will then be further behind, which increases inequality.

14. For these purposes, an increase in opportunities has the same effect as the end of exploitation. The group for which opportunities increase or exploitation ends plays the role of peasants and other exploited groups in a radical political revolution.

15. The correlation between the status of occupations and the average income of people working in them is rarely below .7 (Treiman 1977:112, 114). Calculated over individuals, the correlation between status and income is of course lower (since it reflects differences in age, experience, industry, and other individual characteristics) but generally runs around .4 in a wide variety of societies (Kelley 1978; Kelley and Perlman 1971). For over a dozen countries in the cross-cultural data set described in chap. 2, we found an average correlation of .4, with Bolivia higher than average (see chap. 3). The correlation seems to be equally high in socialist and communist countries, for example .51 in Sweden and .44 in Poland.

16. The correlation between the status of occupations and the average education of people working in them is high, averaging around .7 in various societies (Treiman 1977:114). Calculated over individuals, the correlation between status and education is of course lower (because it reflects individual circumstances, differences between industries, changes over time, and the like) but is very rarely below .5. For over a dozen diverse societies in the cross-cultural data set described in chap. 2, we found correlations averaging .6; Bolivia, at .66, was a little higher than average. The correlations seem to be at least as high in socialist and communist societies, for example .66 in Sweden and no less than .76 in Poland.

17. The correlations average around .6 or .7 (Hammel 1970:660; Gusfield and Schwartz 1963; Rossi 1973). In an (aggregate level) analysis of occupations in the United States, we found high correlations between occupational prestige, on the one hand, and income (r=.8), education (r=.8), and the *Dictionary of Occupational Titles* well-known data-people-things ratings on the other hand (r=.8 for complexity of data manipulations involved in the job, r=.6 for complexity of tasks involving people, and r=.2 for complexity in dealing with physical objects. *See* United States Department of Labor, 1965, for the data-people-things classification and Kelley and Treiman 1978*b* for the analysis). A factor analysis of these and other characteristics of occupations shows a very strong first factor dominated by prestige (with a factor loading of .9), education (.9), income (.8), complexity of tasks involving data (.9), and complexity of tasks involving people (.8).

18. Although there is unanimity as to the importance of occupational status, exactly how to measure it is a matter of lively dispute, particularly between proponents of prestige measures and advocates of some form of socioeconomic status score. But whatever the technical details, prestige and socioeconomic status are highly correlated in practice, typically around .7 or higher, so for the moment we need not trouble with the details. This is taken up in detail in chap. 2 and in App. 3.

19. For these illustrations, we measure status in the cross-cultural status scale defined in chap. 2. Details underlying the following calculations are in Kelley, Robinson, and Klein (1980).

20. Assuming, as we generally will, that the relation between father's and son's status is approximately linear, we have in effect defined inherited privilege as the metric regression coefficient of father's occupational status. Assuming further that the variances of father's and son's status are approximately equal, as often they are, this is equal to the product-moment correlation between father's and son's status. That is now the conventional, and appropriate, measure of inherited status or (low) social mobility. We will usually speak of the "correlation" between father's and son's status rather than, more pedantically, of the "metric regression coefficient."

21. The seminal work is Blau and Duncan (1967) and a long and flourishing tradition follows in that paradigm. See, among many others, Duncan, Featherman, and Duncan (1972); Featherman and Hauser (1976); Haller, Otto, Meier, and Ohlendorf (1974); Kelley (1973); Treiman and Terrell (1975*a* and 1975*b*).

22. Our measure does however differ from the concept of social mobility in that it pays no attention to whether the child rises above the parents' status or sinks below it. So if, for example, children of high status families always got better jobs than children of low status families we would say there was great status inheritance *regardless* of whether all children rose above their parents' status, or stayed the same, or fell below their parents. Whether children will rise above or fall below their parents will depend on two things, first, status inheritance in the sense we have defined it and, second, the nature of the jobs available in the economy. Assuming that the range of jobs available in the economy does not change (and revolutions do not usually change them very much) then most children will be close to their parents' status when status inheritance is high (i.e., there will be little social mobility in the old "rise or fall" sense) but if instead there is no status inheritance, half will be above and half below (i.e., there will be great social mobility in the older sense). This simple link between status inheritance and social mobility will, however, be more complicated if the economy is changing. If the economy is growing so that there are more good jobs than there used to be, then there would be more upward mobility than would otherwise be the case, while if the economy is declining, there will be more downward mobility. With this in mind, it is easy enough to translate from status inheritance to the older concepts of upward and downward mobility, although there is little to be gained from doing so. It is to avoid this confusion that we use the term "status inheritance" rather than the more general term "social mobility."

23. We believe that our theory applies equally to sons and daughters. There is, in fact, substantial evidence in other contexts that the process of status attainment is very much

the same for men and women (see Treiman and Terrell 1975*b*, and the references given there). But for stylistic convenience, we will generally use the masculine pronoun.

24. In exceptional circumstances, a revolution might even increase it, if property played a minor role before the revolution and human capital had a greatly increased payoff afterward. But that is unlikely, especially in the predominantly peasant societies we are considering. Furthermore, property plays a role in transmitting human capital from one generation to the next so economic redistribution will reduce the inheritance of human capital, which tends to decrease status inheritance.

25. Counting personal and corporate savings together (our model does not distinguish between them), a figure in the neighborhood of 10 to 12 percent seems normal for savings in developing societies (Kuznets 1966:236, 406). This does not include investments in skills and human capital, for which we in effect allow another 4 to 6 percent. In the baseline model, a typical poor peasant saves roughly 3 percent of his income, a big peasant 14 percent, the nonagricultural middle classes 15 percent, and the elite 29 percent.

26. Many modern income tax systems have a "standard deduction," an amount below which income is tax free. It is obvious that this tends to make the tax structure progressive since it shelters a large fraction of poor people's incomes from tax but shelters only a small fraction of rich people's incomes. The absence of taxes on income below the subsistence level works in exactly the same way.

27. We posit no change in their savings behavior but rather that they continue to save the same percentage of their incomes above the subsistence line as they did before the revolution. But now that their surplus above subsistence is much larger, the amount of their savings increases both in absolute terms and as a percentage of their total income. However, there are straightforward economic reasons to suppose that they would save a higher *percentage* of their incomes above subsistence (and in most societies the more prosperous do save more than the poor in proportional terms, although not necessarily a great deal more). If that were the case here, it would increase inequality among the previously exploited population even more than in our (more conservative) assumptions.

28. The conceptual issues were discussed at some length earlier in this chapter.

29. There is a difference in this between inequality as measured by the Gini coefficient and inequality as measured by the standard deviation. A simple proportional increase in income will increase the standard deviation proportionately but it also increases the mean income, and by the same proportion. The Gini, which is a measure of deviation divided by the mean, is left unchanged. The rise in the Gini comes about for the reasons noted in the next two paragraphs.

30. There could be exceptions to this, depending on just how the tax burden was allocated. It is possible, for example, that in some parts of Medieval Europe the middle and working class residents of some large towns were politically and militarily strong enough to resist many of the taxes the traditional elite would have liked to impose and wound up paying a lesser percent of their income in taxes than their more vulnerable counterparts in small towns and the countryside. If so, then the end of such exploitation would be likely to increase inequality in the small towns and the countryside but might or might not increase inequality among the combined population of large cities, small towns, and countryside.

31. This is especially true since there is typically great variability in peasant incomes between good years and bad. Hence, peasants may (justifiably) feel that today's surplus is just insurance against tomorrow's privation.

32. This may well be why peasants are so notoriously careful to hide their wealth.

33. We assume that these losses apply to the savings and investments made over the course of a lifetime but not to the basic property and human capital with which one begins life. This has the effect of making the more prosperous, and older, segments of the previously exploited population lose more from disruption and destruction, which seems a reasonable assumption. While our model offers a rather rough and ready

treatment of this complex series of changes, it should suffice as a first approximation.

34. We increase all three by the same proportion, in effect assuming that economic growth increases the returns to unskilled labor at the same rate that it increases the returns to property and human capital. It may well be, however, that economic development increases the returns to human capital faster than those for unskilled labor and, possibly, faster than those for land and other forms of property. If so, that would lead to even greater inequality than implied by our model.

35. Not a doubling of these because the increased income allows more saving and investment, which in turn increases income.

36. In this model, economic growth is at roughly four percent per year for the postrevolutionary generation and the new elite is half as exploitative as the old. The nonagricultural middle and working classes are poor, with incomes averaging only some twenty percent above those of small peasants.

37. In this model, there is no economic growth following the revolution and the new elite is half as exploitative as the old. The nonagricultural middle and working classes are prosperous, with incomes averaging something over twice those of small peasants.

2. Bolivia: The Setting, Data and Methods

1. Unfortunately, survey data are necessary, since experience in other societies clearly shows that well-informed fieldworkers, not to mention less knowledgeable observers, cannot reliably describe patterns of intergenerational mobility either in the sense of agreeing among themselves or in the sense of agreeing with the results of systematic surveys. Even for the United States, to take a conspicuous example, in the days before reliable survey data were available there was a lively debate on the amount of social mobility in comparison with Great Britain and other European societies, with quite diverse opinions expressed but a majority supporting the view that advantages of birth were substantially smaller in the United States than in the older, more tradition-bound European societies. But, in fact Britain is a substantially more open society than the United States, and other European societies are varied, some more and some less open (see fig. 3.5).

2. In the three smaller communities all were included. In the three larger communities samples of between one and two hundred were selected randomly from the census list but the sample snowballed outward from them to include people named in sociometric questions (friends, relatives, people with power or influence, etc.). A few additional men identified as influential by the resident anthropologists were also included.

3. Given the financial constraints and the original investigator's strong interest in community decision making in this male-dominated society, the limitation is not unreasonable. More than two-thirds of the women are housewives or unpaid family workers.

4. We projected forward the age-specific illiteracy rates for 1950 (República de Bolivia 1955:112) to the corresponding cohorts in our data and estimated rates for the younger cohorts by assuming that the secular decline (about 8 percent per decade since the turn of the century) continued.

5. Correlations among the variables with which we will be mainly concerned (education, occupation, father's education, and father's occupation) differ in absolute value by an average of less than .02, under 4 percent of their value, while regression coefficients differ by even less.

6. Exact significance tests for weighted samples are not readily available but since we kept the adjusted number of cases equal to the true one and the unweighted regression results are virtually identical to the weighted ones, the approximation should be close.

7. The income inequality figures referring to the 1960s, which were used in several

secondary sources, were apparently estimated by the Bolivian government largely on the basis of income distributions in other Latin American countries at roughly Bolivia's level of development (Zuvekas 1977:8).

8. We refer to these as "Spanish," although a variety of other terms are used in one or another part of Bolivia to separate them from campesinos and to mark further distinctions among the Spanish group.

9. We are confident that the data used in this classification are reliable. Under the circumstances, anyone who could comfortably have spoken Spanish in the interview would have done so and, in any event, use of Spanish was very closely correlated with self-reports of language used in other contexts.

10. The items are number of domestic servants, presence of electricity in the house, possession of some form of sanitary facilities however simple (the alternative is use of the fields or streets), possession of a wooden or concrete rather than dirt floor, and number of rooms in the house. A principal components factor analysis with communalities estimated iteratively showed only one factor with eigenvalue greater than one. It explained 49 percent of the variance. The items were combined into a scale using the factor scoring weights for this factor.

11. It would make little difference if we had instead used untransformed scores. For comparison, correlations between standard of living in its two forms and various other variables are:

	Untransformed	Cumulative
Father's occupational status	.51	.52
Father's education	.44	.51
Education	.57	.49
Occupational status	.56	.57

12. This refers to different *occupations*, not to different employers, and of course many people with the same job throughout their lives will nonetheless have worked for many different employers.

13. We looked at the mean education and standard of living of incumbents and tried to group only occupations that were reasonably similar in those respects.

14. This was based on the raw standard of living measure instead of the cumulative version in order to stay as close as possible to the original data.

15. The correlations between current occupation scored by the standard of living scale and the same occupation scored by the education-based scale was .9. The two measures had virtually identical correlations with father's occupational status, education, standard of living, and language, the correlations differing by only .03 on the average.

16. We originally had planned to use Treiman's (1977) Standard International Occupational Prestige Scale. It turns out, however, that this does not do justice to the Bolivian situation, for much the same reasons that no prestige scale seems to do justice to the U.S. or Australian stratification systems (Featherman, Jones, and Hauser 1975). Correlations using prestige as a measure of status are consistently lower than corresponding correlations using other measures. Furthermore, a variety of other measures (including those we use) all give similar results, with prestige being the conspicuous exception. This is consistent with the claim (made by Featherman, Jones, and Hauser, among others) that prestige is simply a more fallible measure than the alternatives. But it is also consistent with Treiman's argument that prestige measures an aspect of occupational position close to Weber's status, while the others measure something closer to Weber's class, that it is class rather than status that underlies the correlations between occupation, education, and income and that it is class that is transmitted from one generation to the next. Since we are particularly concerned with the links between occupation, education, and income and with the transmission of advantage from one generation to the next, on either

argument we should not use prestige. For further details and a detailed presentation of the evidence, see Kelley and Treiman (1978:47–59).

3. Prerevolutionary Economy and Society

1. The exact figures vary somewhat from source to source, depending on details of the definitions used and treatments of less than perfect data available. But all agree in placing Bolivia among the more heavily agricultural (and poorer) societies of the world. The figures in table 3.1 which pertain to the total labor force, show a somewhat higher percent agricultural than those of figure 3.1 pertaining to the male labor force.

2. Measuring wealth in other ways gives a similar picture, perhaps slightly more favorable to Bolivia. It ranked,for example, not too far below the medium in per capita kilowatt hours of electricity consumed.

3. We have estimated this from the 1950 census figures (República de Bolivia 1955) but the exact figure is not given there. We assumed that the medium of those with some schooling, reported as 4 years, was the same as the mean and then adjusted for the 46 percent of the population without schooling, obtaining an estimate of 2.2. In our rural survey of the mean for men who came of age before the revolution was, as it happens, also 2.2 years.

4. Exaggeration in the figures supplied to UNESCO is by no means unknown.

5. The census data do not allow a distinction to be made between small farmers and large farmers. As a rough approximation we have estimated them on the basis of our survey data, assuming that in Bolivia as a whole the same proportion of all farmers were actually large farmers as we found in our survey areas.

6. For a detailed description, see McEwen 1975.

7. Fourteen years after the revolution, an out-of-town couple rented an isolated former hacienda house half a mile from the nearest neighbor. The wife complains of loneliness, "besides, the peasants don't want anything to do with the hacienda-house. It is a remembrance of subjugation to them, so I doubt we will ever be friends with the people who live around here."

8. We have defined functional literacy as having four or more years of education. This is a rough and approximate definition but not unreasonable; it differs from the Bolivian census's very generous definition of one year, but is much more realistic given the deficiencies of Bolivian schools and the great difficulties they face.

9. The occupational classification used in these comparative data is Treiman's scheme (1977:203–208). Since the distribution between large farmers, small farmers, and farm workers is not always made in these data, we have combined all farmers for the purposes of this comparison. The data are from Kelley and Treiman (1978:fig. 5).

10. Social race, essentially a measure of linguistic background but one with wide and pervasive implications in the Bolivian setting, is defined in chapter 2.

11. In this, although not in the other matters we are dealing with here, there are noticeable differences between the occupational groups we have combined at status level 32 in table 3.4, but the other groups are quite homogenous. We have, of course, only combined groups in order to have reasonably large categories for the tabular analysis; the correlation and regression analyses reported elsewhere use no such simplification.

12. The income inequality data reported in several secondary sources seem to have been made up out of whole cloth by the Bolivian government (Zuvekas 1977:8).

13. Our data of course do not cover Bolivia's relatively few urban centers. Evidence from other Latin American cities, presented below, suggest that they probably are also characterized by great rigidity, possibly even greater rigidity than in rural areas.

14. We can look at the relation between family background and first job, since our older respondents started their careers before the revolution.

15. Strictly speaking, neither sons nor fathers are a generation, since they are all of quite different ages. But it is convenient to speak of them that way nonetheless.

16. The occupational categories are collapsed somewhat to keep a reasonably large number of cases in each but the categories that were combined were very similar so that little distortion is introduced.

17. Appendix 2 gives a simple description of correlation and regression statistics which may be of interest to those unfamiliar with them.

18. Readers might wish for some standard by which to say whether these figures are large or small. By way of comparison, the correlation between fathers and sons is .50 for traits which are determined genetically (e.g., height). The correlation between father's and son's IQ, a trait for which both environmental and genetic influences seem strong, is also about .50. It is interesting that the correlation between father's and son's occupational status in Bolivia reaches these substantial heights. For a further comparison, the correlation between occupation and income for men in the modern United States is .46 and that between occupation and voting behavior only .16.

19. The cross-cultural data are national samples and are analyzed by methods precisely comparable to those we have used for Bolivia. The Latin American data are mostly urban samples, less representative than national ones, and occupational status is coded differently than we have done although all nine Latin American studies used the same methods and codes and so are fully comparable with each other. The disadvantage of the cross-cultural collection is lack of coverage of Latin America and the fact that son's occupation is current occupation and not first job. This last is probably not, however, of major importance since the correlations between father's occupation and first job are generally very close to those between father's occupation and current occupation, differing by an average of only .01 in absolute value in the eleven countries of the Latin American data set where both are available (Kelley 1978:table 1). The Latin American data are mainly from the Centro Latino-Americano de Demografía's excellent study "Urban Fertility in Latin America," with over 20,000 cases, usually from the capital of each country; details are in Kelley (1978). Bolivia and the United States appear in both collections but the different methods used lead to essentially the same substantive conclusions as is shown in figure 3.5.

20. This appears to come about mainly because the cross-cultural status scores do not capture all the idiosyncrasies of local occupational hierarchies. The scores used in the Latin American study are, in contrast, more clearly adapted to local conditions.

21. In our model, a simple but reasonable and conventional one, we assume that father's occupation and education are both causes of son's education and all three are causes of son's occupational attainments.

22. Appendix 2 provides an informal discussion of the meaning of various regression statistics that may be of interest to readers unfamiliar with them.

23. The calculation is $100 \times .039 = 3.9$ years.

24. This advantage is much less than one might have supposed from the simple averages we saw in table 3.5 where elite white-collar sons got about nine years of education compared to about a year for small farmers' sons at the very bottom of the hierarchy, a difference of seven years. This discrepancy reflects a weakness in the tabular analysis in that it did not take into account the close links between father's occupation and his own education and its influence on his son's education; the regression results show that much of the apparent effect should be attributed to father's human capital rather than his occupational status per se.

25. This is $10 \times .503 = 5.03$ years.

26. The total effect of father's occupation (or any other variable) in models of this sort is always the same whether intervening variables like education are ignored, as in Panel 2, or included, as in Panel 3. This means that our estimates of the advantage of family background are correct even though we have not measured all the intervening links between family and career and, indeed, do not even know what all of them are.

27. It is .346−.253 = .093 which is .093/.346 = 27 percent of the total (for technical details see Alwin and Hauser 1974).

28. Elsewhere we have discussed more fully the ways in which wealth might help and suggested evidence that it is more important in capitalist societies at Bolivia's level of development than it is in more advanced ones (Kelley 1978). Note, incidentally, it turns out that the process linking family background to son's occupation is rather different for Indians (for whom father's occupation is overwhelmingly the dominant factor) than for the Spanish (for whom father's education is more important). We deal with this again at the end of chapter 7.

29. This is in accord with the theory of social mobility presented in chapter 1, which argued that status is passed from one generation to the next through human capital and property but not in other ways.

30. As we have seen, differences between Spanish and Indian are large but so are differences in their parents' education and occupational status and these largely account for the differences in education and occupational status. The remaining advantage of being born into a Spanish family was small with a standardized partial regression coefficient of .08 on education and .07 on occupation, only a small fraction of the corresponding figures for father's education and occupation. There is, however, a complex interaction here and we deal with it in chapter 7.

31. We included a variable measuring farm origin in the analysis together with social race and the usual variables. Farm origin had a path of −.07 on education −.14 on first job. Both of these effects are statistically significant but they are modest in size and omitting them from the model simplifies the analysis without any important conceptual or empirical loss.

32. These data, described in chapter 2, are clearly the best for our purposes. The countries are listed in note 1 of the table. The Latin American data we used in some earlier comparisons lack data on father's education, and so must be omitted here.

33. The Bolivian figures are once again for first job while the others are current occupation. For reasons indicated in note 19 above, this is unlikely to greatly distort the results.

4. The Revolution

1. For further details see Klein (1968) and the references cited there.

2. Some vivid images of the period remained during the fieldwork a dozen years later. A Coroico man recited a tale told him by the wife of an hacendado: "She told me the story about how they got thrown off the finca . . . she told me that right after the Reforma, a group of their indios came to the house and told the family that they must get out of the house by nightfall, otherwise anything could happen to the women. So the family had to clear out, and without taking anything. She was just sick when she told me this, so upset, and losing everything that way." The period was also marked by a certain amount of more random violence. A Sorata woman recounts: "But they killed in broad daylight, right on the corner by the Gunther [the largest store in town]. . . . They shot him, right there. My mother told me that don Alberto and some others were coming out of a cocktailito in doña Emilia's house, and as they came out I don't know for sure, something provoked the peasants—they had been drinking—and they fired a shot into him." The interviewer asked what justice followed: "Justice . . . ha, señorita, not then. Then the government was in favor of the peasants, and nothing happened." But what did the family do, asked the interviewer: "What could they do? And there was the mother screaming, crying right there . . . they couldn't do anything."

3. The estimate of the number of families benefiting from land reform is from Wilkie (1974a:3). We estimate the number of farm families from the proportion of the population in agriculture (Wilkie and Reich 1977:table 105), times the total population in 1960

(a date close to the time of most of the reforms), divided by an estimate of the average family size. We estimate the last somewhat arbitrarily as five, a figure close to the actual average in Bolivia. The estimated proportion of farm families benefiting is then the first of these figures divided by the second. This is a very rough estimate, since all the figures used in the estimate are themselves approximate and the procedure involves further assumptions (e.g., that farm and urban families are the same size). The estimate for Mexico is particularly suspect since the population has grown enormously since the reform and the reform itself was spread over a considerable period of time. Nonetheless, these figures give a rough indication of the extent of reform and clearly show that Bolivia's was among the most extensive in Latin America.

4. Support for the party was probably about twice as high as actual membership, judging by 1966 data. At that time we have data both on preferences and on actual membership. Sixty-six percent of our respondents then indicated a preference for one party or another while at the same time only 33 percent were actually members of a party.

5. The data are from the districts of Punata and Mizaue where 300 and 143 heads of household, respectively, were interviewed (Oropeza and Romero 1972:76, 89, 107, and 110 especially). The figures mentioned in the text refer to peasants only, with some small-town residents in Punata excluded. Except for Lavaud's data (described below) and ours, these seem to be the only survey data yet available. Virtually all observers agree with these conclusions, however, reporting very high rates of participation in ex-hacienda areas of the altiplano. Cochabamba, and the Yungas.

6. Lavaud (1972) interviewed 330 households in the Achachicalo district.

5. Popular Perceptions of the Revolution

1. Spanish language interviews, the majority, were recorded verbatim. Aymara language interviews were recorded in Spanish by the interviewers, all of whom were bilingual.

2. Here and elsewhere we use "rich" and "well-born" to translate the Spanish *ricos* and *gente decente*, respectively. These and related words, with rich connotations in Bolivia, are treated in detail in McEwen (1975).

3. Peasants and nonpeasants had much the same views of this, so we do not show them separately.

4. Up to three comments were recorded for each answer, so the percentages in the table add up to more than 100.

5. Of course some respondents mentioned both reasons. We are saying that a fifth of them mentioned the first reason and that a fifth, including some of the same respondents, mentioned the second.

6. Nor was there popular support for that elsewhere in Bolivia.

7. Very few people gave reservations or qualifications to this question and they were not very informative. The most common were legalistic reservations about the land reform laws and arguments turning on the allegedly poor economic performance of peasants once they got the land (a matter which we deal with later).

8. Some 515 respondents mentioned at least one specific gain or loss from the revolution and percentages are on that basis. Not quite three hundred more thought the revolution led to gains, or to losses, but without going into more detail. We deal with this later in table 5.7.

9. In this context the reference to peasants, *campesinos*, would normally mean Indian peasants of Aymara or Quechua background.

6. Revolution's Effects

1. To answer these questions, we will draw heavily on national accounts data and on a variety of published and unpublished sources which deal with issues not covered in our

survey data. Most of these data go back to 1950, when Bolivia had its first census since the turn of the century; earlier data are scarce and fragmentary. Unfortunately, no retrospective questions on income were asked in the head of household survey, nor would the answers about income a dozen years in the past have been trustworthy even if they had been asked, for reasons explained in chapter 2. So for information on income we are forced to rely on more indirect, albeit not unpersuasive, evidence.

2. There are some figures that suggest that the revolution caused an appreciable decline in inequality in the distribution of land. Land was very unequally distributed before the revolution with a Gini coefficient of inequality of .95. By 1963 that seems to have declined to .87 (Zuvekas 1977:18). The 1963 figures, however, are very dubious (Zuvekas 1977:3).

3. See Simmons (1974) for supporting data for a single village. Our conclusion is, however, not the only possible one, given the rather fragmentary evidence available. Another possibility is that production stayed the same but that less went to the market (since peasants consumed more themselves) and that the increase in home consumption was not well measured in the national accounts statistics (R. Clark 1968; Patch 1967). The national figures do, however, attempt to take this change into account, although improvement in housing ("imputed rental income") is not estimated. It is our best judgment that the national accounts estimates in figure 6.1 are broadly correct, and in this we follow the prevailing view among those who have considered the matter.

4. There was also an enduring decline in Cuba although the implications are clouded by the U.S. economic boycott that was imposed shortly after the revolution (Lewis-Beck 1979).

5. Wennergren and Whitaker conclude that "Trucks, however, provide an inexpensive means of transportation among small villages and to the large urban centers. . . . The system has greatly increased demand in rural areas for manufactured products, promoted more efficient product markets as producers seek buyers in urban centers, and fostered a culturalization process among the campesinos exposed to urban life" (1975:151; see also p. 278).

6. Paul Turovsky has collected and analyzed land ownership data from 400 haciendas before and after the revolution and finds no case in which peasants' customary holdings were redistributed (personal communication).

7. We estimate that primary school enrollment amounted to about 7.5 percent of the total population at the time of the revolution and then grew to twice that by the late 1960s.

8. The main difficulty, especially in a society like Bolivia where people may start their schooling rather late in childhood and may continue it intermittently, lies in making a reasonable estimate of the age at which we assume their education is complete, and hence what cohort they should be assigned to. For reasons set out in chapter 7, we define those who were twenty-six or older at the time of the revolution as the prerevolutionary cohort, those reaching that age in the next nine years as the revolutionary cohort, and the remainder as the postrevolutionary cohort (save that men twenty-three or under at the time of the survey are excluded on the grounds that they may not have completed their education). There is of course some ambiguity in any such classification (e.g., men in their early twenties at the time of the revolution may have considered themselves too old to go to school even though we count them in the revolutionary cohort) but it should suffice to show the main trends. The principal effect of misclassifying people would be to reduce differences between time periods and so make the revolution's effects seem smaller than they actually were, for the reasons noted in chapter 7.

9. The difference between means for the prerevolutionary and the postrevolutionary cohorts is significant at $p<.005$, by a one-tailed t test. That between prerevolutionary and revolutionary cohorts is not statistically significant.

10. The mean for father's education, for example, dropped by over a year from the prerevolutionary to the postrevolutionary period, which in itself implies a drop of half a year in respondent's education if the relation between family background and education

remained the same. While we have no unequivocal data bearing on this surprising change in family background, we believe that it comes about because of the steady (and well-known) shift away from Amerindian languages and toward Spanish. In the first generation, Spanish speakers from Amerindian families are clearly identified in our data (they are the cholos) and their education and occupational status, although higher than those of monolingual Amerindian speakers, are still well below those of Spanish speakers born to Spanish-speaking families. Their children would, however, be classified as Spanish in our data (since we have no information on grandparents). But their parents' low levels of education and occupational status would still be a great disadvantage (see chap. 7), and the children would therefore generally have less education and lower ranking occupations than children whose grandparents spoke Spanish. That would lead to a decline in the education and occupation of the population we (and most Bolivians) classify as Spanish even though every family in Bolivia showed rising levels of education over the generations.

11. These comparisons are based largely on income while consumption-based measures may well be better for societies like Bolivia. But Zuvekas suspects that consumption-based measures would nonetheless show the same pattern (personal communication).

12. Our crucial theoretical prediction is that inequality will first decline following the revolution (Hypothesis 2) and then in the long run increase once again (Hypothesis 5). Changes in the fraction of their production that workers receive in income could mimic that but to do so they would have to follow a complex and implausible pattern. For example, if nonagricultural workers received a high percentage of their product before the revolution, a low percentage in the revolutionary period, and a high percentage again afterward, that would artifactually produce the pattern we predicted. But that set of changes is hardly plausible. And it is almost as hard to imagine any plausible changes for the agricultural labor force that would produce such an artifact. There probably were changes for them at the time of the revolution, namely, an increase in the proportion of agricultural output that they received, which would lead us to overestimate inequality following the revolution. But that is a conservative bias since it is contrary to our prediction.

13. The theory distinguished between inequality in the society as a whole and inequality among the previously exploited population but this distinction, clear enough on theoretical grounds, is not particularly relevant for present purposes. The prerevolutionary elite was able to exploit, to a greater or lesser degree, the vast majority of Bolivians, the hacienda peasants directly but the rest indirectly, by taxes, commercial monopolies, political privileges, and the like. So all stood to gain from the elite's overthrow, save only the small elite itself. But this would now show up in the statistics of this sort. Their agricultural production, for example, would not be distinguished from that of the much more numerous small farmers. Only the broader processes would show up in these data, for example, the expansion of opportunities in trucking and commerce for a large number of small entrepreneurs. But fortunately for our purposes, small enterprises are predominant in Bolivia; even outside of agriculture 60 percent of the labor force is in firms with 5 or fewer employees and in commerce the figure approaches 90 percent (Chirikos et al., 1971:67).

14. See Kelley and Klein 1974 and 1977.

7. Revolution and Inherited Privilege

1. One way in which revolutions can sometimes expropriate at least some of the returns on human capital is by reducing the premium paid to skilled or educated workers. We have argued that these returns cannot be eliminated in the long run, although possibly reduced, since otherwise people will not bother to acquire the educa-

tion and skills needed to run the economy. But in the short run, the premium paid can be reduced even below that level since people educated before the revolution cannot change their minds about investing in human capital, nor can they sell it off to the highest bidder.

2. The people who get married at a very early age, and therefore appear in a head of household sample like ours, are disproportionately those who have little schooling and embarked on their occupational and marital careers at an early age; their limited education condemns them to poor jobs. More successful people of the same age are still in school or have recently taken up jobs but are not yet married, so they do not appear in the sample. A sample of very young people is thus biased in a way that leads to a considerable understatement of the advantages of education and family background. We therefore restricted the sample to an age group old enough that the great majority have already married and established households, a procedure both appropriate and conventional.

3. We do not have data on the income people had at various times in the past, and so unfortunately cannot analyze revolution's effects on income. No retrospective question on income was asked in the survey and the answers would not have been trustworthy even if the question had been asked.

4. The only appreciable reliability problem would seem to be error in reports of family background but for reasons set out in chapter 2 we believe these problems are minimal under the conditions prevalent in rural Bolivia. The major effect of random measurement error in any of the variables we are dealing with would be to reduce the correlations between family background, on the one hand, and respondent's own education and occupational status, on the other, and also (if education is measured with error) to attenuate the estimates of indirect effects through education (see Bohrnstedt and Carter 1971 for an excellent general discussion or Kelley 1973 for an application to the present variables and estimates of measurement error in U.S. data). Given the generally rather high reliability with which occupation and education are measured, however, in the present case the effect of these errors is likely to be modest (the appropriate calculations are in Bohrnstedt and Carter 1971 or Kelley 1973). Crucially, such errors are quite unlikely to be serious for the issues at hand which turn on differences between cohorts. Only if random error was low before the revolution, high during it, and low afterward (a substantially implausible pattern) would there be any difficulty.

5. Ministry of planning figures show 69 percent of the labor force in agriculture before the revolution and 67 percent still in agriculture in 1966, the date of our survey; as late as 1972 the figure had dropped only to 65 percent (República de Bolivia 1974:52).

6. See Treiman's (1977) definitive work, based on data for 55 countries throughout the world including many preindustrial and socialist societies. Using very different techniques, we have developed socioeconomic status scales for 16 societies throughout the world and found that the scores for Bolivia, Poland, and a variety of other societies are essentially the same as those found elsewhere in the world (see chap. 2 and App. 3. sec. 3). If a radical revolution were to change the status hierarchy, the Polish hierarchy would presumably be different than those found in capitalist societies but in fact it is not; the average correlation between the Polish hierarchy and those found elsewhere in the world, .90, is in fact slightly higher than the average correlation among capitalist societies. Bolivia is also very similar to the rest, its hierarchy correlating .92 with Poland's and .93 on the average with the rest of the world. While these results are based on a scoring scheme different from the ethnographic one used in this chapter, the fact that, when applied to Bolivia, it produces results essentially the same as the ethnographic scheme strongly suggests that the results could be safely generalized.

7. Children coming of age just after the revolution would have grown up mainly before it and the father's occupation they report would be the father's prerevolutionary occupation. So children from elite homes would be from prerevolutionary elite homes and they might suffer from discrimination because of that. That would make for a negative correlation in the years just following the revolution. In the longer run this

effect would diminish as the old elite died out and the correlation would reflect conditions of the new society (unless "bad class background" was inherited from generation to generation, as appears to have been the case in China for some decades after the revolution). It would then surely not be negative (for that would mean that children of the revolutionary elite were at a disadvantage) and would be positive if the new revolutionary elite is able to pass advantages on to its children (Djilas 1957).

8. There are several appropriate ways of comparing two correlations and we have chosen a very simple one. The percent reported in the text is simply $(1 - .44/.53 = .17)$ and represents the proportional decline in the correlation from one time period to the next; we are simply saying that .44 is 17 percent smaller than .53. An alternative procedure is to compare not correlations but the corresponding percent of variance explained. That is essentially the same comparison dressed up in an alternative metric. In the present example, the percent of variance corresponding to the prerevolutionary correlation is $.53^2 \cdot 100 = 28$ percent and in the revolutionary period, $.44^2 \cdot 100 = 19$ percent. In these terms, the decline attributable to the revolution is 32 percent. As can be seen from this example, doing the comparison in terms of percent of variance will give the impression of greater change, and hence stronger support for our theory, than the comparison which we focus on. We prefer to focus on the correlations and the closely related metric regression coefficients, however, because they (particularly the metric coefficients) have a clearer substantive meaning; this is illustrated in the text below. The basic results of our analysis are, nonetheless, presented in percent of variance terms in figure 7.2 and the remainder of the analysis is given in that form in table 6.5A. In any event, the difference is a matter of style and not of substance and we beg the indulgence of those readers who would have preferred the discussion to be in terms of percent of variance explained.

9. Metric regression coefficients (variously called unstandardized regression coefficients, b's, or simply regression coefficients) are more appropriate for comparing different periods since they are unaffected by differences in the standard deviations in the two periods. The standardized coefficients are, however, useful since they permit a comparison of variables measured in a different metric (for example, occupation and education) and many readers will find them more familiar. In practice the standard deviations in all three time periods are much the same, so standardized coefficients can be compared in different periods with little risk.

10. These figures are from a simple regression equation predicting the status of son's first job from his father's occupational status alone.

11. Unfortunately we do not have reliable measures of mother's education or occupation. But given the high correlation between spouses' education in most societies, the small number of rural and small-town Bolivian women who work outside the home, and the general dominance of men in Latin society, this will not be a serious bias for present purposes.

12. In models where we are predicting on the basis of a single variable, the percent of variance explained, R^2, is just the square of the correlation coefficient and is therefore just an alternative way of reporting the same fact reflected in the correlation (see n. 8 above), which in turn is the same thing as the standardized regression coefficient. When there are several predictor variables, R^2 has an analogous meaning. In the case at hand, for example, if we made a combined measure of father's status by averaging his occupation and education, weighting each in a way that best predicts his son's occupation, then R^2 would be exactly equal to the square of the correlation between that combined status measure and son's occupation.

13. These estimates are obtained from the metric regression equations. We start with an equation predicting the son's occupational status, say:

$$\text{son's status} = a + b_1 \text{ father's status} + b_2 \text{ father's education}$$

$$+ b_3 \text{ father's social race} + C$$

We estimate the status of sons from privileged families by inserting appropriate values for father's occupation, education, and social race into the equation (namely, 100 status points, 11.6 years of education, and 1 for social race; details on this are in the text), doing the multiplication, and adding up the result. Then we estimate the status of sons from poor peasant families by inserting appropriate values for their fathers (i.e., 0 status points, 1.2 years of education, and 0 for social race). Then we subtract the figure for privileged sons from the figure for sons born into peasant families. That is our estimate of the advantage of being born into a privileged family.

14. There are a variety of reasonable ways of summarizing the results of a regression analysis like ours and no clear consensus as to which is best. But this is not a matter of much moment since in practice one usually reaches the same conclusions no matter which summary is used. That is certainly the case in this analysis, as may be seen by inspecting the full regression equations, which are shown in tables 6.2A and 6.5A.

15. These estimates are from a regression model in which the status of son's first job is predicted on the basis of his father's education and occupational status. Details are in Appendix 6, section 2.

16. These estimates are from a regression model predicting the status of son's first job on the basis of his father's education, father's occupational status, and social race (See App. 6, sec. 2).

17. This is essentially an application of the mobility model we presented in chapter 1, where we argued that occupational mobility was to be explained only by the transfer of property and human capital from parent to child. In this model if *both* property and human capital are directly measured, father's occupation will have no direct effect on son's occupation. But if either one of the intervening variables, property and human capital, is omitted it is easy to show that its effect will reappear as a direct effect of father's occupation.

18. There is a stylistic dilemma here. Some readers might understandably object to reading about the effect of father's "property" when that attribution is only an inference and would prefer to have the effect explicitly labeled as the direct effect of father's occupational status controlling for education and social race. But other readers, also understandably, might object to such seeming pedantry, especially in a technical discussion which is not exactly light reading to begin with. We have preferred the stylistically simpler, if technically less precise, solution and hope that readers who would have preferred the other alternative will bear with us.

19. These estimates are from Model 3, in which the status of son's first job is predicted on the basis of his father's occupational status, education, and social race. The partial regression coefficient for father's occupation is, we have just argued, a plausible estimate of the effects of father's property. Details are in Appendix 6, section 2.

20. The definition of direct and indirect of course depends on the model. In our analysis we have explicit measures of the son's education so the direct effects are by definition those not involving education.

21. The standardized partial regression coefficient for father's education was .49 before the revolution, .57 during the revolution, and .56 afterward. The corresponding figures for father's occupational status were .24, .17, and .26.

22. This is calculated from the metric regression coefficient of father's education in a model predicting the status of son's first job from his father's education, occupation, and social race (Model 3). It is simply a way of expressing the regression coefficient, 1.31, in a more intuitive form. For the elite son the calculation is $11.6 \cdot 1.31 = 15.2$ status points and for the poor peasant son, $1.2 \cdot 1.31 = 1.6$ status points; the difference beween 15.2 and 1.6, rounded to the nearest point, is the 14 reported in the text.

23. In this section we will focus entirely on education, ignoring social race even though it has elements of human capital in it, especially with respect to language skills. But it also has strong elements of ethnicity, discrimination, and structural differences since the cleavage between "races" is in Bolivia defined mainly in terms of language. A detailed treatment is given in the next section. However, for present purposes language in fact

has only modest effects on son's first job (see table 6.2A) so that we in fact lose little by equating father's education with his human capital. Thus the effects of father's education that we discuss are those that exist apart from the connections between education and language.

24. This sort of problem in the reporting of first job is a common one. It was a major problem in, for example, Blau and Duncan's otherwise definitive Current Population Survey data on the United States (Duncan, Featherman, and Duncan 1972). There is also some direct evidence in that the correlation between first job and current occupation is lower in the postrevolutionary period than earlier (.67 compared to .70 and .73) even though the first jobs could have been only a few years in the past for men in the postrevolutionary period.

25. The uncertainties about first job in the postrevolutionary period are of no consequence for the results of the last section. The alternative estimates of the effects of father's education give results virtually identical to the ones we discussed in the text.

26. This is our usual comparison between a father with an elite white-collar job (100 status points) and 11.6 years of education (the average for such men) on the one hand, and a landless llama herder (0 status points) with little education (1.2 years). Here we of course assume that both are Spanish speaking, as indeed many poor peasants are.

27. The estimate is the partial regression coefficient associated with father's occupational status in an analysis where son's status is predicted from father's occupation and education. Since this analysis is for the Spanish population only, social race is controlled implicitly and this is essentially the same as Model 3. With the modest size of the sample, the decline was not statistically significant (see note 28).

28. Significance tests must, however, be treated with more than usual caution in this section because our sample size is decidedly modest once we analyze Spanish and Indians separately. For the Spanish, there are 245, 94, and 63 cases before, during, and after the revolution, respectively.

29. These are estimated from a regression model in which father's occupation, father's education, and son's education are used to predict the status of son's first job. Details are in Appendix 6, section 2.

30. For reasons given earlier, we have some reservations about the reporting of first job in the postrevolutionary period. Using the alternative estimate based on current occupation for this group of young men suggests that an elite son would enjoy a 22 point advantage, fractionally higher than he enjoyed during the revolution.

31. Note that results for the population as a whole are *not* simply some weighted average of the results for Spanish and Aymara (even though our population is made up of only those two groups) but also depends on the (large) differences in the mean values for Spanish and Aymara. It is possible, to take an extreme example, for there to be no correlation between father's and son's status among either Spanish or Aymara taken separately but nonetheless a high correlation for the population as a whole, that correlation arising out of a large difference in the mean status of Spanish and Aymara.

32. The sample size is 368, 169, and 103 before, during, and after the revolution, respectively.

33. It is also possible that our results are due to some unique feature of Bolivia's revolution apart from this. We do not think that this is especially likely, if only because the unique aspects would have somehow to account for the decline of inequality followed by a rise again barely a decade later; for the dramatic drop in the effect of father's property followed by an even more dramatic increase a decade later and all that juxtaposed with a simultaneous increase in the effects of father's human capital during and after the revolution; it would have to account for the sharp decline followed by rapid increase in the direct effect of father's wealth while the indirect effects through education remain. To be fully persuasive it would also have to account for the results on education and income, and on inequality in education and income, that we presented in the last chapter. It is easy enough to cite one or another seemingly special feature of Bolivia and the

Bolivian revolution to account for one or two of these facts, but that is unlikely to be persuasive counterargument; the strength of the argument lies in the whole pattern of predictions and a series of individual, *ad hoc* counterarguments are unlikely to be a viable alternative.

34. His analysis focused on different issues than those we raise and came to different conclusions and he is, of course, in no way responsible for the uses we have made of the data. Our figures are computed from his table 2 (p. 7).

35. We have omitted farmers since no status distinctions can be made among them and their rank with respect to white- and blue-collar workers is unclear. Including them as blue collar, the best guess, leads to the same substantive conclusions as those given in the text.

36. The figures for other societies are based on detailed and accurate measurement of occupational status whereas Poland's is based on a crude dichotomy, so there is surely much more measurement error in the Polish data. Hence status inheritance in Poland is probably even higher than these comparisons suggest.

37. Worsnip (1979) briefly summarizes reports from an unpublicized seminar focusing on these questions held by more than 100 academics and journalists in Poland in 1978. Most speakers agreed that inequality was increasing and several explicitly mentioned the link between economic growth and growth in inequality.

8. Conclusion

1. The theory was formulated in our original grant proposal (Kelly and Klein 1974) before we had done any quantitative analysis and appeared in print virtually unchanged just as our analysis was getting well under way (Kelley and Klein 1977).

2. Such rewards exist in, among others, Pharaonic Egypt, classical Greece, the Roman empire, tribal Africa, medieval Europe, thirteenth-century Nepal, colonial Latin America, the Ottoman empire, the USSR and other eastern European communist societies, communist China, Cuba, and throughout the contemporary third world. Differentials exist because skills are necessary. Neither ancient kings nor modern nation-states can keep track of taxes without literate clerks; skilled technicians are needed to make boats and gold jewelry, iron caldrons and airplanes, chain mail and atomic bombs; it takes skilled managers to provision a modern army, run a large farm, or direct a steel industry. Those with skills and technical training will have to be rewarded—whether in money or other perquisites—in order to motivate them to acquire the training and to apply their skills diligently. Their skills also give them a stronger bargaining position than unskilled workers even if all power is concentrated in the hands of the state.

3. For an elegant analysis of why these new opportunities lead to economic growth, see Olson (1978).

Appendix I

1. Without changing our conclusions, the aggregate could be any function which increases whenever any of its components increases and whose variance increases whenever any of their variances increase. Assume, plausibly, that having one resource (education, skills, property, motivation, ability, luck, etc.) does not systematically entail a loss of others, so that the correlations among resources are positive or zero. Then any (positively weighted) average of them, a multiplicative Cobb-Douglass function of them, and a variety of other specific functions all have the required characteristics. We assume that the correlations among human capital, property, and other resources are all positive or zero, i.e., that having one resource is not a disadvantage in terms of acquiring others.

This seems intuitively obvious and, indeed, is true in every society for which we have the appropriate data. This assumption ensures that an increase in the variance of H, P, or O will also increase the variance of the combined resource (H+P+O), i.e., that an increase in inequality of human capital, property, or other resources will increase inequality in the combined resource. The model in the text could easily be developed with all three of these resources specified separately rather than combined into a single aggregate but that would only complicate things unnecessarily.

2. The sum of $(1 + r + r^2 + \ldots + r^{n-1})$ is $(r^{n-1})/(r-1)$ in general or $[(1+\text{save·int})^n -1]/(1+\text{save·int}-1)$ in this case.

3. Both expressions are of the general form a·WEALTH $+ b + c$·(H+P+O), where a, b, and c are constants and WEALTH and (H+P+O) are variables. The standard deviation, our measure of inequality, of the sum is a function of the means and standard deviation of each variable and the covariance between them. We assume that inherited wealth is either positively correlated with human capital, property, and other resources, or uncorrelated; it follows that wealth in the nth year also has a positive or zero correlation. Hence the standard deviation will be an increasing function of a, of c, and of the variance in wealth, human capital, and other resources.

4. If we are just talking of literacy versus illiteracy, the argument is clear. If p is the percent literate before the revolution, the standard deviation will be $\sqrt{p(1-p)}$ and that obviously will grow as p increases from zero percent literate to 50 percent and decrease thereafter. When we measure education in years of schooling, the argument is not as neat but essentially similar. Only when the average level of schooling among peasants is very low, will increases in education increase inequality; this is, however, the usual situation.

5. Suppose the classes have n_1, n_2, n_3, and n_4 members, respectively, and that the income (or wealth) of each member is w_1, w_2, w_3 and w_4, respectively. Then the average income (or wealth) in the society as a whole is simply the weighted average for each class and income (or wealth) inequality, measured by the standard deviation, is a simple function of the squared deviation from the mean, $\Sigma/i \; (n_i w_i - \text{mean})^2$. As the income or wealth of each class moves closer to the mean, this declines and conversely as income or wealth moves away from the mean, inequality increases. Allowing heterogeneity of income or wealth among classes (i.e., some variance in w_i) does not change matters appreciably and income remains an analogous function of the squared deviation from the mean.

6. This is not to say that other factors are unimportant or unpredictable by other theories but rather that they are, to a reasonable approximation, unrelated to the explanatory variables we are dealing with, and so can be ignored for present purposes.

7. Namely, $c = (a^2 \, \sigma w^2 + b^2 \, \sigma h^2 + 2ab \, r_{hw} \, \sigma h \, \sigma w + b_2 \, \sigma O_2{}^2 + b_1 \, \sigma O_3{}^2 + \sigma O_1{}^2)$.

8. All these terms drop out because each involves the correlation between father's status and the son's other resources (for example, r_{so}) and these are by earlier assumptions all zero.

9. Both partial derivatives are of the general form $(k_1 X + k_2)/(k_3 X^2 + k_4 X + k_5)^{3/2}$, where the k_i are various combinations of constants from Eqs. 5–7 and X is the standard deviation of physical or human capital, respectively; by earlier assumptions all these terms are positive and hence both derivatives are positive.

Appendix 3

1. If prestige varied a great deal from one society to another, this way of dividing up major groups could create problems of comparability. But Treiman (1977) has shown that prestige is essentially invariant throughout the world, so this is no problem.

2. The countries are Australia, Denmark, Finland, West Germany, Great Britain, the Netherlands, Northern Ireland, Norway, Poland, and Sweden among more developed countries and Kenya, Malaysia, the Philippines, and Taiwan among less developed. The

Polish and Kenyan data are for single cities while the others are the national samples described in chapter 2.

3. The results are not quite in the conventional zero to 100 range, so we rescaled them to that range for convenience. The scores are high professional = 100, administrative and managerial = 75, low professional = 70, high clerical = 60, high sales = 51, low clerical = 38, low sales = 32, high production = 37, high service = 33, medium production = 24, low service = 18, low production = 14, high and medium farm = 10, and low farm = 0.

4. In the few countries where they can be distinguished in the data, large farmers are above average in status, often, as in Bolivia, well above average.

5. The local and cross-cultural canonical scores are correlated .98. This is a slight overestimate of the similarity between Bolivia and the world, because the Bolivian scores were one of the sixteen averaged to produce the cross-cultural score.

References

Adelman, Irma, and Cynthia Taft Morris. 1971. "An Anatomy of Income Distribution Patterns in Developing Nations." *Development Digest* 9 (October):24–37.

Albó, Xavier. 1979. *Achacachi: medio siglo de lucha campesina.* La Paz: Ediciones CIPCA.

Alker, Hayward R., Jr., and Bruce M. Russett. 1964. "On Measuring Inequality." *Behavioral Science* 9 (July):207–218.

Allison, Paul D. 1978. "Measures of Inequality." *American Sociological Review* 43 (December):865–880.

Alwin, Duane F., and Robert M. Hauser. 1975. "The Decomposition of Effects in Path Analysis." *American Sociological Review* 40 (February):37–47.

Anderson, Barbara A. 1975. "Social Stratification in the Soviet Union: Equality, Excellence and Other Issues." *Studies in Comparative Communism* 8 (Winter):397–412.

Andorka, Rudolf. 1978. "Tendencies of Social Mobility in Hungary: Comparisons of Historical Periods and Cohorts." In *Social Mobility in Comparative Perspective.* Edited by Włodzimierz Wesołowski, Kazimierz M. Słomczyński, and Bogdan W. Mach. Warsaw: Ossolineum, The Polish Academy of Sciences Press. Pp. 305–319.

Averango Mollinedo, Asthenio. 1974. *Aspectos generales de la población boliviana.* La Paz: Editorial "Juventud."

Bailey, F. G. 1963. *Politics and Social Change: Orissa in 1959.* Berkeley and Los Angeles: University of California Press.

Becker, Gary S. 1964. *Human Capital: A Theoretical and Empirical Analysis with Special Reference to Education.* New York: National Bureau of Economic Research.

Blau, Peter M., and Otis Dudley Duncan. 1967. *The American Occupational Structure.* New York: Wiley.

Bohrnstedt, George W., and T. Michael Carter. 1971. "Robustness in Regression Analysis." In *Sociological Methodology.* Edited by Hubert L. Costner. San Francisco: Jossey-Bass. Pp. 118–146.

Bolivia, República de. CONEPLAN. 1973. *Plan quinquenal de desarrollo económico y social, 1972–1977.* La Paz.

―――. Dirección General de Estadística y Censos. 1955. *Censo demográfico, 1950.* La Paz.

―――. Dirección Nacional de Estadística y Censos. 1950. *Censo agropecuario.* La Paz.

―――. Ministerio de Asuntos Campesinos y Agropecuarios, Oficina de Planeamiento. 1974. *Diagnóstica del sector agropecuario, 1974.* La Paz.

————. Ministerio de Planeamiento y Coordinación de la Presidencia de la República. 1976. *Plan nacional de desarrollo económico y social, 1976–1980.* 4 vols. La Paz.

————. Instituto Nacional de Estadística. 1977. *Censo nacional de población y vivienda 1976. Resultados anticipados por muestra.* La Paz.

Burke, Melvin. 1967. "An Analysis of the Bolivian Land Reform by Means of a Comparison between Peruvian Haciendas and Bolivian Ex-Haciendas." Ph.D. dissertation, Department of Economics, University of Pittsburgh.

————. 1971 "Land Reform in the Lake Titicaca Region." In *Beyond the Revolution: Bolivia Since 1952.* Edited by James M. Malloy and Richard S. Thorn. Pittsburgh: University of Pittsburgh Press. Pp. 301–339.

Camacho Saa, Carlos. 1970. *Estudio de caso en el Valle bajo de Cochabamba (Caramarca, Parotani, Itapaya).* La Paz: Servicio Nacional de Reforma Agraria.

Cancian, Frank. 1965. *Economics and Prestige in a Maya Community.* Stanford: Stanford University Press.

Carter, William E. 1964. *Aymara Communities and the Bolivian Agrarian Reform.* University of Florida Monographs, Social Sciences, No. 24. Gainsville: The University.

————. 1971. "Revolution and the Agrarian Sector." In *Beyond the Revolution: Bolivia Since 1952.* Edited by James M. Malloy and Richard S. Thorn. Pittsburgh: University of Pittsburgh Press. Pp. 223—268.

CEPAL. 1958. Comisión Económica para América Latina, Nacimes Unidas. *El desarrollo económico de Bolivia.* Analisis y Proyecciones del Desarrollo Ecónomico, no. 4. Mexico.

Chevalier, François. 1967. "The *Ejido* and Political Stability in Mexico." In *The Politics of Conformity in Latin America.* Edited by C. Veliz. New York: New York University Press. Pp. 158–191.

Chinn, Dennis L. 1978. "Income Distribution in a Chinese Commune." *Journal of Comparative Economics* 2 (September):246–265.

Chirikos, Thomas N., S. Clifton Kelley, G. Gene Lamb, Donald P. Sanders, John R. Shea and Associates. 1971. *Human Resources in Bolivia: Problems, Planning and Policy.* Columbus: Center for Human Resources Research, Ohio State University.

Clark, Evelyn Kiatipoff. 1970. "Agrarian Reform and Development Change in Parotani, Bolivia." Ph.D. dissertation, Indiana University.

Clark, Ronald J. 1968. "Land Reform and Peasant Market Participation on the North Highlands of Bolivia." *Land Economics* 44 (May):153–172.

————. 1971. "Agrarian Reform: Bolivia." In *Land Reform in Latin America: Issues and Cases.* Edited by Peter Dorner. Land Economics Monographs, No. 3. Madison: Land Tenure Center, University of Wisconsin. Pp. 129–164.

Collins, Randall. 1971. "Functional and Conflict Theories of Educational Stratification." *American Sociological Review* 36 (December):1002–1019.

Comitas, Lambros. 1966. "Anthropology." *The Americana Annual, 1965. Yearbook of the Encyclopedia Americana.* Pp. 56–58.

Craig, Wesley W., Jr. 1969. "Peru: The Peasant Movement of La Convención." In *Latin American Peasant Movements.* Edited by H. Landsberger. Ithaca, N.Y.: Cornell University Press. Pp. 274–322.

Dahrendorf, Ralf. 1959. *Class and Class Conflict in Industrial Society.* Stanford: Stanford University Press.

Dandler, Jorge. 1969. *El sindicalismo campesino en Bolivia: los cambios estructurales en Ucureña*. Mexico: Instituto Indigenista Interamericano.

Djilas, Milovan. 1957. *The New Class: An Analysis of the Communist System*. New York: Praeger.

Dobson, Richard B. 1977. "Social Status and Inequality of Access to Higher Education in the USSR." In *Power and Ideology in Education*. Edited by Jerome Karabel and A. H. Halsey. New York: Oxford University Press. Pp. 254–275.

Dorsey, Joseph F. "A Case Study of the Lower Cochabamba Valley: Ex-Haciendas Parotani and Caramerca." Research Paper No. 64. Madison: Land Tenure Center, University of Wisconsin.

Duncan, Otis Dudley. 1961. "A Socioeconomic Index for All Occupations." In Albert J. Reiss, Jr. et al. *Occupations and Social Status*. New York:Free Press of Glencoe. Pp. 109–138.

———. 1966. "Path Analysis: Sociological Examples." *American Journal of Sociology* 72 (July):1–16.

Duncan, Otis Dudley, David L. Featherman, and Beverly Duncan. 1972. *Socioeconomic Background and Achievement*. New York: Seminar Press.

Duncan-Jones, P. 1972. "Social Mobility, Canonical Scoring and Occupational Classification." In *The Analysis of Social Mobility: Methods and Approaches*, edited by Keith Hope. Oxford: Clarendon. Pp. 191–210.

Erasmus, Charles J. 1967. "Upper Limits of the Peasantry and Agrarian Reform: Bolivia, Venezuela, and Mexico Compared." *Ethnology* 6 (October): 349–380.

Featherman, David L. and Robert M. Hauser. 1976. "Changes in the Socioeconomic Stratification of the Races, 1962–1973." *American Journal of Sociology* 82 (November):621–651.

———. 1976. "Prestige or Socioeconomic Scales in the Study of Occupational Achievement?" *Sociological Methods and Research* 4:403–422.

Featherman, David L., F. Lancaster Jones, and Robert M. Hauser. 1975. "Assumptions of Social Mobility Research in the United States: The Case of Occupational Status." *Social Science Research* 4 (December):329–360.

Ferragut, Castro. 1964. *Informe al Gobierno de Bolivia sobre reforma agraria*. FAO Report No. 1856. Rome: Food and Agriculture Organization.

Fields, Gary S. 1979. "A Welfare Economic Approach to Growth and Distribution in the Dual Economy." *The Quarterly Journal of Economics* 93 (August): 325–353.

Frolic, Michael B. 1978. "Reflections on the Chinese Model of Development." *Social Forces* 57 (December): 384–418.

Goldberger, Arthur S. 1968. *Topics in Regression Analysis*. London: MacMillan.

Goodman, Leo A. 1979. "A Brief Guide to the Causal Analysis of Data from Surveys." *American Journal of Sociology* 84 (March):1078–1095.

Gusfield, Joseph R., and Michael Schwartz. 1963. "The Meanings of Occupational Prestige: Reconsideration of the NORC Scale." *American Sociological Review* 28 (April):265–271.

Haller, Archibald O., Luther B. Otto, Robert F. Meier, and George W. Ohlendorf. 1974. "Level of Occupational Aspiration: An Empirical Analysis." *American Sociological Review* 39 (February):113–121.

Hammel, E. A. 1970. "The Ethnographer's Dilemma: Alternative Models of

Occupational Prestige in Belgrade." *Man: The Journal of the Royal Anthropological Institute* 5 (December):652–670.

Havens, A. Eugene, and William Flinn. 1975. "Green Revolution Technology and Community Development: The Limits of Action Programs." *Economic Development and Cultural Change* 23 (April):469–481.

Heath, Dwight B. 1969. "Bolivia: Peasant Syndicates among the Aymara of the Yungas: A View from the Grass Roots." In *Latin American Peasant Movements.* Edited by Henry A. Landsberger. Ithaca, N.Y.: Cornell University Press. Pp. 170–209.

———. 1973. "New Patrons for Old: Changing Patron Client Relationships in the Bolivian Yungas." *Ethnology* 12 (January):75–98.

Heath, Dwight B., Charles J. Erasmus, and Hans C. Buechler. 1969. *Land Reform and Social Revolution in Bolivia.* New York: Praeger.

Heyduck, Daniel. 1971. "Huayrapampa: Bolivian Highland Peasants and the New Social Order." Latin American Studies Program Dissertation Series, No. 27. Ithaca, N.Y.: Cornell University.

———. 1974. "The Hacienda System and Agrarian Reform in Highland Bolivia: A Re-Evaluation." *Ethnology* 13 (January):71–81.

Inter-American Development Bank. 1973. FAO-IDB Cooperative Program. *Prioridades de inversión en el sector agropecuario de Bolivia.* Documentos sobre desarrollo agrícola, No. 12. Washington, D.C.: Inter-American Development Bank.

International Bank for Reconstruction and Development. 1971. *World Tables.* Washington, D.C.: International Bank for Reconstruction and Development.

International Labor Office. 1958. *International Standard Classification of Occupations.* Geneva: International Labor Office.

———. 1971. *Labor Force Projections.* Geneva; International Labor Office.

Jackson, Elton F., and Richard F. Curtis. 1972. "Effects on Vertical Mobility and Status Inconsistency: A Body of Negative Evidence." *American Sociological Review* 37 (December):701–713.

Jencks, Christopher, et al. 1972. *Inequality: A Reassessment of the Effect of Family and Schooling in America.* New York: Basic Books.

Johnston, J. 1963. *Econometric Methods.* New York: McGraw Hill.

Kelley, Jonathan. 1971. "Social Mobility in Traditional Society: The Toro of Uganda." Ph.D. dissertation, Department of Sociology, University of California, Berkeley.

———. 1973. "Causal Chain Models for the Socio-Economic Career." *American Sociological Review* 38 (August):481–493.

———. 1978. "Wealth and Family Background in the Occupational Career: Theory and Cross-Cultural Data." *British Journal of Sociology* 29 (March): 94–109.

Kelley, Jonathan, and Herbert S. Klein. 1974. "Social Mobility in a Developing Society." Research proposal to the National Science Foundation, subsequently funded as Grant SOC74–21514.

———. 1977. "Revolution and the Rebirth of Inequality: A Theory of Stratification in Postrevolutionary Society." *American Journal of Sociology* 83 (July): 78–99.

Kelley, Jonathan, and Melvin L. Perlman. 1971. "Social Mobility in Toro: Some Preliminary Results from Western Uganda." *Economic Development and Cultural Change* 19 (January):204–221.

Kelley, Jonathan, Robert V. Robinson, and Herbert S. Klein. 1980. "A Theory of Social Mobility, with Data on Status Attainment in a Peasant Society." In *Research in Social Stratification and Mobility*. Vol. 1. Edited by Donald J. Treiman and Robert V. Robinson. Greenwich, Conn.: JAI Press. Pp. 27–66.

Kelley, Jonathan, and Donald J. Treiman. 1978*a*. "Social Stratification in Cross Cultural Perspective: Extensions of a Basic Model." Research Proposal Submitted to the National Science Foundation. February.

———. 1978*b*. "Occupational Differences in Marriage and Child-Bearing among Women: Final Report to the National Institute of Child Health and Human Development on Contract NO1-HD-22744." New York: Center for Policy Research. Pp. 1–209.

Kelley, Jonathan, Donald J. Treiman, Robert V. Robinson, Patricia A. Roos, and J. L. P. Thompson. 1980. "Social Stratification in Cross-Cultural Perspective: A Preliminary Analysis of Survey Data from Fourteen Societies." Paper presented to the Annual Meetings of the American Sociological Association. Pp. 1–75.

Khrushchev, Nikita. 1970. *Khrushchev Remembers*. Boston: Little, Brown.

Kieniewicz, Stefan. 1969. *The Emancipation of the Polish Peasantry*. Chicago: University of Chicago Press.

Kim, Jae-On, and James Curry. 1977. "The Treatment of Missing Data in Multivariate Analysis." *Sociological Methods and Research* 6 (November): 215–240.

Klatsky, Sheila R., and Robert W. Hodge. 1971. "A Canonical Correlation Analysis of Occupational Mobility." *Journal of the American Statistical Association* 66 (March):16–22.

Klein, Herbert S. 1968. "The Crisis of Legitimacy and the Origins of Social Revolution: The Bolivian Experience." *Journal of Inter-American Studies* 10 (January):102–106.

———. 1969. *Parties and Political Change in Bolivia, 1880–1952*. Cambridge: Cambridge University Press.

———. 1971. "Prelude to Revolution." In *Beyond the Revolution: Bolivia Since 1952*. Edited by James Malloy and Richard Thorn. Pittsburgh: University of Pittsburgh Press. Pp. 25–52.

Kondor, Yaakov. 1975. "Value Judgements Implied by the Use of Various Measures of Income Inequality." *The Review of Income and Wealth* 21 (September):309–321.

Kornfeld, William J. 1969. "Concepto de cultura y cambio social en un pueblo bilingue de los Andes." *América Indígena* 29 (October):983–1027.

Kuznets, Simon. 1965. *Economic Growth and Structure: Selected Essays*. New York: Norton.

———. 1966. *Modern Economic Growth: Rate, Structure, and Spread*. New Haven: Yale University Press.

LaBarre, Weston. 1948. *The Aymara Indians of the Lake Titicaca Plateau, Bolivia*. Memoir No. 68 of American Anthropology Association. Menaska, Wisconsin.

Lane, David Stuart, 1971. *The End of Inequality? Stratification under State Socialism.* Harmondsworth, England: Penguin.

Lavaud, Jean Pierre. 1972. *Organisation sociale et attitudes politiques dans un quartier marginal de La Paz.* Thesis 3ᵈ cycle (Paris V) U.E.R. de Sociologie.

Layard, Richard, and George Psacharopoulous. 1974. "The Screening Hypothesis and the Returns to Education." *Journal of Political Economy* 82 (September/October):985–998.

Lenin, V. I. (1920). 1967. *Selected Works,* vol. 3. New York: International.

Lenski, Gerhard E. 1966. *Power and Privilege: A Theory of Social Stratification.* New York: McGraw-Hill.

Lewis-Beck, Michael S. 1979. "Some Economic Effects of Revolution: Models, Measurement, and the Cuban Evidence." *American Journal of Sociology* 84 (March):1127–1149.

Lipset, Seymour Martin, and Richard B. Dobson. 1973. "Social Stratification and Sociology in the Soviet Union." *Survey* 19 (88):114–185.

Lyle, Norris B., and Richard A. Calman, eds. 1966. *Statistical Abstract of Latin America.* Los Angeles: UCLA Latin America Center Publications.

McEwen, William J. 1975. *Changing Rural Society: A Study of Communities in Bolivia.* New York and London: Oxford University Press.

Malloy, James M. 1970. *Bolivia: The Uncompleted Revolution* Pittsburgh: University of Pittsburgh Press.

Malloy, James M. 1970. *Bolivia: The Uncompleted Revolution.* Pittsburgh: University of Pittsburgh Press.

Matthews, Mervyn. 1978. *Privilege in the Soviet Union: A Study of Elite Life-styles under Communism.* London: Allen and Unwin.

Mincer, Jacob. 1974. *Schooling, Experience, and Earnings.* New York: National Bureau of Economic Research, distributed by Columbia University Press.

Miracle, Marvin P., and Bruce Fetter. 1970. "Backward-Sloping Labor-Supply Functions and African Economic Behavior." *Economic Development and Cultural Change* 18 (January):240–251.

Moore, Wilbert E. 1966. "Changes in Occupational Structures." In *Social Structure and Mobility in Economic Development.* Edited by Neil J. Smelser and Seymour Martin Lipset. Chicago: Aldine. Pp. 194–212.

Muratoria, Blanca. 1969. "Participación social y política de los campesinos de Nor Yungas." *Revista Mexicana de Sociología* 31 (October-December).

Olson, Mancur. 1978. "The Political Economy of Comparative Growth Rates." Department of Economics, University of Maryland. MS. Pp. 1–96.

Omran, Abdel R., William J. McEwen, and Mahfouz H. Zaki. 1967. *Epidemiological Studies in Bolivia.* New York: Research Institute for the Study of Man.

Oropeza, Maria Inés Pérez, and Salvador Romero Pittari. 1970. "Cambio y tradicionalismo." *Aportes* (Paris) 17 (July):81–120.

Overall, John E., and C. James Klett. 1972. *Applied Multivariate Analysis.* New York: McGraw-Hill.

Paglin, Morton. 1975. "The Measurement and Trend of Inequality: A Basic Revision." *The American Economic Review* 65 (September):598–609.

Patch, Richard W. 1967. "Peasantry and National Revolution: Bolivia." In *Expectant Peoples—Nationalism and Development.* Edited by Kalman H. Silvert. New York: Vintage. Pp. 27–126.

Patrick, George F., and Earl W. Kehrberg. 1973. "Costs and Returns of Education in Five Agricultural Areas of Eastern Brazil." *American Journal of Agricultural Economics* 55 (May):145−153.

Paukert, Felix. 1973. "Income Distribution at Different Levels of Development: A Survey of Evidence." *International Labour Review* 108 (August-September):97−125.

Pescosolido, Bernice A., and Jonathan Kelley. 1979. "Taking a Second Look: Regression Analysis, Goodman's Log-Linear Models and Comparative Research." Revised version of a paper read at the Annual Meetings of the American Sociological Association.

Petras, James, and Hugo Zemelman Merino. 1972. *Peasants in Revolt: A Chilean Case Study, 1965−1971.* Austin: University of Texas Press.

Pirenne, Henri. 1936. *Economic and Social History of Medieval Europe.* New York: Harcourt, Brace and World.

Reiss, Albert J., et al. 1961. *Occupations and Social Status.* New York: Free Press of Glencoe.

Reyeros, Rafael. 1949. *El pongueaje, la servidumbre personal de los indios bolivianos.* La Paz.

Robinson, Sherman. 1976. "A Note on the U Hypothesis Relating Income Inequality and Economic Development." *American Economic Review* 66 (June):337−340.

Rossi, Peter H. 1973. "Comment." In *Social Stratification and Career Mobility.* Edited by Walter Müller and Karl Ulrich Mayer. Paris: Mouton. Pp. 374−375.

Ryder, Norman B. 1965. "The Cohort as a Concept in the Study of Social Change." *American Sociological Review* 30 (December):843−861.

Schuman, Howard, Alex Inkeles, and David H. Smith. 1967. "Some Social Psychological Effects and Non-Effects of Literacy in a New Nation." *Economic Development and Cultural Change* 16 (October):1−14.

Sen, Amartya. 1973. *On Economic Inequality.* Oxford: Clarendon Press.

Simkus, Albert A. 1980. "Historical Changes in Occupational Inheritance under Socialism: Hungary 1930−1973." In *Research in Social Stratification and Mobility.* Vol. 1. Edited by Donald J. Treiman and Robert V. Robinson. Greenwich, Conn.: JAI Press.

Simmons, Roger A. 1974. *Palca and Pucara: A Study of the Effects of Revolution on Two Bolivian Haciendas.* Publications in Anthropology, Vol. 9. Berkeley, Los Angeles, London: University of California Press.

Stinchcombe, Arthur L. 1961. "Agricultural Enterprise and Rural Class Relations." *American Journal of Sociology* 67 (September):165−176.

Szelenyi, Ivan. 1978. "Social Inequalities in State Socialist Redistributive Economies." *International Journal of Comparative Sociology* 19 (March-June):63−87.

Tellenback, Sten. 1978. "The Logic of Development in Socialist Poland." *Social Forces* 57 (December):436-456.

Thorn, Richard S. 1971. "The Economic Transformation." In *Beyond the Revolution: Bolivia Since 1952.* Edited by James M. Malloy and Richard S. Thorn. Pittsburgh: University of Pittsburgh Press. Pp. 157−216.

Thurow, Lester C. 1975. *Generating Inequality: Mechanisms of Distribution in the U.S. Economy.* New York: Basic Books.

Treiman, Donald J. 1975. "Problems of Concept and Measurement in the

Comparative Study of Occupational Mobility." *Social Science Research* 4 (September):183–230.

———. 1977. *Occupational Prestige in Comparative Perspective*. New York: Academic.

Treiman, Donald J., and Jonathan Kelley. 1974. "A Comparative Study of Status Attainment." Research proposal to the National Institute of Mental Health, subsequently supported as Grant 1-RO1-MH26606.

Treiman, Donald J., and Kermit Terrell. 1975a. "The Process of Status Attainment in the United States and Great Britain." *American Journal of Sociology* 81 (November):563–583.

———. 1975b. "Sex and the Process of Status Attainment: A Comparison of Working Women and Men." *American Sociological Review* 40 (April): 174–200.

United Nations. 1961. *United Nations Report of the World Social Situation*. New York: United Nations.

United States Department of Commerce. 1977. *Social Indicators 1976: Selected Data on Social Conditions and Trends in the United States*. Washington, D.C.: United States Government Printing Office.

van Ginneken, Wouter. 1976. *Rural and Urban Income Inequalities*. Geneva: International Labour Office.

Vellard, Jehan A. 1963. *Civilisations des Andes, evolution des populations du haut-plateau bolivien*. Paris.

Volgyes, Ivan. 1978. "Modernization, Stratification, and Elite Development in Hungary." *Social Forces* 57 (December):500–521.

Wagley, Charles. 1952. *Race and Class in Rural Brazil*. Paris: UNESCO.

Welch, Finis. 1975. "Human Capital Theory: Education, Discrimination and Life Cycles." *American Economic Review* 65 (May):63–73.

Wennergren, E. Boyd, and Morris D. Whitaker. 1975. *The Status of Bolivian Agriculture*. New York: Praeger.

Whitehead, Laurence. 1969. "Basic Data in Poor Countries: The Bolivian Case." *Bulletin of the Oxford University Institute of Economics and Statistics* 31 (August):205–227.

Wilkie, James W. 1969. *The Bolivian Revolution and U.S. Aid Since 1952: Financial Background and Context of Political Decisions*. Los Angeles: UCLA Latin American Center Publications.

———. 1974a. *Measuring Land Reform*. Statistical Abstract of Latin America Supplement. Los Angeles: UCLA Latin American Center Publications.

———. 1974b. *Statistics and National Policy*. Statistical Abstract of Latin America Supplement 3. Los Angeles: UCLA Latin American Center Publications.

Wilkie, James W., and Peter Reich. 1977. *Statistical Abstract of Latin America*. Vol. 18 (1977). Los Angeles: UCLA Latin American Center Publications.

Wolf, Eric R. 1956. "Aspects of Group Relations in a Complex Society: Mexico." *American Anthropologist* 58 (December):1065–1078.

———. 1966. *Peasants*. New York: Prentice-Hall.

———. 1969. *Peasant Wars of the Twentieth Century*. New York: Harper & Row.

Worsnip, Patrick. 1979. Reuters news article reported in the *Los Angeles Times*. 11 May 1979.

Wright, William E. 1966. *Serf, Seigneur, and Sovereign: Agrarian Reform in Eighteenth-Century Bohemia*. Minneapolis: University of Minnesota Press.

Yueh, Hai. 1976. "Communist Party Members Must Work for the Benefit of the Majority and Persist in a Continuous Revolution under the Proletarian Dictatorship." *Red Flag* (April):40–44.

Zagorski, Krzysztof. 1971. "Social Mobility in Poland." *The Polish Sociological Bulletin* 2 (24):5–16.

Zedong, Mao. 1965. Interview with Andre Malraux reported in the *New York Times*, 10 September 1975.

Zuvekas, Clarence, Jr. 1977. "Rural Income Distribution in Bolivia: A Summary and Evaluation of Quantitative and Qualitative Information." Economic Research Service, U.S. Department of Agriculture.

Index

Age: and income, 147; measurement of, 59, 146–148

Agriculture: advances in, 191; in Altiplano Valley, 44, 45–46; compared to other countries, 89, 126; in Cordillera Real Valley, 46–47; marketing changes in, 126–127, 255 n. 5; occupational opportunities in, 126–128, 142; occupational status of, 263 n. 4; population involved in, 62, 67, 68, 73, 123, 149, 251 n. 1, 253 n. 3, 257 n. 4; prewar conditions in, 69–70, 71–89; productivity decline in, 69, 99, 117, 124, 125, 131, 141, 253 n. 3; recovery of, 124, 125, 131. *See also* Land reform

Altiplano Valley, Bolivia, 44, 45–46, 47, 51

Andes Mountains, 43–44

Army: peasant uprisings suppressed by, 77; seizes government, 92–93, 94

Aymara Indians. *See* Indians

Barrientos, René, 102

Baseline model. *See* Research Institute for the Study of Man (RISM) survey

Blau, Peter M., 260 n. 24

Bolivian National Revolution: aims of, xii; beginnings of, 93–94; compared with other revolutions, 95, 104, 119; data on, xii, xiv, 42–43, 105; U.S. aid to, 42; violence during, 253 n. 2. *See also* Movimiento Nacionalista Revolucionario

Busch, Germán, 92

Catavi massacre, 93

Cattle ranches, 149

CBF (state development corporation), 94

Chaco War, 91–92

Chinese Revolution, 104, 179; destruction of private property during, 40, 41; and elites, 37, 172, 258 n. 7; government intervention during, 10; and human capital, 185; and inherited privilege, 14, 145, 188

Cholos: political involvement of, 93, 102; social status of, 51; Spanish characteristics of, 51, 58

Clark, Ronald J., 124

COB (Bolivian Labor Center), 95

COMIBOL (state tin monopoly), 94, 128–129. *See also* Tin industry

Compi, Bolivia, 46, 97

Communist revolutions: and elites, 37, 172; and inequality, 35; and inherited privilege, 144, 179, 185. *See also* Chinese Revolution; Cuban Revolution; Poland

Cordillera Real Valley, Bolivia, 46–48

Coroico, Bolivia, 97

Correlations: determination of, 207, 261 App.1, n. 1

Cuban Revolution, 40, 104, 185, 255 n. 4